The Shimmering Heat
Memories of a Bush Doctor in East Africa

The *Shimmering* Heat

Memories
of a Bush Doctor
in East Africa

Besv wishes

David Webco

David Webster

The Shimmering Heat
David Webster

Published by Aspect Design 2013
Malvern, Worcestershire, United Kingdom.

Designed, printed and bound by Aspect Design
89 Newtown Road, Malvern, Worcs. WR14 1PD
United Kingdom
Tel: 01684 561567
E-mail: allan@aspect-design.net
Website: www.aspect-design.net

ISBN 978-1-908832-46-7

To Rosemary
the love and companion of my life

CONTENTS

The Northern Frontier

The rugged hills, the bush, the sand;
    Sansievra and cactus guard the land.
The doum palms rustle by the river's verge
    Where the streams from the hills and the desert merge.
Haunt, where the stately kudu strides;
    A range of proud, nomadic tribes.
Ancestral home of the elephant host,
    From Rudolf's blue waters to Archer's Post.
The shimmering heat of the day at noon,
    The peace of the night by the light of the moon;
And when the pink glow tinges the slopes clad in thorn
    Comes the beauty of sunset, the glory of dawn.

Mervyn Cowie 1953

GLOSSARY

AIM	Africa Inland Mission
AMRF	African Medical Research Foundation, the Flying Doctor Service of East Africa founded by the surgeon Michael Wood
Baraza	A meeting to discuss topical issues
Bwana	'Sir', a respectful title for a man
Ayah	A children's nurse or carer
BCMS	Bible Churchmen's Missionary Society, an evangelical Anglican society, now called Crosslinks
DC	District Commissioner, the senior administrative officer in charge of a district.
Dhambi	A wild fig tree
Duka	A shop
Kiswahili	The language of the Swahili tribe of Kenya's coast, now spoken widely throughout East and Central Africa, having been 'carried' inland by traders, including slave traders
Kwa Heri	Goodbye, literally 'For happiness' (Kiswahili)
MAF	Missionary Aviation Fellowship, a mission agency which flies planes to support the work of other mission and charitable agencies
Manyatta	A tribal village, comprising temporary huts surrounded by a thorn stockade, and usually containing an enclosure for cattle
Maskini	The poor, beggars
Matatu	A taxi used for journeys between towns, and usually packed tight with passengers and luggage

Memsahib	'Madam', a respectful title for a woman
Mishkid	A child of missionary parents.
MOH	Medical Officer of Health, the government doctor in charge of the health services of a district
Mzungu	A white person (plural – *Wazungu*) (Kiswahili)
Panga	A machete
PC	Provincial Commissioner, the administrative officer in charge of a province, with several DC's under his charge
PMO	Provincial Medical Officer, in overall charge of the health services of a province
Shamba	A plot of maize or other crops, a garden or smallholding
Shifta	Bandits, active in northern Kenya, often Somali, sometimes with political motivation, sometimes robbery
Shuka	A loose cloth, knotted at the shoulder, worn by a Pokot man
Tef	Small-grained cereal used to make sour pancakes
Tororut	The Pokot word for God
Wazungu	Plural of *Mzungu*
Woya	The white robe of a Boran or Gabbra man

FOREWORD

Amudat and Marsabit – what wonderful memories they conjure up in my mind! Having been always deeply in love with the African wilderness, where better to go than these two places? I am delighted that David Webster has written this memoir of his and his family's time in East Africa, part of which coincided with my tour of duty with Oxfam there; and feel very flattered that he has asked me to write this foreword.

Amudat was a remote centre in eastern Uganda and a major staging post for travellers venturing from Kenya to Karamoja District in Uganda or Turkana District in Kenya. With both Karamoja and Turkana being areas of considerable priority for Oxfam, I made the journey many times and I always relished the thought of overnight hospitality with the Websters, who ran a most excellent medical programme – both inpatient and outreach – from Amudat. It was a prayerful and welcoming place and I just loved being there. The fact that Oxfam was playing a major role in helping to fund both capital and outreach programmes was another reason for Amudat being really rather special.

As someone who would rather run a mile than have a needle anywhere near me, it always amazed me that the Pokot so loved inoculations that they would have one and then queue up for a second dose, necessitating the dipping of a thumb in gentian violet in order to avoid the double dose! I also remember the commemorative tree I planted, which died of a surfeit of goat manure – a story recorded in this book.

In Marsabit, way to the east of Lodwar in central northern Kenya, the urban centre and its rural outreach presented a most interesting series of challenges. The Websters handled them with great sensitivity and care, and their deep faith enabled them to seek guidance in all they did. The need for preventive medical care was very evident and David gave priority to teaching the local population that health could be helped as much through preventing illness as through a purely curative programme.

What happy days they were – and how full of confidence we were that, with independence, countries had entered a new and progressive era! The fact that this was far from universally the case did not dim our optimism for the future. It was a privilege and a pleasure to be working in East Africa, and inspirational to be partnering the Websters and others of their ilk.

Malcolm Harper
(Oxfam Field Director in Eastern Africa, 1968–71)

INTRODUCTION

The birth of this book was unexpected. Some years ago I wrote, for the interest of family only, a record of my parents' time as missionaries in Kenya, and my memories of my childhood as a *mishkid* in colonial Kenya. It then seemed logical to write, again for the purpose of family records, an account of Rosemary's and my years working in Uganda and Kenya. However when our friend and Associate Vicar, the Reverend Doctor Mary Barr, read this latter account she encouraged me to publish it. So it is Mary who must take the credit – or the blame!

I have combined a much abbreviated account of my parents' lives and my childhood with the story of our Amudat and Marsabit years. (For a more detailed account of my childhood you will have to read my book *Mishkid*). Rosemary and I were privileged indeed to live and work, and to bring up our family, in those remote and fascinating parts of Uganda and Kenya, at a time when the people were still mostly living their traditional way of life. It was, in many ways, the end of an era. We were there for only nine years, yet such a lot was packed into those years that I now wonder how we coped.

I kept a daily diary, so have not had to rely entirely on memory. But if any facts relating to other people are not correct, I can only apologise. I have checked them in so far as I am able. I hope the reader gets a little taste of, and enjoyment from, this story of our life in the bush, with its family, social, church and medical aspects. They were rich years, largely due to the wonderful people we worked with and among.

I love biographies, and I believe in the importance of one's 'story', and of passing that story on from generation to generation. So I would echo the words of the Psalmist who said:

> Let this be written for a future generation,
> that a people not yet created may praise the Lord.
> Psalm 102:18

ACKNOWLEDGEMENTS

A number of people have assisted in the birth process of this book. My thanks to the Reverend Doctor Mary Barr for encouraging me to publish in the first place, and for thoroughly searching out my split infinitives and other misdemeanours. Thanks also to the late Reverend Robin Denniston, formerly of Oxford University Press, who was kind enough to take an interest and to give me wise advice; to Trisha Hutchison and Roy Knightley for reading the script, and making helpful comments; to Dr Andrew Ferguson and Dr Peter Armon of the Christian Medical Fellowship, who likewise read the script and advised and encouraged me. I am grateful to my son, Andrew, who scanned my transparencies on to disc, and also to Lynette who helped to guide me through the mysteries of scanning. What a technological boon sons and daughters are to those of us who were born too soon! Thanks too to Aspect Design of Malvern, who have been such a help in producing this second edition. To all these I am so grateful. Last, but not least, I thank Rosemary who has not only spurred me on, and kept me supplied with coffee during long hours at the computer, but has also, together with Andrew, Paul, Stephen and Lynette, been so much a part of the story.

Malcolm Harper, one-time Oxfam Field Director in East Africa, and a great friend to us and our work, has – in the midst of his very busy 'retirement' – done me the honour of writing the Foreword. I had to catch him between visits to the Congo, Uganda and Afghanistan, in his work with the United Nations Association, Landmine Action, Friends of Northern Uganda and other worthy charities and NGO's. What an example of 're-tyrement'! Thank you, Malcolm.

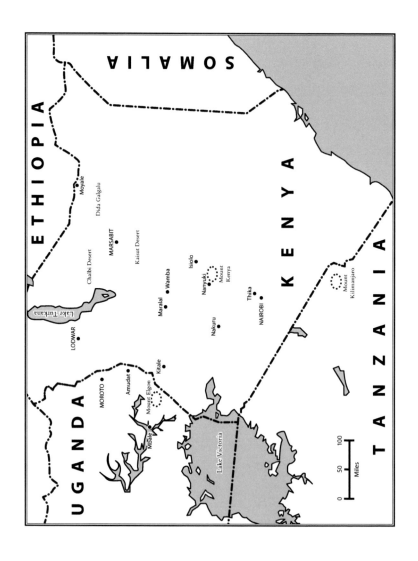

SOMALIA

ETHIOPIA

KENYA

TANZANIA

UGANDA

Moyale

Dida Galgalu

MARSABIT

Chalbi Desert

Kaisut Desert

Isiolo

Lake Turkana

Wamba

Nanyuki
Mount
Kenya

Maralal

Mount
Kilimanjaro

Thika

LODWAR

Nakuru

NAIROBI

Kitale

Amudat

MOROTO

Mount Elgon

Mbale

Lake Victoria

100

50

Miles

0

Chapter 1
ROOTS

I was standing on the edge of memory. The date was 11 June 1970. It was fourteen years since, at the age of fifteen, I had left my childhood home on Marsabit mountain, in northern Kenya, when my parents started a new life in Nairobi. Now I was back again, visiting old haunts. Below stretched the familiar valley, clothed on one side with thickly forested slopes, the trees festooned with trails of grey-green lichen, or 'old man's beard' as we used to call it; on the other an open hillside, rippling with windswept grass the colour of honey. At its lower end the valley opened on to rolling plains of brown thorn scrub, interspersed with conical hillocks – the outpourings of long past volcanic eruptions. These foothills of the mountain shimmered in the heat. And way beyond and below them, in a distant haze, stretched the desert, its surface glistening faintly with a snow-white crust of salt. So much was the same – the forest surrounding the old mission site; the steep hill rising behind the mission, its eastern-facing, mist-catching slopes covered with dense forest, its western slopes bare of trees; the wind-swept avenue of jacarandas which once proudly lined the drive up the mission compound; the wild fig or *dhambi* tree under which my father and companions had first pitched their tents in 1931, its massive trunk made up of a coil of intertwined aerial roots; the red soil, blue sky, scudding clouds, and the echoing bark of baboons in the forest canopy. So much was the same. But so much had changed. The mission, its church and houses, its life and purpose, had long since moved, following the people to the centre of population, to the shops and administrative offices on the other side of the hill. No more scattered huts and *shambas* on the hillside. No longer did people live at Karantina. It had reverted to bush. It had become, once again, as it was before 1931, the haunt of elephant and buffalo and the shy, stately greater kudu. The wilderness and the swirling Marsabit mists had reclaimed their territory.

In my mind's eye I could see my father in his khaki shorts running down the grass drive to his mud-walled office. He always ran, as though life was short – the people affectionately called him 'Mirta', (the Runner). I could see my mother, coming home from the school, striding erect through the eddying mist, in one of those bright floral dresses that she loved to wear. I was standing on the cement floor of what was once our house – the house that my father had built. The mud walls and corrugated iron roof were gone – taken as salvage and flattened by rain and elephants. But the outline of the house, the cement floor, remained like a footprint in the soil, the evidence of what had once been. I traced each room, remembering how it was, where the furniture stood, where we placed each bucket when the roof leaked in the rains. Relics of my mother's beloved garden remained – bougainvilleas gone wild, straggling into trees; a tecomaria bush, with its vivid orange flowers, defying the wild; oleanders, and even the odd unkempt rose bush. The stumps of custard apple, guava, lime and avocado pear trees were all that had survived the depredations of elephants. Bravest and brightest survivor of all was the sprawling golden shower which had once graced the wooden house where my parents began their married life in 1937. No trace of the wooden house itself remained. In the branches of a severely mauled fir tree one large rusty nail protruded – all that was left of a tree house built proudly by my brother Dennis, our African friends and me. As I stood on what had been my childhood home, and as those memories flooded back, I felt a deep sense of loss for what had been – an idyllic childhood that could not be recovered; parents who had died; a past gone for ever. And I wept.

A short way from what had been our house was the site where the church had once stood. Thatched roof it had, and mud walls, built low on the side that overlooked the valley. I could hear in my mind the clanging of the church 'bell' – a piece of railway line suspended in a tree, and beaten with an iron bar. I was once allowed to ring it, and it deafened me for days. As the sound used to echo down the valley and across to the opposite hillside, calling the people to worship, they began to emerge from their scattered mud houses, wearing their best *woyas* and robes, to converge along the winding paths that led to the mission. Soon they would be singing the familiar hymns in Borana, accompanied by my mother on a wheezy harmonium, or by my father on his concertina. Meanwhile my eyes and mind used to roam from the incomprehensible

Borana service to the forested hillside opposite, scanning it for signs of baboons, or monkeys, or possibly elephants.

Childhood friends provided a strong link with the past, on that nostalgic visit to Marsabit in 1970, some of them among the first converts to Christianity. Philippo Mato, tall and solemn and dignified; and the Reverend Petro Oce, the first local person to be ordained priest; Dube, our much-loved gardener, with his grizzled hair, and soft-spoken voice; Samson Gedde, short and squat and bandy-legged, strong as his Biblical counterpart; and gentle Diramu, who was *ayah* to baby sister, Marilyn, while our mother taught in the school. There were hugs and tears at the memories of what our parents had meant to them – how much they owed to them, and how much they had loved them. And always the same question – the challenge – 'When are you coming back to live with us and to be our doctor?' So how did I come to be in this remote and outlandish part of northern Kenya?

My family story goes back to the grey streets of Glasgow in 1876 with the birth of Caleb, a son to John Webster. In due course Caleb became a travelling cutlery salesman, and he moved to Sheffield. He also, at some point in his early life, became a devout Christian. At his church in Sheffield, St Thomas's, Caleb met and fell in love with a young lady, Gertrude Bentley. Born in 1878 Gertie was the eldest of eleven children. Her father, James, was a commercial traveller, and her mother, Charlotte, ran a shop. When Caleb fell for Gertie she was in her early twenties. Caleb asked her father for her hand in marriage, but James Bentley said that she was too young, and insisted that they did not see one another for two years. They kept to this promise, and meanwhile Gertie trained as a teacher. After two years they resumed their friendship, and the marriage was finally allowed to go ahead. In 1904, at the age of forty-eight, Gertie's mother, Charlotte, developed breast cancer. A mastectomy was carried out in their home, in Buckingham Street, Sheffield. The kitchen table was dragged to the window to give the surgeon a better light, and there Charlotte was operated on. She developed pneumonia postoperatively, and died. Gertie, aged twenty-six, and now with her own first child, Harold, took on the responsibility for her younger, school-age siblings. She was a coper. In due course her father re-married, to Amelia Gallimore, the nurse who had looked after Charlotte. But his second wife never took to her stepchildren, and Gertie remained their mother-figure. The children never called Amelia 'Mother', but always 'Auntie Kitty'. She discouraged the children from attending church, or taking part in any religious activity. Gertie did her best to counteract that negative influence.

In 1905, the year following her mother's death, Gertie gave birth to their second child, Eric John (my father). Edith followed, then a daughter who died in infancy, and finally Ella. The family was complete. When World War broke out in 1914 Caleb, always rather frail in health, was declared unfit for military service. He joined the Territorial Army, and was posted as munitions inspector to Glasgow, returning to Sheffield after the war. Caleb and Gertie, both passionate in their Christian faith, brought up their four children to be equally committed. It was a home with much laughter, and not much money, but Caleb and Gertie always looked to God in the certain belief that He would provide, not for their wants but for their needs. Theirs was an open home, with many visitors. Always there was a generous welcome, but the welcome was not necessarily matched by the amount of food in the larder. When food was short Caleb and Gertie would ask God for help, and time and again the doorbell would ring and a friend, unaware of their predicament, would be standing there with a basket of goodies. This was the sort of living, practical faith that the Webster children grew up with. (Caleb was a licensed Lay Reader in the Church of England. For many years he was paid assistant at the parish church in Tibshelf. In the latter half of his life he and Gertie led a small mission church at Thornton Cleveleys, near Blackpool. This was an unsalaried job, and they lived there by faith.) At the age of fourteen my father very nearly died in the post-war influenza epidemic. Much prayer was offered for him and he survived but never returned to school. So ended his formal education. He became apprenticed to a bookbinder, and attended evening classes in Latin. It seems a strange choice of subject, but later it stood him in good stead when he found himself working out from scratch the grammar and vocabulary of an as yet unwritten African language.

Though a close family, the Websters' closeness took second place to what each of them considered to be God's call on their lives. My father's older brother, Harold's, calling was to be a missionary to the Eskimo (Innuit) in the Arctic. After his departure for the Arctic in 1928 he and Eric would only ever meet once again. He spent his life there, at first in the remote northern trading post of Coppermine, then in Aklavik. He and later his family experienced all kinds of privation and danger. He travelled vast distances with his dog sled, bringing the Gospel to the Innuit people. In later years he was made Archdeacon of the Arctic, and was awarded an honorary doctorate of divinity, and also the Order of Canada.

My father's calling was to hotter climes. In 1928 he was inspired by the impassioned plea of a Christian visionary, Alfred Buxton. Buxton had given up medical training at Cambridge to go as a missionary to the Congo. He joined the famous cricketer and Congo missionary, C.T. Studd, and married his daughter Edith. In due course AB (as Buxton was always known) moved east to Uganda and Kenya. There he became aware of the vast tracts of desert and semi-desert stretching across the north of Uganda and Kenya, home to nomadic tribes who had never heard the Gospel. AB was a pioneer looking for a cause; a visionary looking for a purpose. Here lay his challenge. He returned to England in search of fifteen men willing to rough it, willing to give their lives to the people of this vast, desolate, and as yet unreached area. Eric was one of those who heard and responded to that call. So too did a newly formed evangelical Anglican missionary society, the Bible Churchmen's Missionary Society (BCMS) – an offshoot of the Church Missionary Society. Eric was accepted for training for ordination at the BCM Training College, Tyndale Hall, in Bristol. And so it was that in 1930 he was ordained deacon in the chapel of Tyndale Hall by the Bishop of Bristol, acting on behalf of the Bishop of the Upper Nile. On 29 September 1930, his twenty-fifth birthday, Eric and sixteen other BCMS recruits were commissioned at a service at Church House, Westminster. A group of them were destined for northern Kenya, and set sail soon afterwards for Mombasa, in the company of the man who had inspired their calling, Alfred Buxton. Eric's commission was, along with Charles Scudder, to establish a mission on Marsabit mountain, in the deserts of Kenya's Northern Frontier District. It was a tough but exciting challenge for this young man who had so nearly died, whose health was considered to be 'frail', and whose formal education had been terminated so prematurely.

Chapter 2
MARSABIT

Marsabit is beautiful and mysterious. A low, sprawling mountain, pitted and scarred with volcanic craters, it rises almost imperceptibly from the desert wastes which surround it in northern Kenya. To the south lies the arid scrub of the Kaisut desert. To the southwest the Koroli desert. To the west the salt-encrusted sands of the Chalbe desert, stretching for one hundred miles to the barren shores of Lake Turkana (formerly Lake Rudolf). To the north, between Marsabit and the southern Ethiopian hills, lie the forbidding lava plains of the Dida Galgalu. To the east lies nothing but flat, featureless desert and scrubland, stretching for five hundred miles through Kenya and Somalia to the shores of the Indian Ocean. And here lies the secret of Marsabit. Although the volcanic peaks of the mountain rise to only just over five thousand feet, it is the first high land to be met by the moisture-laden trade winds, as they blow in from the Indian Ocean. As the winds are forced up over Marsabit's range the moisture condenses, and thick mists clothe the higher peaks. The very name 'Marsabit' means 'The place of black mist'. The mist is Marsabit's life-blood, sustaining the cool, green forest which clothes the peaks and east-facing slopes of the mountain. Wild olive trees are festooned with trailing grey-green lichen. Springs emerge from the rocks and trickle down fern clad valleys. It is a haven for birds and colourful butterflies – myriads of which drink from the muddy edges of streams, and feed from rich elephant droppings. The forest is an oasis for wild life – noisy troops of baboons and vervet monkeys; shy and elusive bushbuck; and herds of buffalo. But the two animals for which Marsabit mountain is renowned are the greater kudu, with its graceful, spiralling horns; and particularly large and long-tusked elephants. These enormous creatures can often be seen moving like silent shadows through the forest undergrowth. Deep in the forest lie two crater lakes, a precious source of water for the wildlife.

Just as Marsabit mountain has been for centuries an oasis for wild life, so too it has been an oasis for the nomadic peoples of the surrounding deserts. For generations Boran, Gabbra, Rendille and Samburu people have brought their camels, cattle and goats to the watering holes and wells of Marsabit. Whereas down in the desert these tribes would think nothing of raiding one another to steal cattle, Marsabit seems to have been, by and large, a place of truce, where the tribes recognised and respected one another's need of water. Two further tribal groups occupy the mountain. The Burji are an agricultural people from the southern Ethiopian highlands, who sought refuge on Marsabit from their aggressive Galla neighbours in Ethiopia. Since the nineteenth century Burji have grown their crops of millet, sorghum and *tef* on the relatively fertile upper slopes of Marsabit. Somalis comprise the last group, overflowing westward from Somalia, and claiming that part of Kenya. They are the tradesmen of the bush – proud and shrewd businessmen, they trade in livestock, and run small shops (*dukas*) in any settlement of population.

The first white man to set foot on Marsabit was Dr Arthur Donaldson Smith, a twenty-nine-year-old American medic. In 1895 he followed the route that Count Teleki had taken to Lake Rudolf ten years previously, and on his return journey saw the distant outline of Marsabit mountain to the east. He diverted to visit this as yet unexplored territory. He found the beautiful crater lakes, and camped on the shore of the larger one, collecting animal and bird specimens. Lord Delamere was the next white visitor, in 1897. On his way south from Somalia and Ethiopia he crossed the cauldron of the Dida Galgalu, skirted the edge of the Chalbe desert, and then with relief trudged up into the welcoming cool of Marsabit's forest. He camped there for three weeks while a young British surgeon in his party shot no less than twenty one elephants. The first European to live for any length of time on Marsabit was the Marquis Ralph Gandolfi Hornyold. He left the family Blackmore Estate, near Malvern in Worcestershire, to set up with a friend a livestock trading company, the Boma Trading Company, in the East African Protectorate, in 1906. The company's first outpost was at Marsabit, and here the Marquis camped in the forest, on the shore of the crater lake, and set about trying to persuade the local tribes to sell him cattle. He built mud houses for himself and his staff, and lived there for a year. The venture failed, amidst growing government suspicion and opposition. In 1922 an American adventurer and wild life photographer, Martin Johnson, with his wife Osa, arrived at the shore of Marsabit's crater lake. They were so overwhelmed by its beauty that they called it 'Lake Paradise', and settled down to live there for the next four years. To read their accounts of that time one would think that they had discovered the lake. A 'first' that Osa could genuinely claim was to be the first white woman to live in Marsabit. The vestiges of their house can still be seen.

It was to this remote mountain that Alfred Buxton brought his two young recruits, my father Eric Webster and Charles Scudder, in 1931.They borrowed a lorry and a driver, Funga Funga, from the obliging missionary doctor, Dr Clive Irvine, at the Church of Scotland Mission at Chogoria, on the slopes of Mount Kenya. Then, heavily laden with supplies, they set off on the arduous journey to Marsabit. From the cool heights of Mount Kenya they descended into the hot bushland of the Northern Frontier District. One can only imagine Eric's and Charles' feelings as they caught their first sight of herds of gazelle, and zebra, and giraffe; and flat-topped acacia trees festooned with weaverbird nests; and towering earth-red termite hills; and rugged mountains rising out of the shimmering heat of the plains. There was the choking dust, and interminable bone-shaking of the lorry on the rough road. There were dry riverbeds to cross, with the risk of the lorry wheels sinking into the soft sand. Most exciting of all would have been their first glimpses of tribesmen, in their finery and armed with spears, herding their camels and goats through the bush. These were the very people for whom they had come.

On 19 January 1931, precariously balanced on top of their luggage on the back of the lorry, the three men arrived in Marsabit. The Government allocated them a plot at Karantina, a mile from the administrative centre. There, on the edge of the forest, they pitched their tent at the base of a large wild fig, or *dhambi* tree, and began to make friends with the local populace. It was decided that Boran was the predominant language, and the one they would learn. Eric, with his knowledge of Latin from his night classes, began the laborious process of working out the vocabulary and grammar of an, as yet, unwritten language. It was a process fraught with misunderstandings, and the cause of much laughter with the local people. Soon their tent gave way to grass huts. Eric was alarmed more than once when he was woken at night by an elephant eating his house. One night his shoes were taken from beside his camp bed by a hyena.

AB had never intended to stay long with Eric and Charles. He had accompanied them to see them settled. But he was a restless pioneer at heart, and more and more his eyes wandered towards the distant hills of Ethiopia one hundred miles to the north. A new challenge was already drawing him. In his diary he wrote, 'Usually of an evening I go out… looking to Abyssinia, over the great plain, and have some prayer.' Within two months he was on his way north, travelling with camel men and eight camels, three of them to carry water. Charles Scudder accompanied him to Mega, beyond the Ethiopian border. It took them seven days to cross the Dida Galgalu and reach Moyale. They walked at night, and rested up in the scorching heat of the day. When the time came to part AB continued north towards Addis Ababa, while Charles turned back to Marsabit. It was an emotional parting, and as the distance between them grew they called out Scripture verses to encourage one another, their voices echoing among the hills, until at last they could hear one another no more.

Charles had a hard journey back. They found little vegetation for the camels, and water ran short. He finally staggered in to the Karantina site on Marsabit to find that Eric had not been idle – he had already compiled an extensive Borana vocabulary and a tentative grammar. Within months he had started the first translation into Borana of St Luke's Gospel. A school was started, and forty pupils enrolled – varying in age from young children to men of fifty. More substantial buildings began to rise. Eric, who would have loved to study medicine if he had not had to leave school so young, found himself doctoring people and their animals for all sorts of conditions. He and Charles began to make safaris down the mountain, to visit Boran *manyattas* (tribal villages) on the lower slopes, to befriend the people. They were treated to Boran delicacies such as 'ititu' (rancid milk from which drowned flies had been skimmed) and 'buna' (roasted Ethiopian coffee beans floating in sweetened warm fat and milk). Eric developed quite a liking for them. He immersed himself in the life of the Boran, and in due course became an authority on their language and their culture.

Towards the end of that first year Charles Scudder moved to Maralal, in Samburu country, one hundred and fifty miles to the southwest. My father was joined by a pharmacist – the nearest thing to a doctor that the mission could find at the time. A dispensary was built from stone quarried in the nearby forest, and during 1932 over seven thousand patients were treated. A mud walled, thatched church accommodated the growing congregations. The number of converts was rising steadily, and Eric encouraged these young Christians to take leadership roles in the church. The pharmacist, Wesley Haylett, was joined by his wife – the first white woman to live in Marsabit since Osa Johnson had lived at Lake Paradise. Mrs Haylett gave birth to a baby boy, but then developed pneumonia and died – the first tragedy to strike the new missionaries. Her body was laid to rest at the edge of the forest, her grave surrounded by a thorny kei-apple hedge to keep off wild animals.

In May 1932 Eric, with six young Christians, a train of camels and a mule, made an extended safari to the Rendille and Gabbra people in the desert to the west of Marsabit. They moved from *manyatta* to *manyatta*, befriending, sharing the Good News of Jesus Christ, and treating the sick. At a place called Oloma Eric had a significant meeting with a group of Rendille chiefs, who listened to what he had to say. 'We know little about God,' they confided, and thought that whenever the moon 'died' God had died. This was an opening for Eric to talk about Jesus who did indeed die and rise again. Eric rather grandly named this important meeting with Rendille chiefs 'The Oloma Conference'.

The safari continued north, across the burning, featureless, salt-encrusted Chalbe desert. Walking in the relative cool of the mornings and evenings they reached the oases of North Horr and Kalacha. Here thickets of rustling doum palms grew around pools of brackish water. They began to meet up with Gabbra and Boran people, whose response to the Gospel was much more hostile. At Kalacha Eric's camels were attacked at night by lions. Two were mauled, two broke free. He was left with just one serviceable camel. Some of his men became separated from the main party, and were missing for two days. But none of this disheartened him. At last they made their way back up into the cool and mists of Marsabit, one month, two hundred miles, and a pair of boots later.

Nineteen thirty-three was a year of beginnings – the first baptisms, the first Christian marriage, the first church council, the first translation of Scripture into Boran – St Luke's Gospel. Those early Christian converts in Marsabit turned out to be remarkable men, pillars of the church. One of the most outstanding was Daudi Dadacha. Blind from childhood, once he became a Christian he had a passion to share his faith with his people. He spent the rest of his life as an evangelist. Led on a stick by one of his children, or some willing friend, he walked thousands of miles, from *manyatta* to *manyatta*, preaching. Many people came to faith through Daudi's ministry. And so the Church in Marsabit grew.

Eric was due for his first home leave in 1936. Before he left for Africa in 1931 he had become engaged to Eileen, a nurse at the Bristol Royal Infirmary. Although post each way took many weeks, he and Eileen had written regularly to one another during those long five years. It was at that time mission policy that marriage was not allowed until the prospective husband had mastered the local language, and completed a five year tour. Eric had now satisfied both requirements, and he looked forward eagerly to returning to England to claim his bride. As the time approached her letters became less and less frequent, but he put that down to the imminence of their meeting again. As his ship from Mombasa docked at Southampton he scanned the quay for Eileen, but she was not there. He took the boat train to Victoria, where surely she would be waiting on the platform. But she was not there either. It was only then that the news was broken to him – that Eileen was engaged to a doctor at the B.R.I. The wait for him had been too long. He was heart-broken. He had just eight months to find himself a wife, if he was not to remain a bachelor.

Eric's sister, Edith, had trained as a teacher in Sheffield, and there had met another Christian teacher trainee, Ruby Bloor. Like Edith, Ruby came from a strongly Christian family. But her background was that of the strict 'exclusive' variety of the Plymouth Brethren. When Ruby's parents, in Derby, heard of her new friendship, and that Edith was (of all things) 'C of E', they were concerned. They were even more concerned when Ruby said that Edith had invited her to stay at her home. Ruby's parents, Fred and Rosa Bloor, set off forthwith to visit Caleb and Gertie Webster, to vet them. They had an eye-opening visit. They discovered to their enormous surprise that these Anglicans had a dynamic faith, that was based on the Bible, and was, in all essentials, no different from their own. They discovered that even C of E members can be Christians! Ruby loved her visits to Edith's home. It was a breath of fresh air – the fun and laughter, the warmth of friendship and the relaxed atmosphere. And so it was that Ruby met Edith's older brother on his return from Africa. Events moved apace, and Eric and Ruby became engaged during his furlough. Ruby's parents had to make the further mental adjustment to the prospect of having, not just an Anglican son-in-law, but an ordained one. The idea would at one time have been unthinkable. Ruby's older sister had already married a Pentecostal minister, and that had been adjustment enough. By the time Eric was due to return to Kenya, Ruby had been interviewed and accepted as a prospective missionary by BCMS, but on the condition that she do a one year missionary training course at their women's college in Bristol, Dalton House. Eric returned to Marsabit single, but with the prospect of Ruby joining him in 1937.

While her best friend, Ruby, was doing her training in Bristol, Edith (who by now had also felt God's calling to Africa) joined Eric in Marsabit. Edith had had a proposal of marriage from an eligible and attractive young clergyman, with whom she had fallen in love. But his calling was to parish ministry in England, while Edith felt that God was calling her to Kenya. She wrestled in prayer with the dilemma, and her missionary calling won. A life-time of dedicated missionary work followed, during which she was also an outstanding aunt and spiritual mentor to her various nephews and nieces. Edith took over the mission school in Marsabit, with the proviso that when Ruby came she would move to Maralal, to work among the Samburu. In October 1937 an excited Eric met Ruby off the Mombasa boat train, at Nairobi station. She had come complete with trousseau, and just two days later she and Eric were married in St Stephen's church, Nairobi. Edith was a bridesmaid, and was the only person at the wedding (apart from the bridegroom) that Ruby knew. She was given away by a kindly friend of Eric's. None of the parents or other family members could be present. It must have been a bitter-sweet day for Ruby. After a honeymoon at Naivasha, in Kenya's Rift Valley, they set off for Marsabit.

Ruby, who must already have been in overload with new adjustments, now faced another challenge. In addition to the mission boxbody car, a lorryload of supplies had to be got to Marsabit. Ruby, who had never driven, would have to drive the car, and Eric the lorry. During the honeymoon Eric gave her a 'crash' course in driving. She took her driving test in Isiolo, on the way to Marsabit. (Eric, who was sitting in the back seat while the police officer conducted Ruby's driving test, leaned forward and surreptitiously released the hand brake, which Ruby had forgotten to do.) She passed the test, and then drove the open-sided boxbody over that most appalling road to Marsabit, while Eric followed in the lorry. Corrugations, deep ruts, sandy river beds, rocks – all made for a steep learning curve in driving for Ruby. By the time they reached Marsabit mountain it was dark. As they wound their way up the mountain road Ruby could hear a padding noise beside the open-sided car. She did not dare take her eyes off the road. It was only when they reached the mission that Eric told her that, for a while, a lion had been trotting alongside her. So Ruby came to her new home, a wooden house with golden shower creeper sprawling over its verandah. The pressure lamps were lit, and tea brewed up on the Dover stove. She went to sleep to the sound of the wind in the forest trees, and the sharp barking of a baboon disturbed by a prowling leopard. England must have seemed a very long way away.

Chapter 3
CHILDHOOD

Eric and Ruby's early days together in Marsabit were somewhat overshadowed by events to the north. In 1935 Mussolini's aspirations for empire had led to his invasion of Ethiopia. His army ruthlessly and cruelly suppressed the Ethiopian people, and Emperor Haile Selassie fled to Britain. Many Ethiopian refugees poured south in to Kenya, passing through Marsabit. What with Mussolini's fascist Italy, and the rise of Nazi Germany, it was an unsettled time. But Eric and Ruby were encouraged by the progress of their work, and not least by the arrival of a doctor, Reginald Bunny, and his physiotherapist wife Mary. One of Dr Bunny's first cases sadly ended in tragedy. Daudi Danabo, one of the very first Christians in Marsabit – a tall, striking man, and a born leader – developed what Dr Bunny thought was acute appendicitis. He operated on him, and Daudi died on the operating table. It was a sore blow to the church in those early days, especially as the time was rapidly approaching when the Christians were going to have to fend for themselves, without missionaries.

On 23 July 1939 Ruby gave birth, in Nairobi, to their first child Dennis. Just six weeks after his birth (although not as a result of it!) the world was plunged into conflict. On 3 September war with Germany was declared. Initially Italy declared itself to be neutral, but its fascist sympathies were with Hitler, and the occupation of Ethiopia was being pursued with vigour. The border town of Moyale, just one hundred miles north of Marsabit, was now occupied by Italian troops. Invasion of Kenya was threatened, and the situation in Marsabit was increasingly tense. It became more and more difficult for Eric to engage in safari work. On 10 June 1940 Italy declared war against the Allies. Italy had territorial ambitions, and invasion became increasingly likely. Marsabit would be their first target. Italian bomber aircraft had been seen in Moyale. The missionaries in Marsabit were ordered to evacuate and the church was left in the hands of the African Christians. Soon afterwards a bombing raid on Marsabit's airstrip was carried out. A goatherd was killed. The British retaliated. No bombers or bombs were available, so a small aircraft dropped the most offensive refuse possible onto Italian Moyale! Troops of the King's African Rifles were moved to Marsabit. Eric and Reginald Bunny were allowed back for a short time, and then once again ordered out, so they decided to enlist with the King's African Rifles, Eric as a chaplain. It was not long before he was posted back to Marsabit with the troops. The mission houses had meanwhile been commandeered by the army, and for a spell, when he was ill with malaria, he found himself admitted as a patient to his own bedroom.

Ruby had meanwhile found herself a job as tutor to the Hopcraft family, on their pyrethrum farm on the shores of Lake Naivasha, in Kenya's Rift Valley. She subsequently moved to a small bungalow at Dagoretti Corner on the outskirts of Nairobi, and taught at the local Kilimani Primary School. Here she spent the rest of the war. Meanwhile with the aid of South African troops, the Italians were steadily pushed back from their bases in southern Ethiopia. By the end of April 1941 Eric was writing to Ruby from Addis Ababa.

I was born in the Eskotene Nursing Home in Nairobi on 18 June 1941, and was baptised in All Saints Cathedral. Soon after my birth, but again not as a result of it, the tide of war began to change. In Europe the Battle of Britain was at its height. Eric, now a Major, and the proud father of two sons, set off once more with his KAR regiment, this time to Madagascar, Ceylon and Burma. I would not meet him again until nearly the end of the war. At last the great day of his return came. I was by now three years old. We stood on the platform of Nairobi station watching the long troop train pull in, belching clouds of steam after its long climb from the coast. Hundreds of men in khaki uniform began to spill out. Then one detached himself from the crowd, and took the liberty of embracing my mother, and hugging Dennis and me. As the Unknown Man in khaki drove us home I whispered to my mother, 'Mummy, who that man who come in chuff chuff?' It took a while to make up for those early years of absence.

Eric and Ruby were able to make a short visit to Marsabit. They were greatly encouraged by all that they found. The Christians had taken it on themselves to build a new, larger mud and thatch church. It had cost them five hundred shillings, which they had raised amongst themselves – a lot of money in those days. More important than the building, the Church had grown. Eric baptised eight adults, and nine children from Christian homes. Twelve others stood up in church to make a profession of faith. Stephen Dere, one of the church elders, was that day, by permission of the bishop, licensed as a Lay Reader. The Church in Marsabit was alive and well, and growing.

War ended with the surrender of Japan on 14 August 1945. It was nine years since Eric had last had home leave, and Ruby had not been back to Britain since their wedding. But all ships to England were heavily booked, and it was not until late 1946 that we obtained passage on the SS *Cameronia*. It was a troop ship, packed to capacity. The men all slept in hammocks slung in every available space. Ruby, Dennis and I were in a crowded cabin, shared with another family. The Red Sea, Suez and Mediterranean had not yet been cleared of mines, and we had two close encounters. There were regular lifeboat drills. I recollect docking at night at Genoa next to the Queen Mary (also drafted as a troop ship), and looking up and up at her lights, and being overawed by her immensity. We arrived to a drab, post-war Britain, with its bomb sites and rationing, and the severe winter of 1946–47. A high-light was two precious weeks, when Uncle Harold and family from the Arctic, my Aunt Edith from Kenya, and ourselves were all staying at Eric's parents at the same time – the only time after 1928 that brothers Harold and Eric ever met again. We were in England for Eric's sister, Ella's, wedding – and she was advised against having me as a page boy because of my unpredictability. (I was reputed for my moodiness and stubbornness, and was very likely to turn my back on the cameras). We spent much of that bitter winter with Ruby's parents, Fred and Rosa Bloor, in the Derbyshire hills, in the pretty village of Bonsall. Each morning we had to dig ourselves out of Alpine Cottage, tunnelling through the snowdrifts which built up against the front door. That was my overriding memory of Britain, and what, throughout my childhood, I thought normal winters in Britain are like. I also have memories of my mother's much loved Derbyshire in the spring and summer – of bluebell woods and meadows of cowslips; of

Dovedale, and jumping its famous stepping stones; of Blue John cavern, and an underground boat trip in Speedwell, the walls of the old lead mine lined with flickering candles. These were the memories of England that I took back to Kenya, on the Llangibby Castle, in 1947.

I was now six years old, and it was time for some serious schooling. Dennis and I started together as boarders at Nairobi Primary School in January 1948. It was a Government school for white children, in those pre-independence days of segregated education. Our parents drove us down to Nanyuki, at railhead, and there we joined other white children, mostly the sons of settler farmers from the Nanyuki area, on the school train. Once settled into our bunks on the train, under the supervision of a teacher, the novelty of the journey began to wear off, and the truth began to dawn. The regime at Nairobi Primary School was marginally friendlier than a modern-day boot camp. I found myself in a dormitory with twenty other little boys, and a dormitory matron who would have done well on the staff of a boot camp. Miss E. was a sadist. The smallest infringement of the rules – such as talking after lights-out, an untidy bedside locker, or being heard to be crying under the blankets at night – was rewarded with a beating with a gym shoe. More serious offences, such as swearing, earned a caning from the housemaster. I spent many a night, tucked in the privacy of my mosquito net, stifling my sobs as I longed for home. The school was set on a hillside overlooking Nairobi, and sometimes at night I would gaze from the toilet window onto the lights of the town, and listen to the plaintive whistles of the steam trains down at Nairobi station, and long to catch one back to Nanyuki and home. In those early days the one glimmer of kindness was from Ma Simpy, the catering matron. She was a tiny, white-haired lady with a huge heart of love. After 'little boys' supper' she would line us up, and give us each a goodnight kiss – a moment of physical contact that was not hostile, a gesture of love that I treasured. Half way through that first term, our parents came down from Marsabit for meetings and supplies, and visited us. I was so happy to see them, but very homesick, and had to be prised off my mother when it was time for them to go.

It was not all bad at Nairobi Primary School, and in due course my homesickness grew less. My strongest memories are of Saturdays, when we were free to roam the school playing fields in the hot sun, in our shorts and regulation felt hats. My friends and I played endless games of Cowboys and Indians; we built dens, and played dinkies and marbles; we scrumped loquats from the garden of a neighbouring house; and we taunted large hairy baboon spiders by poking grass stalks down their holes. I developed a great interest in ants, and spent hours lying on my stomach studying their habits, and watching them dismember grasshoppers in order to carry the parts down into their ant holes. At the age of seven I wrote an account of my observations, and produced a little book called (appropriately) *Ants*. I kept ant lions and baboon spiders in tins in my bedside locker. On Sundays we filed in a long crocodile down the hill to All Saints Cathedral for morning service. Sunday afternoons were taken up with Crusaders, run by a saintly little Scotsman, Mr Craig, who called us his 'jewels'. On Sunday evenings we had evensong in the school hall, and the poetry of Cranmer's 1662 liturgy became engraved on my soul. 'Lighten our darkness we beseech Thee O Lord . . . '

We regarded our journey between Marsabit and school in Nairobi, at the beginning and end of every term, as an adventure. We often camped somewhere in the bush between Marsabit and Isiolo. We would put up our camp beds next to the car, and sleep under the stars. On one occasion we found ourselves surrounded, in the dark, by a herd of elephants. Never was the car repacked so rapidly. Sometimes as we travelled to Marsabit we would see ahead a large, black cloud, low and swirling. As we hit the cloud, and entered it, the sun would be blotted out, and the windscreen became an orange-yellow mess of wings and legs. Locusts! Those were the days of vast swarms of locusts, which bred in the Arabian peninsular or Somaliland and then headed southwest into Kenya, leaving a trail of total devastation. Sometimes our journey was blocked by floods on the desert, or a washed-away bridge. This was always welcome if it was on a journey to school, but most unwelcome if we were trying to get home for the holidays. Sometimes our parents took us to Nairobi, sometimes to railhead at Nanyuki. On occasion we were entrusted to the driver of a lorry. A memorable trip was on a sheep lorry. Dennis and I travelled in the cab, but our school trunks shared the back of the lorry with scores of sheep on their way to market. The trunks arrived at school plastered with a thick layer of sheep dung, and I recall being most unpopular as my trunk reposed at the foot of my bed while I unpacked it, filling the dormitory with the pungent smell of a farmyard. Sometimes we took with us to Nairobi an African assistant, and as often as not they had never travelled beyond Marsabit. They were astonished by such mundane things as tarmac roads, electric lights, traffic and traffic lights, and, above all, lifts. To step into a small room, and then step out moments later to find yourself high in the sky, was a cause for much clicking of the tongue. On one occasion we found our companion helpless with laughter outside a clothes shop. 'I have been watching those *memsahibs* and *bwanas* in the window', he said. 'And they are standing so still! They haven't moved at all!'

A highlight for Kenya in 1952 was the royal visit by Princess Elizabeth and the Duke of Edinburgh. The royal party stayed with the Governor at his residence just across the road from our school. On Sunday 4 February the Princess and Duke set out from Government House to stay at Sagana Lodge to the north – a hunting lodge in the Aberdare Forest given to them as a wedding present by the people of Kenya. Ruby was down in Nairobi from Marsabit, and she and we joined the crowds outside Government house to wave to the royal couple as they set out on their journey. Two days later I was in a Latin lesson with the Headmaster, the Reverend Barton, when a grave-faced boy came in with a message for him. We overheard the words. 'Please sir! The King is dead!' King George VI, already ill with lung cancer, had died in his sleep from a thrombosis. At the same time his daughter was viewing game in Treetops Hotel, near Sagana. Thus she became the only British sovereign to accede to the throne while in a tree. The news reached Sagana Lodge next day via the press, and it fell to the Duke to break the news to her, and that she was now Queen of Great Britain and her Dominions. The Kenya visit was cut short.

My missionary parents lived on a shoestring. We could not afford 'proper' holidays. Then, in 1952, a British farmer at Timau, on the slopes of Mount Kenya, offered us the free use of their farmhouse for a holiday, if we would keep an eye on the farm. That was a blissful time – pony riding, wandering free over the vast farm, damming streams, helping to dip the sheep. The only slightly troubling factor was the rather unfriendly attitude of the African farm supervisor. It was the following term, on the evening of 21 October, that a message came round the dormitories at bath time. We were all to assemble in the common room. The austere headmaster, the Reverend Barton, was there himself to announce to us, in solemn tones, that a State of Emergency had been declared by the new Governor of Kenya, Sir Evelyn Baring. A seditious and violent Kikuyu organisation called Mau Mau, whose aim was to expel all whites from Kenya, had been uncovered, we were told. Its ringleader, Jomo Kenyatta, had been arrested under emergency powers that very day. A new set of school rules was announced to comply with the emergency situation. We were not allowed out of the boarding houses after dark. We must at all times move around the school compound in groups of no less than five. Leave-outs and shopping trips were to be restricted.

Marsabit was safely remote from the tensions and violence that central Kenya was experiencing. But driving through Kikuyu country, to and from northern Kenya, there was always a feeling of apprehension. Cars were ambushed (on one occasion my parents very nearly met an ambush, but a last minute decision took them by another route). We never stopped the car while in Kikuyu country, and took care never to drive there after dark. Most Europeans carried guns at all times, although my father refused to on principle. One of the first outbreaks of violence by Mau Mau occurred on the farm adjacent to the one where we had stayed at Timau. It turned out that the farm supervisor on our farm, who had been unfriendly to us, was a Mau Mau oath administrator, recruiting members throughout the time we were there. There was a fear in the land. White settlers were savagely hacked to death, including the father of a boy at our school. One of our fellow pupils was murdered. But the suffering of whites was as nothing compared with that of those Kikuyu people who opposed Mau Mau, and who refused to be oathed. It was Christians who suffered most.

But in Marsabit there was none of this. Dennis and I roamed free and bare foot during school holidays, with our band of African friends – Luka, the son of blind evangelist Daudi Dadaca; Elisha son of Danieli; Solomon and Daniel, sons of Daudi Danabo who had died on the operating table; Mattayo son of Yonah; and Ali, a Muslim who was later baptised Kenneth. We played soldiers, and built ourselves a mud headquarters. We built tree houses, and a raft to float on the small dam in a nearby valley in the forest. Our parents treated our friends as part of the family – something quite unusual in those days of racial segregation. Dennis and I put on plays to entertain our parents, and conjuring shows to astound our African friends. We also played 'church', Dennis always the preacher, and I the congregation. At the end of each blissful day it was into the tin bath, and a wash down with water heated in a kerosene tin on the wood-burning Dover stove. Then a session around the hissing pressure lamp as, with safety pins, we dug jigger fleas from our toes, and roasted them on the hot lamp.

In 1949 a much longed for sister, Marilyn, was born. Ruby had miscarried on hearing news of her mother's death in England, and it was some time until Marilyn came along. When old enough she attended our mother's school. She spoke Borana fluently as a small child. Another addition to our family was a baby baboon. It's mother had been speared, and the baby was found clinging to her back. We named her Daigo, after the man who brought her to us. She lived for much of the time in the roof of our verandah, where she would scamper up and down, her tail, like a length of ragged rope, dangling over the edge of the verandah ceiling. It was Christmas, and as was the custom at Christmas and Easter, Eric conducted a service in English for the British Government officials. It was held in our sitting room, which had a polished cement floor. Ruby played the harmonium for the service, and on this occasion had placed the harmonium on a mat on the polished floor. Her chair was not on the mat. She was broadside on to the congregation, with Eric, in his robes, conducting the communion service from the sideboard. As Ruby started to pedal away for the first hymn the harmonium began to slide away from her. Between verses she had to pull her chair forward to catch up with it. It was a long hymn, and she was steadily advancing across the room between the congregation and the sideboard. Meanwhile Daigo (of whose presence the District Commissioner and other officials were unaware) chose to hang her ropy tail over the ceiling, and to parade up and down. The congregation was mesmerised. In front of them the organist was moving steadily across the room. To the side of them a piece of rope with a life of its own was moving backwards and forwards along the edge of the ceiling. It was a Christmas service to remember.

In 1953 I joined Dennis at one of the two secondary schools for white boys, the Prince of Wales School, Nairobi. Junior House was a wooden ex-army construction, very vulnerable to arson. By then the Mau Mau emergency was at its height. Threats had been made to boarding schools for white children. We spent the games periods of our first term building a protective mud wall around the boarding house. On the outside of the mud wall a barbed wire fence was erected, and adjacent to each boarding house a watchtower was constructed. These were manned at night by armed guards. The same rules applied as at primary school – no leaving the school compound, no going about after dark, always walking in groups of five. Cross-country racing was discontinued after a boy was attacked in a coffee plantation. Our teachers wore revolvers at their waists at all times, and senior boys were given weapons training. At night we lay with our crystal sets tuned to the nearby radio broadcasting station, to catch the latest news. But it was not only Mau Mau fighters who posed a threat – there was a degree of violence from fellow pupils within the school. Bullying was rife, and during that first year my fellow juniors and I experienced some intense sadism from one prefect in particular – a boy who found himself in prison soon after leaving school.

The saying goes that God has many children, but no grandchildren. To be a Christian is not to do with genes and background, but with 'rebirth'. If it was to do with genes then I had little chance of being anything else – I came from a strongly Christian background, for which I am eternally grateful. This provided a fertile environment, but it did not automatically make me a Christian. Of course we had school services, and I joined Crusaders because I knew that would please my parents. Even better, one got an excellent tea at Crusaders, which was a serious consideration in the light of school food. (The Nairobi Crusader class was the largest in the world, and was run by three wonderful, dedicated Nairobi doctors – Jarvis, Winteler and Calcott). But being a Crusader did not make me a Christian either. It was all a matter of going through the motions, without any real commitment to Christ. Then, in 1954, our outstanding

Headmaster, Philip Fletcher, himself a devout Christian, announced that there was going to be a series of voluntary 'special meetings' with a local vicar, the Reverend Silberbauer, talking about Christianity. Our school chaplain (who had been Eric's Best Man) encouraged us to go. I went. And I found, as John Wesley put it, 'my heart was strangely warmed within me'. The speaker was not particularly charismatic or persuasive. There was no stirring of artificial emotions. What he had to say was nothing new. But it came to me in a new way. This Jesus Christ, whose name had so often and so glibly fallen from my lips – what did He really mean to me? Did I truly know Him – or did I just know about Him? Was my Christianity first hand or second hand? Had my head knowledge ever done the 'twelve inch drop' and become 'heart' knowledge? Was I a child of God, or just a grandchild? I responded to the Reverend Silberbauer's invitation to meet him privately one afternoon. And there, on my knees in the Headmaster's study, I experienced for the first time that indescribable elation and sense of peace and of God's presence that comes when you open up your heart and life to Him. As I walked back to the dormitory I knew that life would never be the same again. Telling my friends about what had happened was a challenge, and there was the inevitable derision: 'Webby's gone religious!' I felt I must kneel at my bedside to pray after lights out, and this invited a hail of well-aimed shoes. I tried to take it in good part, and by the end of that term eight of us from my dormitory were meeting each week in the housemaster's flat to pray and (in our amateurish way) study the Bible together. I had said 'Yes!' to God, and I felt that, from that day onwards, my life was His.

Caleb

Gertrude

Ruby

Eric

Roadside repairs on the way to Marsabit

Eric, Charles Scudder and Funga Funga
at their first camp site at Marsabit

Eric's first house

Eric on return from Chalbe safari

Karantina mission

The wooden house

Ruby and Eric setting out on safari

Blind Daudi Dadacha, evangelist

Myself with a friend

The family on leave in England, 1947

My childhood home built by Eric

Elisha, Solomon and Daniel

The Prince of Wales School, Nairobi

Our last time together as a family in Nairobi, 1960

St Thomas's Hospital

Dr and Mrs Bennett with medical students at MMA Hostel.
I am in the third row, third from the left.

Rosemary at the time of our engagement

Our wedding day

Chapter 4
A BUDDING DOCTOR

For as long as I could remember I had wanted to be a doctor. There were no doctors in the family, although my father would have loved to study medicine if he had not had to leave school so young, and if his parents could have afforded it. My decision to be a doctor was made at the tender age of four. My mother was admitted to hospital, and children were not allowed to visit. I decided there and then that if you can't beat a system join it. I remember telling my mother that one day I would be a doctor, and then I would be able to visit her in hospital every day, and take her grapes. Such was the profound reason that motivated me to study medicine. Once made, I never questioned the decision for a moment. I never contemplated any other career. My six years at the Prince of Wales School were much happier than those at Nairobi Primary School. I did well academically, but my best subjects were the arts rather than the sciences. I did not excel in games but I redeemed myself on the rifle range. We had a school .22 range, and we went further afield for .303 shooting. This was my sort of sport. I won the cup for best shot in the school, and captained the school team which won the Kenya Interschools Shooting Competition.

In 1956, the year I sat the Cambridge School Certificate examinations, Eric was asked by his old friend Leonard Beecher, now a bishop, to leave his mission work at Marsabit and to take up the post of senior chaplain to the Kenya Prisons Department. The Mau Mau uprising had virtually ended, and there were forty thousand Mau Mau detainees in camps. There was also the usual population of civilian prisoners. But there was no chaplaincy work in the camps or prisons. It was seen by the Church as an urgent priority to set up a chaplaincy service, with a minister or evangelist in every camp and prison. Eric was considered to be the person to organise this. It meant painful farewells, after twenty five years, to the people of Marsabit, and a move to the suburbs of Nairobi. It proved to be a huge undertaking for Eric. There was an active programme of rehabilitation for Mau Mau detainees, and it was important that the scars left by the obscene and cruel rituals of Mau Mau, and the violence that had been perpetrated, should be healed. The Christian Gospel had much to offer. Over a period of time Eric installed some outstanding clergy and Church Army workers in the prisons and camps. Two particular responsibilities he felt very much to be his, as Senior Chaplain. One was to spend time with prisoners who had been condemned to death, and then to be present with them before and at their execution. Eric was a gentle person, opposed to violence in any form, and this aspect of his work wreaked a heavy toll on him emotionally. He would leave for the prison the evening before the execution, and spend the night there, returning home shattered after the dawn hanging. I believe his subsequent illness arose from this stress.

The other responsibility which Eric felt to be his was to visit the alleged leader of Mau Mau, Jomo Kenyatta, in prison at Lokitaung, in the deserts of the far northwest of Kenya. Eric made two official visits to Lokitaung. The first was in January 1957. Eric did not find Kenyatta to be the monster that he had been led, by propaganda, to expect. Instead Kenyatta was friendly and receptive, and showed an intelligent interest in spiritual matters. Eric warmed to him. Another Mau Mau leader in detention there, 'General' China, was also friendly. The other leading prisoners were hostile, and refused to see him. In August 1957 Eric made the second visit. On this occasion he took with him Bishop Obadiah Kariuki, who like Kenyatta and the other prisoners, was Kikuyu. He was in fact distantly related to Kenyatta. Bishop Obadiah was a gentle and deeply spiritual man, the first African Anglican priest to be consecrated bishop. He had shown enormous courage during the atrocities of the Mau Mau uprising. Kenyatta was delighted to see Bishop Obadiah, and was moved to know that many were praying for him. Kenyatta had a long discussion about the Christian faith, he was glad for Bishop Obadiah and Eric to pray with him, and he accepted the gift of a Bible, which he resolved to read from cover to cover. Eric was convinced that Kenyatta had a transforming spiritual experience while at Lokitaung, and this would seem to be confirmed by Kenyatta's biographer, Jeremy Murray-Brown. Certainly Kenyatta emerged from his imprisonment without any bitterness, and determined that Kenya should be a multiracial and harmonious society. Who knows how much Kenya's stability under Kenyatta's presidency was owed to what happened at Lokitaung?

Once my parents were settled in Nairobi, our new house being only three miles from the school, I realised how much I wanted to spend some time living at home. Eric had been absent for most of the war years; I had boarded at school since the age of six; and at seventeen I would be off to England, hopefully to study medicine, and would then see my parents only very occasionally. Dennis had already gone to England, to study English at Cambridge, and it had made me realise what a final sort of departure that had been. Air travel was then not so cheap and easy as it is now. Much to my Housemaster's disapproval I became a day boarder for my last year at school – he had had me lined up to be Head of House. I also found myself in conflict with my esteemed Headmaster, Philip Fletcher. He wanted me to do arts subjects for Higher School Certificate, as these were my best subjects. I wanted to do science for the simple reason that I hoped to study medicine. He tried to dissuade me, but my mind was made up – there was no other career that I was prepared even to contemplate. When he realised that I was determined he supported me to the hilt, and before long, and on the basis of his recommendation, I was offered a provisional place at St Thomas's Hospital, London. I finished my Cambridge Higher School Certificate examinations in December 1958, and a week later left for London.

My Aunt Edith had returned from leave in England to her work among the Samburu people shortly before I departed. She was most concerned that I would not survive the cold in London. It would be my first time to visit England since 1947. I was not acclimatised. She thoughtfully brought me from England two pairs of long, woolly combinations. I had never seen such items of clothing, and had never imagined that men with any sort of self-esteem wore such things. But I heeded her advice about the perils of death from hypothermia. I had never flown before either, and did not know how practical it would be to don such clothing on the plane. I decided to put it on before leaving home. Saying goodbye to my parents and Marilyn at Nairobi airport was not easy. We had no idea when we would next meet. I was a naïve seventeen year old, setting off to a strange and distant land, and to a new life at medical school.

That day we got no further than Entebbe airport, in Uganda. The plane, a Constellation, broke down, and we were taken to a hotel in Kampala, twenty miles away, for the night. The next day the plane was still undergoing repairs. We were taken for a tour of the tombs of the Kabakas in Kampala. It was December, the hottest time of the year, and I was still wearing the life-saving combinations supplied by Aunt Edith. As we traipsed round the tombs I got hotter and hotter. The thick material pricked and itched. Finally I could stand it no more. With my last cents I bought a newspaper, found a public toilet, and removed my precious underwear, wrapping it in the newspaper. I arrived the next day at Heathrow, at the Nissen hut which then served as the Africa Terminal, with my underwear under my arm, wrapped in The East African Standard. Contrary to Aunt Edith's predictions, I survived the cold.

It was not the cold but the smog which shocked me. As our plane had approached London I was agreeably surprised by the blue sky and bright sunshine. England could not be that bad after all. It did not occur to me that below us was an ominously unbroken layer of cloud. As we descended to land we entered a thick, yellow-grey blanket – and I did not see the sun again for many days. In those early days in London I could not understand how human beings survived there. The constant smog was not only all-enveloping and choking – it was also filthy. The collars of my shirts were black by the end of the day. Nor could I understand why everyone seemed so unfriendly. In the twilight world of the Underground people sat staring blankly ahead, their heads rocking to the motion of the train. Nobody greeted anybody, nobody spoke, as they would have done in Kenya. People seemed to be moving like zombies in their private worlds, hurrying here and there. Who were they all, I wondered; and where were they going; and what were they doing? So many people, and, to my surprise, so many black faces. I was tempted to greet them in Swahili – it was probably as well that I did not! It was not until four months later – when the Spring came, and the warmth brought out nodding daffodils in profusion, and the trees in the London parks were weighed down with blossom, and the scent of wallflowers filled the air – it was not until then that I realised that England was not only survivable; it was incredibly beautiful.

For the next six years I lived at a hostel in Bedford Place, run by the Medical Missionary Association. There were twenty four of us, all male, all medical students at different London medical schools, and many either (like me) the sons of missionaries or themselves prospective medical missionaries. It was a very happy place to be, especially for a student like me, so far from home. There was warmth and friendship and fun. There was also a very strong work ethic, and we helped and encouraged one another in the long and demanding medical course. The warden, Dr Bennett, was a former missionary doctor in Uganda. Until my arrival he and his wife, when they wanted to communicate confidentially at mealtimes, would speak to one another in Swahili. Before long they realised that I understood exactly what they were saying, and that put a stop to that. I spent my first months in London studying at a rather seedy crammers, Borlands, behind Victoria Station. At the Prince of Wales I had studied biology, but St Thomas's required an A-level in zoology, which I now acquired. Meanwhile I made myself known to the medical school secretary at St Thomas's, Dr Crockford. As I walked over Westminster Bridge for the first time – with St Thomas's Hospital stretched along the embankment before me, and facing it across the River Thames the Houses of Parliament – and then along Lambeth Palace Road, I could not believe that it was for real. My dreams had come true. Here I was at what was to me the centre of the world. An exciting but daunting future lay ahead. I felt an enormous sense of privilege, of trepidation, of anticipation, and of thanks to God that I, a bush kid, had come to this. I also felt a deep sense of gratitude to my parents for their encouragement all along the way.

In October 1959 I started my medical training. It was a baptism of fire. The professor of anatomy, Professor Dai Davies, a taciturn Welshman, explained to us that the party was over. Life was going to consist of work, grind and sweat for the foreseeable future. And so it did. We nervously approached the bodies we were to dissect – for most of us the first dead bodies we had ever seen. And with those first tentative incisions of the scalpel our medical careers began. The next eighteen months, leading up to the Second M.B. examinations in anatomy, physiology and biochemistry, were sheer hard graft. One wondered when medical students had the time to get up to all the pranks for which they were reputed. We sat our gruelling examinations to the timing of Big Ben, and it was a relief to get that part of the course over. We could now turn from shrivelled bodies preserved in formalin to real people.

Before starting Clinical Medicine there was our last long summer vacation to enjoy. In that summer of 1960 Dennis and I returned home to Kenya. It was a shock to see our father. Our mother had warned us in letters that he was becoming very slow and absent minded. Though only fifty-five years old he looked seventy. He had become white-haired and stooped, and quite forgetful. Nevertheless we had a wonderful family holiday, including a whole month on the coast at a remote location south of Mombasa, exploring the reef and snorkelling. I returned to St Thomas's eager to start on the wards.

Three full and happy years, 1961–64, followed. Each discipline of medicine was equally fascinating, and I resolved in turn to specialise in almost every branch of medicine that we studied – which is probably why I ended up as a general practitioner. I remember the long, open, airy Nightingale wards, looking on to the river and the Houses of Parliament. I recall ward rounds with awesome consultants, some of whom considered themselves to be somewhere above God in the pecking order. I remember even more awesome ward Sisters, in whose presence even the consultants trod warily – and to whom we medical students were insignificant irritants. I remember my first patients, and the nervousness with which I approached them, and the diffidence with which I asked them to remove clothing to be examined. They were so long-suffering, and often went out of their way to put me at ease. They also taught me quite a lot about their own illnesses. I remember 9 p.m. on the wards. A hush would fall, as the chimes of Big Ben rang out across the river. The ward sister and nurses, in their frilly Nightingale caps, would kneel around the central desk in the ward, and evening prayers would be said. 'Lighten our darkness we beseech Thee O Lord . . .' My mind would go back to Evensong at Nairobi Primary School, and in All Saints Cathedral. Across time, and across continents, we were once again gathering up the day before God. Sadly the relentless march of secularism did away with the St Thomas's tradition of ward prayers soon after my time there.

The quickest way to get around London, in particular from my hostel in Bedford Place to St Thomas's, was by bicycle. A departing student bequeathed me his bicycle, which I named 'George' after him. George was an entirely unpredictable velocipede. It had four main faults – it steered constantly to the right (causing the rider to have to steer constantly to the left); the back wheel was slightly oval in shape (giving rise to a gentle undulating motion); the right pedal was bent outwards (causing the right foot to be inverted); and it had no brakes (compensated for by a foot on the back wheel). I would ride George at speed, down Kingsway, around Aldwych and over Waterloo Bridge, weaving in and out of the London traffic, my skeleton or medical kit strapped to the carrier. It took me just eleven minutes to get from hostel to hospital. On one memorable occasion I was returning to St Thomas's from a gynaecology clinic at the Women's Hospital in Westminster. I was late for a lecture. As I sped through Parliament Square a very thoughtless traffic policeman raised his hand to stop the stream of traffic. Now George could not cope with sudden changes of plan. Some advance warning was needed. Still rising gracefully up and down in the saddle, and steering to the left, I took my foot off the bent pedal and jammed it hard on to the rear wheel. We eventually came to a juddering halt in no-man's land. The policeman stopped the traffic in every direction, and advanced ominously towards me. I had brought the centre of London to a halt. The policeman stood before me and eyed me up and down. I smiled weakly at him. Then he said, 'It's Webster isn't it?' My heart missed a beat. Was I that notorious? He continued: 'Prince of Wales School, Nairobi? Don't you remember me?' And then I did. He looked very different in uniform and helmet from school shorts and shirt. While the traffic waited we had a hurried reminiscence, exchanged telephone numbers, then he waved me on. 'By the way, get your brakes fixed!' he called after me.

In the summer of 1962 I flew home to Nairobi again, for a short holiday and to celebrate my twenty-first birthday. That birthday was memorable, not for any celebration, but because on that day Eric was diagnosed as having Parkinson's disease with also a degree of pre-senile dementia – a combination of diagnoses that nowadays would probably be called Lewi Body dementia. He had become increasingly unable to care for himself, needing help with dressing and washing. He was still working at prison headquarters, but he was struggling – and having a succession of minor accidents with the car. He was fifty-six years old. Medication for the Parkinson's disease was commenced, but the outlook was worrying. I was also concerned about Ruby. Soon after Marilyn's birth in 1949 she had had a mastectomy for breast cancer. In 1956 she had had recurrence in her neck glands, and had flown to England for treatment at the Royal Marsden Hospital in London. Now again she was experiencing pain, possibly exacerbated by lifting Eric. I returned to England deeply worried about both of them.

Chapter 5
GAIN AND LOSS

In the spring of 1962, shortly before my visit to Kenya, an event occurred which was to have a profound effect on my life. The combined St Thomas's Hospital Christian Unions (student medics, physiotherapists and nurses) held their annual house party at Ashburnham Place in Sussex. Our missionary speaker that year was a former St Thomas's student, Dr Peter Cox. He was working at a remote bush hospital at Amudat, in northeast Uganda. I knew quite a lot about him – in fact we had met briefly at Nairobi Cathedral in 1958, at about the time of his marriage to Liza, and just before I departed for England. As a Christian Union we had supported his work with prayer, and also with a supply of refurbished surgical instruments which we rescued from the bins of St Thomas's operating theatres. Peter spoke to us that weekend about his work. As talks go it was chaotic. He put slides in upside down, and without a thought displayed pictures of naked tribes people that even medics found embarrassing. But his story was gripping, and he challenged us all to consider serving God in a rural hospital in the third world. I had long since made up my mind that, whatever I did with my life, it would not be as a missionary. I had seen too much of my parents' struggle to live on a pittance. I was not averse to going back to Africa, but it would have to be in government or private work. Or so I had decided until that weekend at Ashburnham Place. As I listened to Peter Cox I felt a growing conviction that this was what God wanted of me – to work in a rural hospital, as a missionary doctor. A 'calling' is difficult to explain. It was a deep, inner sense of purpose; of having been shown the way ahead; of having been spoken to by God. It was accompanied by an inner excitement and yet of peace. Certainly it was a conviction that I could not duck or suppress, and I left Ashburnham with a very different idea about my future from that with which I had come.

A year later we were back at Ashburnham Place. In order to reduce the cost of our Christian Union house party we had all agreed to do some work on the buildings and grounds. A pretty and vivacious physiotherapy student, Rosemary Roundhill, and I were allocated a rose bed to weed. Not a lot of weeding got done. It was love at first sight. Over the following weeks, as our friendship grew, it became apparent to us both that this was 'it'. But Rosemary came from a sheltered background, from a comfortable home in leafy Surrey, where her father owned a motor business. As marriage became a real possibility I was afraid that if I were to tell her about my calling to be a missionary in the African bush she might be well and truly put off. For a while I said nothing, but when I did finally bite the bullet Rosemary revealed to me that she too had felt a similar calling at the very same meeting at which Peter Cox had spoken the previous year. She, like me, had not mentioned it in case it put me off. That mutual sense of vocation, given to each of us in the same room, at the same time, but quite independently, and a year before we met, stood us in good stead at difficult times in the years ahead. After all, God couldn't have got it wrong twice.

During that summer of 1963 my father decided to fly to England to seek treatment for his worsening condition. He was no longer fit to do his Prisons Chaplaincy work, and my mother and fourteen year old Marilyn were having to do more and more for him. His departure for England was at very short notice. Rosemary came with me to meet him in at Heathrow. He was a heartbreaking sight – a white-haired, hunched figure in a wheelchair, able only to speak in a whisper. It was hard to believe that he was only fifty-eight years old. We had discovered a last-minute problem – having left the missionary society, BCMS, for his prisons work he no longer qualified for treatment on the National Health Service. St Luke's Hospital for Clergy in London came magnificently to our rescue, and a consultant neurologist at St Thomas's, Dr Kelly, generously saw him for free. The conclusion, as we feared, was that no treatment was possible. My father had set his hopes on some form of brain surgery, and he was very disheartened. It cheered him when the Reverend John Stott, rector of my church, nearby All Souls Langham Place, visited him and prayed with him. He was subsequently moved to a nursing home for clergy, Manormead, at Hindhead in Surrey. There he shared a crowded room with three other very elderly and confused clergymen, and he was desperately lonely and unhappy. He kept asking for Ruby, and he also wanted the scripts of the Borana translation of the Bible, which he had been working on, to be sent from Kenya – a task that was by now clearly beyond him. Ruby and Marilyn were meanwhile packing up at the Kenya end, and they sailed to England that autumn. We found them an ideal little cottage in nearby Farnham, from where they could visit Eric daily.

I proposed to Rosemary in style, on one knee, that August, and to my great joy she said 'Of course!' We did not announce our engagement at the time, as some might have thought it too soon into our friendship. But we met regularly during our lunch breaks on the embankment in front of St Thomas's, or, if wet, in a quiet part of the hospital corridor. There Rosemary was observed one day by the Principal of the Physiotherapy School. For a student physiotherapist to be seen actually talking to a medical student was an appalling breach of etiquette and decency! Rosemary was summoned to the principal's office, and was given a severe telling off. I leapt to her defence, and wrote a fairly blunt letter to the Principal. We decided that we had better announce our engagement sooner rather than later. Eric's deterioration was another reason for doing so. So it was that on Boxing Day we told our families. With difficulty Eric mouthed the words, 'This is an auspicious occasion!' He died a few days later, on 2 January 1964, and we laid him to rest in the lovely churchyard in Hindhead, high above the Devil's Punchbowl.

I qualified, aged twenty-three, in June 1964, and drove straight down to Farnham to tell my mother, and also her father, Fred Bloor, who was visiting. It was a proud day. Rosemary qualified as a physiotherapist soon afterwards. We were married in St Giles Church, Ashtead, on 19 September. We spent the first night of our honeymoon at the Hind's Head Hotel in Bray. It had not at that time achieved its current fame, as a place where royalty and celebrities dine, though I would like to think that our stay there helped it on its way to fame. We continued our honeymoon on a small cabin cruiser, Ma Cherie, on the River Thames, chugging up-river from Bray to Lechlade and back over the course of a fortnight. We experienced perfect autumn weather – the early mists over the water, the warm sunshine breaking through, the rich autumn colours of the trees along the river banks. It was a blissfully happy time.

Then we came back to reality. At that time very few hospitals in Britain provided married accommodation for Housemen. At St Thomas's even the spouses of resident Housemen had to be out of the building by 10 p.m. We had no intention of starting our married life in this way, and I applied to a hospital which did provide flats for couples – Swindon. My first eight months was as a house surgeon in Swindon's old Victoria Hospital. It was slave labour. I worked (or was on call – which was much the same thing) for one hundred and ten hours a week, and was paid eight pounds a week (less than a hospital porter). It was considered a privilege to be a Houseman. I was there to learn, and to gain experience – and that I most certainly did, under the guidance of the Registrar. I then moved to the brand-new, state of the art, Princess Margaret Hospital to do six months as a house physician, and that was followed by a year of obstetrics and gynaecology at the Kent Road Maternity Hospital. My consultant there, Mr 'Dad' Rowarth, was quite eccentric. In the event of an obstetric emergency he would cycle in to hospital from his nearby home in his carpet slippers. If an anaesthetic was called for he delighted in beating the anaesthetist to it. He would prepare the patient for theatre, and only then call the anaesthetist. Meanwhile he, or I, would give the patient a spinal anaesthetic and start surgery. The aim was to have the baby out by the time the breathless anaesthetist arrived. 'Too late!' 'Dad' would boom. 'We couldn't wait!' By the time I left Swindon I had given several hundred spinal anaesthetics – invaluable experience later for Africa.

Two major family events occurred during our time at Swindon. At about the time of our wedding my mother's breast cancer had recurred again, this time in her spine and other bones. She hardly walked again after the wedding day, and she spent the last year of her life bed-bound. Marilyn, who was at school in Guildford, did most of the day-to-day care, returning from school not only to homework, but also to housework and nursing care. She was only fifteen years old. Neighbours were also very supportive. Never once did Ruby complain. Friends would visit to cheer her up, and instead find themselves being cheered up. People would call to discuss Ruby's problems and instead find their own problems being discussed. My days off were few and far between, but at every opportunity Rosemary and I drove to Farnham to visit and do what we could – as did Dennis and Priscilla, who by now were in a Curacy at Herne Bay in Kent. It was a stressful time for us all. Ruby died on 11 April 1966 after sustaining a pathological fracture of her femur. I was not there when she died because nobody was willing or able to cover my duty in the maternity hospital. On a bitterly cold, snowy day we laid her to rest with Eric at Hindhead. She was fifty-seven years old. The epitaph on Eric and Ruby's grave reads, 'They spent their life in missionary service', and the word 'spent' aptly describes the way in which they had given themselves totally to serve God and the people of Kenya.

The other major family event that year was the birth of our first child, Andrew, on 11 September. Before she died Ruby knew that both of her daughters-in-law were pregnant, but she did not live to see either grandchild. Andrew was born in the maternity ward adjacent to our hospital flat. 'Dad' Rowarth delivered him. 'Humph!' he said. 'Looks just like a poached egg! Just like his father!' Thus was heralded our precious son!

While my mother was ill and dying we could not make any definite plans to go abroad. But we began to explore possibilities, and in due course we applied to BCMS – the missionary society with which my parents had worked, and with which Peter Cox at Amudat was serving. We had to complete extensive and searching application forms. We had interviews, both with the BCMS General Council and with individual advisers. We were supposed to have thorough medical examinations. Our GP in Swindon scanned the forms sceptically, put a finger on Rosemary's pulse, and asked me to take my own. He then rapidly ticked the various questions without the tedium of further examination, and marked us both as being 'Exceptionally fit for service in the tropics.' Our acceptance by BCMS on health grounds was based on Rosemary's pulse. A plan began to emerge. We would go to Bristol, myself to Tyndale Hall Theological College (the very same where my father had trained for ordination) and Rosemary to Dalton House women's college (where Aunt Edith and my mother had trained), for six months of missionary training. We would then, after a short time of induction with Peter Cox at Amudat in Uganda, return to Marsabit, the place of my childhood in northern Kenya. There I would be seconded by BCMS to the Kenya

Ministry of Health as the District Medical Officer of Health. We were following in my parents' footsteps all the way.

In a way we were sad to leave Swindon. We had made many friends both in the hospital and at our church, St Mary's, Rodbourne Cheney. Our final departure was uneventful, but on a previous occasion, on my last day on the medical wards, the nurses had marked the occasion by dumping me – white coat, stethoscope and all – in a bath of cold water that they had prepared for me on the ward. Revenge was called for. I got the nurses in the Accident and Emergency Department to bandage my face. I then rang the medical ward and told the sister that I was admitting, from A&E, a man who had had a serious epileptic fit, and who had injured his face. A porter was called to wheel me up to the medical ward on a trolley. It so happened that the two consultants for whom I worked were waiting for the lift. Fortunately they did not recognise my heavily bandaged face, and clearly I was a medical priority. They stepped aside. The porter and I ascended to the medical ward. I had forgotten about visiting time. The lobby outside the ward was seething with visitors waiting for the ward doors to open. The crowd parted, glancing anxiously at me as I was wheeled into the ward. The nurses rolled me on to a bed they had prepared, and drew the curtains round. 'Page Dr Webster and tell him that his patient is here,' said the ward sister to a nurse. 'Meanwhile we'll get the man undressed.' Now that was something I had not bargained for. They began to undo my shirt. Clearly another fit was called for. I began to shake convulsively, and the nurses immediately stopped. The fit stopped. They tried again. Another fit. 'Draw up an injection of Paraldehyde,' ordered the sister. 'And bleep Dr Webster again. Tell him his patient keeps fitting.' While this was being done the nurses stood gazing down at me. By rolling me on to the bed the less bandaged side of my face had come uppermost. 'Funny thing!' said one of them 'But who does he remind you of?' 'He looks rather like Dr Webster!' said the other. I was overcome with another convulsion, but this time it was of laughter. 'It is Dr Webster!' they cried in chorus. I leapt from the bed, pursued by the two nurses, and fled down the ward, my bandages trailing – to the shock of patients and their visitors. The so recently moribund patient had made a most remarkable recovery. Staff and patients talked and laughed about it for some time afterwards, but I was given to understand that Matron, when she heard about it, was, like Queen Victoria, 'not amused'.

On 10 January 1967 our service with BCMS began with a pre-sailing conference – we and our fellow recruits were advised on such things as how to pack, what to take, culture shock, health in the tropics, and language study. We would sail from the London Docks to Mombasa in the autumn. The Reverend Stephen Houghton, who had succeeded my father in Marsabit, and who was an accomplished linguist, would give us Swahili lessons on the voyage. On 13 January Rosemary and I began our missionary training in Bristol. Andrew was by now a lively four month old, and Dalton House – under its rather daunting Principal, Miss Weeks – was not accustomed to small children. It was thanks to a rota of fellow student 'aunties' that Rosemary was able to participate in the course. Rosemary's course was relevant to Mission, mine at Tyndale Hall less so. In effect I did two terms of the three year ordinands' training. Church History and Liturgy were not my priorities. But there was also opportunity to study for the Bible Diploma, and to preach at local churches. This was preaching with a difference – a group of critical colleagues and a staff member formed the 'sermon class'. They would be in the congregation, and afterwards, over a cup of coffee, would analyse and pull to pieces the sermon. It was all very salutary, and good experience. I learned a lot from the Principal, the Reverend Stafford Wright (a contemporary of my father), and from the Reverends John Wenham, Colin Brown and Anthony Thistleton. I also studied, while at Tyndale Hall, for the Diploma in Obstetrics and Gynaecology (DRCOG), an exam which I passed that April.

A theological 'hot potato' at that time was the issue of 'Renewal' – baptism in the Holy Spirit and spiritual gifts. Christian leaders such as Michael Harper and David Watson were leading lights in the Renewal movement, which was influencing not only evangelicals, but all branches of the church. It was exciting, and bringing fresh spirituality and life into the church. Students at Tyndale Hall were divided over the issue, though the staff tended to take a conservative point of view. Rosemary and I tried to keep an open mind, and to be ready for whatever God wanted to give us.

A gift God did give us was the expectation of another baby. By March we realised that Rosemary would be due in November. We were, of course, delighted, but the situation was not without its problem – we were due to sail for Kenya in the autumn. Plans might have to change. We broke the news to the BCMS Home Secretary, Jim Seddon, who said philosophically, 'Ah well! Man proposes but God disposes!' Even Miss Weeks, whom Rosemary dreaded telling, took the news stoically. It was perhaps the first time in history that one of her 'girls' had got pregnant.

We left Bristol in early July. We were homeless, but Rosemary's parents had offered to put us up until such time as we left for Africa. This was generous of them, and convenient for us. But it was also a recipe for rising tension. I did locums for a local GP, and in A&E at Kingston Hospital. We attended the Keswick Convention. We had our Valedictory Service in London in September. But for much of the time we were in Ashtead, packing and preparing for our sailing. We were booked to sail on the BI *Kenya*, from the Royal Docks, on 6 October. (Significantly this would be thirty years to the day from when my mother sailed for Kenya, to join and marry my father.) We began to accumulate trunks and packing cases – we were planning to make our home in Marsabit for an indefinite period, and there was much to take. Some wedding presents had never been used. Into the trunks they went. We had been given the window sizes of what was to be our house in Marsabit, so there were curtains to be made. We tried to make ourselves useful to Rosemary's parents. But always there was a tension. It was understandable – they really did not comprehend our motivation for going to the wilds of Africa. The problem had come into the open when we sent them a copy of our first Prayer Letter from Bristol. The language in it, the concept of God's calling, of 'doing God's will', offended Rosemary's mother in particular. She contacted the friends who had offered to send out our Prayer Letters and asked them never ever to send them another. Rosemary's parents thought our plans to be foolhardy, irresponsible and lacking in any consideration for themselves. Their ideal for our future was a practice in England, with a good income and security. For me to take their pregnant daughter, let alone their small grandson, to a remote, hot, unhealthy, godforsaken spot in Africa, in order somehow to 'do good' to the native population, was sheer crassness. What was wrong with 'doing good' in our own country? It was, inevitably, my fault, my obsession, my influence on their daughter, which caused us to be doing this. More hurtful was the suggestion that we had waited for my parents to die before going, but that I did not care about my parents-in-law. Rosemary's mother often told her that she would never see her father again, as he was a sick man. (To an extent this was true, but there was no reason to think that he would die in the foreseeable future.) This was the constant, though often subtle, background to that time of waiting in Ashtead. Hurtful comments would often be made to Rosemary in my absence. She found it very hard, because in truth she did dread leaving her parents and homeland. I was returning to the land of my birth. For Rosemary it was a huge and rather scary step into the unknown.

The original plan was that we would sail via Suez, a voyage of three weeks. This would mean arriving in Kenya about three weeks before the baby was due. Special permission was required from BI, but it was granted on the grounds of my being a doctor with an Obstetric diploma. Then things began to go wrong. The Six Day War in June had led to the closure of the Suez Canal. We would have to take the longer Cape route. Still BI was agreeable for Rosemary to sail. Then in mid-September, with just three weeks to go, a dock strike began. At first it was thought that it would not affect our sailing, but with just one week to go the sailing was delayed by a week, and then on 4 October it was delayed indefinitely. Either we had to fly immediately, or wait until Rosemary had had the baby. For two reasons the latter was not acceptable – I was needed in Kenya; and the rising tension at home made the prospect of another two or three months in Ashtead difficult to contemplate. I went up to London, obtained cancellation bookings on an East African Airways flight for the very next day (10 October), and returned to Ashtead to break the news to Rosemary and her parents.

The situation was too hectic for much emotion. Cases had to be repacked to keep within the weight limit. There were visitors calling and hurried goodbyes to be said. Suddenly the time had come to depart for Heathrow. Rosemary's parents gave her a bunch of roses and violets, a precious reminder of England and of home. Our luggage, including all the accoutrements for Andrew, was overweight. Rosemary looked enormously pregnant, and I rather optimistically urged her to 'hold your tummy in', lest airline staff would consider her too pregnant to fly. But soon we were up and away, on an EAA VC10. Rosemary had never flown before, and was nervous, but the surge and comfort of the VC10 reassured her. We flew via Frankfurt and Rome, and arrived Nairobi the next morning. Archdeacon Robert McKemey, the BCMS Field Representative, was there to meet us. As he watched us stagger across the tarmac, laden with hand luggage, little Andrew's sleeping bag stuffed with surplus items, and Rosemary's tummy leading the way, he remarked in his warm Irish brogue that we looked like 'a couple of Christmas trees'. So a new phase of our life began – for me a coming home; for Rosemary a strange land, far from home. Exhausted, stressed, homesick, for her the last straw was when a customs officer took the precious bunch of roses and violets off her, and told her 'No flowers!' That last link with home and parents was tossed into a bin.

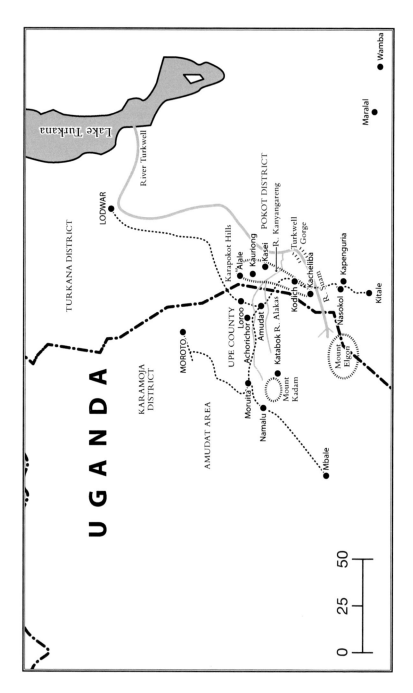

Chapter 6
CULTURE SHOCK

The one hundred mile journey from Nairobi to the McKemey's home in Nakuru was, for me, pure nostalgia. We ascended through the green, fertile Kikuyu uplands, past scattered villages on the hillsides, past roadside vendors of woven baskets and fruit and live rabbits, past *shambas* of maize and coffee, banana trees, and red, red soil. Then suddenly we were at the forested edge of the Great Rift Valley. Stretching from the Dead Sea in the north to central Africa, this two-thousand-foot-deep rift in the earth's surface is spectacular. As the road wound its way down the eastern escarpment we looked out over the vast plains of the valley base to the distant blue Mau escarpment on the western side of the valley. Between lay the dormant volcanic craters of Longonot and Suswa, and lakes Naivasha, Elementaita and Nakuru, teeming with bird life. I wanted Rosemary to see everything. I wanted her to fall in love with 'my' Kenya. But for much of the journey the poor exhausted soul slept. We stopped in Naivasha for refreshments at the Bell Hotel, and there to my delight was my godfather, Dr Reginald Bunny, former colleague of my father in Marsabit, and now the GP in Naivasha. Finally we reached Nakuru, where Robert and Cathy McKemey made us so welcome to their home, and immediately recognised our need of time and space to rest and acclimatise. Their house, on the slopes of Menengai crater, looked out over Lake Nakuru, with its shore-line of flat-topped yellow-green fever-thorn trees, and smudges of pink around the lake edge – vast flocks of flamingos in the shallow alkaline waters. For the next few days we unwound in the McKemey's garden, while Rosemary endured from me a tutorial on the garden plants of Kenya. We also got down to some serious Swahili study.

The plan had always been that we would go first to Amudat, in northeast Uganda, where I would spend two or three weeks with Dr Peter Cox, learning some tropical medicine and how to run a bush hospital. We would then return to Kenya, and proceed to Marsabit, where I would take up the post of Medical Officer of Health for the district. Our sea luggage had already been despatched to Marsabit. Events, however, began to take a different turn. Robert McKemey broke the news to us that Peter Cox was ill, and in hospital in Kampala. He was suffering from bilharzia, and also from an unidentified viral illness that was called, for want of a better name, 'the Amudat virus'. He had been unwell for some time, and his specialist in Kampala had strongly recommended that the Coxes should leave the unhealthy environs of Amudat and move to somewhere cooler – such as Marsabit. The obvious way for this to happen was for the Websters to replace the Coxes in Amudat. This idea came to us as something of a shock and a bitter disappointment. If Amudat was so unhealthy why should we, with baby Andrew and another due in four weeks, take that risk? And surely it was so logical for me to return to Marsabit, the place of my childhood. And anyway our luggage was already on its way there, and the curtains were made for there. We, the new missionaries, supposedly eager to do God's will, felt angry and rebellious. It all seemed so unfair. We had heard tales of Amudat – its remoteness and primitiveness – and I wondered how Rosemary would cope with that sort of life and isolation. We had words with God during those days at Nakuru, but had to accept that this was how it was going to be. It was a lesson in obedience, and we had to trust that God knew best – something which the next six years proved to be true.

The day came for our departure for Amudat. We would take the 'back door' into Uganda. Amudat lies only just inside Uganda proper, and close to a strip of land, Karapokot, which, though technically part of Kenya, due to its inaccessibility from the Kenya side was at that time still administered by Uganda. This was a left-over arrangement from colonial days, when it was a simple administrative convenience, but which had become a political hot potato since independence. A back road, with no border controls, led from Kitale, in Kenya, to Amudat, in Uganda – and then on northwards back into Kenya, to the remote town of Lodwar, in Kenya's Turkana district. Our entry into Uganda was to be by this unofficial route. We set out from Nakuru to the small farming town of Kitale in a *matatu* (a taxi). Awaiting us there with the Amudat Hospital Landrover was Ruth Stranex, one of the two nurses at Amudat. It began to rain heavily, and Amudat lay eighty-five miles of rough earth road to the north. We set off without delay. As we slid and bumped our way Ruth told us about herself, and something about Amudat. She came from South Africa, a straightforward person, quite tough, and very committed to the work in Amudat – someone we knew we would get on well with. After twenty miles we reached the BCMS mission at Nasokol, where my other godfather Canon Lawrie Totty and his wife Annette had served for many years. At Nasokol the road to Amudat plunges down a steep and rough escarpment, from a cool, green altitude of seven thousand feet to the hot thornscrub plains at three thousand feet. Darkness was falling, but away to the north, rising out of the plain, we could see the majestic, rugged outline of a ten-thousand-foot mountain, Kadam. 'Amudat is twenty miles to the east of Kadam', Ruth told us. We had a long way yet to go. The African night descends suddenly. We drove on and on, the headlights of the Landrover picking out the corrugated red earth road and the interminable thornbush on either side. Occasionally we saw the red reflection of an animal's eyes – a dikdik, or eland, or jackal. Ten miles before Amudat we reached a seasonal riverbed, the Alakas. It was dry, but deeply rutted. With Rosemary's advanced pregnancy in mind Ruth eased the Landrover through the humps and hollows, the Landrover's headlights bouncing drunkenly over the thornscrub ahead. Another few miles and we passed a solitary building near the road. 'Amudat!' announced Ruth. We passed a larger building which Ruth told us was the hospital. And before long the headlights picked out a wooden shack apparently in the middle of nowhere. A faint flickering glow emanated from its window. We had arrived at the Cox's house – or, as we now realised, at what was to be our home for the foreseeable future.

Liza Cox welcomed us warmly to their bush home. The generator had broken, she explained, and with Peter away in Kampala they were having to make do with paraffin lamps and candles. Our eyes took in the scene. The wooden building was clearly infested with termites. Parts of the celotex lining of the walls had been eaten away. The ceiling was propped up in one corner with a pile of kerosene tins. On the table bowls of mashed potato and minced meat awaited our arrival. On the same table were tin lids containing a pink fly poison. Dead and dying flies lay around each tin lid. Moths and beetles and sausage flies meanwhile made kamikaze dives at the sputtering candles. A large, orange, hairy-legged Solifugid spider scuttled across the cement floor, seizing hapless prey in its jaws. I sensed a severe dose of culture shock coming over Rosemary. The saving grace was that there in the room were old friends, Drs Michael and Adrienne Winter, visiting Amudat from their hospital at Ngora, further south in Uganda. How wonderful to see familiar faces.

Liza took us to the small guesthouse in the garden, which was to be our home for the next three months. That night, although tired from the travelling, sleep did not come easily. The night was so hot. Mosquito nets added to the stuffiness. Andrew was miserable. The unborn baby was very restless. And the night was filled with unfamiliar sounds – the distant chant and throb of singing in a nearby Pokot *manyatta*; the eerie howl of a hyena; the sharp bark of a jackal. Not that night, but on many nights to come, we would hear the grunt of lions on the hunt, or the strange sawing sound of a leopard. A puzzling noise was a loud scrabbling on the ceiling above us. Only later did we discover that a three-foot monitor lizard lived in our roof, and he came out to hunt each night. And always there was the whine of hungry mosquitoes. This, I reassured Rosemary, was the real Africa.

We awoke from our fitful sleep to a most wonderful dawn chorus – barbets calling to one another, superb starlings, weaver birds, hoopoes, so many colourful birds, all celebrating the cool of the new morning. By the light of day our feelings about our future home rose somewhat. The main house was surrounded by trees – a huge wild fig tree shaded the bedroom end, its spreading branches the home of many birds (and the odd boomslang snake). There were indigenous terminalia trees, with their horizontal branches, and iron-hard, termite-proof trunks. The Coxes had planted cassias and flamboyants and franjipanis. The surrounds of the house were like a small oasis in the midst of a desert of thornscrub. The wooden house itself looked no better in the light of day. It was in a very bad state of repair – in fact, we were given to understand, it had been condemned as unfit for habitation some time previously. But Peter and Liza Cox had felt that it was unjustifiable for money to be spent on improving their accommodation when the local people had so much less. We could only admire them for this, but were not at all sure that we could live up to such high principles. The house was in fact in two quite separate parts – the collapsing wooden structure (an old colonial Government rest house) contained living room, kitchen and study; a separate concrete block structure contained the bedrooms and bathroom. This part was fine. The bathroom even had a flush toilet – though water was too precious to actually flush. The toilet we used was a 'long-drop' down a winding path, about fifty yards from the house. The hole was not very deep, and had been blasted out of the rocky ground. The little corrugated iron toilet house that perched above the hole was a fascinating refuge for beetles, flies, lizards, hornets, mason wasps and the occasional snake. There was always some natural curiosity to watch when perched on the toilet.

Water for the house came from a borehole in a nearby gulley, and the water had to be pumped daily by hand. Later an electric pump was installed. The water was metallic in taste, orange in colour, and the supply frequently broke down. Baths had to be very shallow. The whole family in turn washed in the same water, then the laundry, then nappies, and finally the water was directed to the small, struggling vegetable patch. The hot water supply came from a forty gallon drum, heated by a log fire, which was lit and tended each day by Songa Karibu ('Come Closer'), a toothless character with a wooden plug in his lower lip. Perhaps the best thing about the house was its view – it faced Kadam mountain, which rose, stark and purple, from the plain twenty miles to the west, to a height of ten thousand feet. It boasted two forest-clad peaks, one a vast plateau, the other a series of jagged rocky outcrops. It was a view that we never tired of, and a mountain that I immediately longed to explore.

But there were much more immediate and pressing matters than mountain exploration. With Peter Cox away ill in Kampala a locum doctor had been keeping an eye on things. Now it was up to me. As I set off for the hospital, which lay a mile from the house, the heat of the sun was beginning to burn. By midday the temperature would rise to the upper nineties Fahrenheit. Beyond the cool shade of the house one was struck by the white glare. A shimmering heat-haze lay over the landscape. I left Rosemary on that first morning to the tender care of Liza Cox. Liza, who abounds in energy and enthusiasm, was all for taking Rosemary for a walkabout through the bush to a Pokot village, to meet the local people. Rosemary, suffering from pregnancy, heat and culture shock, and with one year old Andrew to look after, weakly excused herself, and wondered if she was, after all, cut out for this kind of life.

The concept of Amudat Hospital had begun following the visit of the British Governor of Uganda in the 1950s. Disgruntled local Pokot tribesmen threw mud at him. They were not happy at paying poll tax to the Government and getting little back in return. So how about a hospital? An agreement was reached between the then colonial Government and BCMS (who already had work in the area) that the Government would fund a hospital, if the Mission would staff and run it. It was to be a unique joint venture. So it was that Peter Cox arrived in Amudat in 1957, and he began to hold medical clinics under a thorn tree while the first hospital buildings went up. By the time we arrived, in 1967, Amudat Hospital was a thriving little hospital, with a reputation far and wide. It served an area of about five thousand square miles of remote bush country. Its main clients were the semi-nomadic Pokot people who populated the area. But at that time the workload had been increased considerably by a refugee camp of twenty thousand Sudanese, twenty miles away at the foot of Kadam. They were in poor health, and needed a lot of medical attention.

As I stepped into the hospital for the first time I had mixed feelings – excitement, nervousness, inadequacy. It was all so different from an English hospital. The two open-sided twelve-bedded wards, male and female, were virtually empty. Apart from very ill patients everybody – patients and the relatives caring for them – was outside. Scattered under the acacia trees around the hospital were groups of people, patients and carers, cooking on open fires. The hospital provided a basic diet of maize meal, but everybody cooked for themselves. And then there was the smell and the dirt. The walls of the wards were distinctly grubby, smeared by dirty hands and greasy heads. The bed linen (originally white) was various shades of brown. It soon became obvious that, in a culture where water is very short and where washing is not the custom, where animal fat is used to oil the hair and where the dress of the women was goatskins, it was unrealistic to expect the wards to be pristine. They were washed down daily with Lysol, to minimise bed bugs, but one had to adopt a realistic standard of cleanliness.

The hospital was staffed by two BCMS nurses – Ruth Stranex, who had met us in at Kitale, and Lilian Singleton. Lilian, from Lancashire, had already been in Amudat for some years. She was gentle and quiet – an introvert, in contrast to Ruth, the extrovert. Lilian was the sort of person whom you would not expect to find roughing it in the bush, but who was enabled to do the unexpected because of her quiet faith in God. There were six 'dressers' – local young men who had been recruited after a few years of Primary schooling, and had then been trained on the job. This small band of staff was caring for about one and a half thousand in-patients a year, and thirty-six thousand out-patients. The wards were always over-full, with patients and their relatives sleeping at night in, under and between the beds. It was the custom of Pokot men to wear very little – usually just a *shuka* (a cloth knotted loosely over one shoulder, and concealing little). But their pride and glory – especially the young warriors – was their hairstyle. The hair would have mud worked into it and plastered onto it, forming a skullcap that was an integral part of them. This would then be decorated with pigments and crowned often with an ostrich feather. Such a headdress could not be lain on, for fear of it breaking. At home in their villages men would therefore sleep with their necks resting on a small wooden stool. In hospital they soon discovered that the metal bedstead at the foot of the hospital beds made an ideal neck rest. At night, therefore, the aisle between the beds in the men's ward was obstructed by the plumed and mudded heads of sleeping Pokot men, their necks resting comfortably on the bed ends.

Outpatients to the hospital were all first seen, and most of them treated, by one of the dressers. Patients with more complex problems were referred to the doctor. When I arrived at Amudat there was no consulting room for the doctor. Patients waiting to see me were lined up on a bench on a verandah, and, squatting on my haunches, I hopped from one to the next. Only a cursory examination was possible in such circumstances. There was a small operating theatre. The nearest hospital of any size was one hundred and ten miles away, so most surgical problems had to be dealt with on the spot. The Flying Doctor Service flew in a surgeon from time to time, to deal with non-urgent but more complex cases. The operating table was illuminated by a single light bulb, or, if the generator was not working, a pressure lamp. I was, on many an occasion, profoundly grateful for a set of volumes of Practical Operative Surgery, complete (more or less) with dotted lines showing where to cut. I carried out many an operation, in the years ahead, that I had not only never done, but had never even seen done. I would operate with the book open. Fortunately patients considered me doubly clever not only to be able to do operations, but also to read a book that told me what to do.

Another aspect of hospital work in which my learning curve was steep was that of the laboratory. We had to do all our own investigations, including blood counts; staining and microscopy for malaria parasites, T.B., Leishmaniasis and meningitis; serology tests for Brucellosis; and grouping and cross-matching of blood. It was all so new and so different. On that first day in hospital I saw diseases that I had never seen before; and I saw medical conditions in their grossest forms. Patients abounded with huge livers and spleens; with enormous fungating tropical ulcers on their legs; people with TB and meningitis; and children in the last stages of malnutrition. Where did one begin? A child with meningococcal meningitis died on the second day – just as little Andrew developed a high temperature. I became acutely aware that my own family was going to be at risk of all sorts of tropical and potentially lethal diseases, and that it was up to me alone to diagnose and treat them. There was no other doctor to call on. Perhaps Rosemary's parents had been right after all.

Most patients came to hospital only after first trying traditional medicine, and making a sacrifice to *Tororut*. The village treatments sometimes gave the symptoms away, and I soon learned to recognise them. A patient with a strip of green sansievra leaf tied around the head had a headache, which might well be due to malaria. A patient with a strip of sansievra around the chest had chest pain, and could well have pneumonia with pleurisy. Multiple cuts to the skin might indicate that fits had occurred, and were an attempt to let evil spirits out. Babies were often smeared from head to foot with herbal concoctions, and as likely as not they were suffering from gastroenteritis. Bark tied around a leg was probably concealing a tropical ulcer. Under the bark would often be a poultice of cow dung, or of wood ash. Thongs of goat or cow skin, around the wrists or body of a patient, were an indication that an animal had been sacrificed. I began to read the signs.

Sunday came. It was not, for me, a day off, as there was always the hospital to keep an eye on. But there was time for church. Amudat Anglican Church came at that time under the auspices of the vast Kenyan Diocese of Nakuru. Later it would be taken over by Uganda's Soroti Diocese. The church was a mud building with low-walled open sides and a corrugated iron roof. The seating consisted of planks laid on tree-trunk supports. The pastor was the Reverend Timothy Oluoch, who lived with his wife Mary and family next to the church. Timothy was assisted by one of the local shopkeepers, Daudi Chebtwey (a lay reader), and also by the headmaster of the primary school, Solomon Mworor. They all became our close friends. The service officially began at 10 a.m., but Timothy would keep an eye out from his house towards the open-sided church until he felt that a sufficient quorum had gathered. Then, and only then, would he come across and start the service. We, with our western obsession with time, found this practice very irritating. The services were very long anyway, and to spend time sitting waiting before them seemed to us wrong. But as we were often reminded, Westerners have clocks, Africans have time. That first service in Amudat was memorable. From time to time Pokot, in their traditional dress (or lack of it) would wander up to the open sides of the church, peer in, and greet everyone. The service would pause while respectful greetings were returned. The service was often interjected with loud clearings of the throat, and fruitful spittings onto the church floor. Mothers breast fed their babies. People came and went. Dogs and chickens wandered in and out. The sermon (preached in both Pokot and Swahili) went on for a very long time, and was mostly incomprehensible to us. And the relentless sun blazed down onto the iron roof of the church. How grateful we were for the open sides, and gusts of breeze, though warm. It was a lesson to us that worship is not about being entertained, or even necessarily about enjoying oneself, but is an attitude of heart and mind.

On our fifth day in Amudat we received news by the Flying Doctor radio that Peter Cox was now out of hospital in Kampala, and would I drive down in the hospital Volkswagon Beetle to collect him? Liza was a bit uncertain as to how far it was and how long the journey would take, but I was determined to go there and back in the day. I did not want to leave Rosemary in Amudat, in her condition, with no doctor present. I left Amudat at 5 a.m. and drove non-stop the two hundred and sixty miles to Kampala – the first one hundred and ten miles being on a rough earth road. But having arrived there, I could not find Peter. I finally tracked him down to the Medical School library. He was appalled that I had promised Rosemary to return the same day, but there was no way of letting her know otherwise. We set off from Kampala to Amudat at 4 p.m., Peter driving. It was probably the scariest journey of my life. Peter drove very fast. He wanted to do as much of the journey as possible in the light. We drove through a torrential thunderstorm at high speed, and nearly collided with an on-coming lorry, barely visible in the rain. We skidded on a bend. And meanwhile, as if to reassure me, Peter recounted to me stories of near-misses he had had in the past at various places on the way. The journey did have its high points – we saw porcupine, eland and, near Kadam mountain, a beautiful leopard in the road. We arrived back late that night to an apparently unconcerned Liza, and an anxious Rosemary.

Chapter 7
APPRENTICE BUSH DOCTOR

With Peter Cox's return to Amudat my apprenticeship began in earnest. He was warmly welcomed by everyone, and it was immediately apparent how much he was loved and respected. Peter was known locally as 'Coggis', the Pokot pronunciation of 'Cox'. Ruth, the nurse, was called 'Chepocoggis', the daughter of Cox. In the early days I was referred to as 'Wericoggis', the son of Cox. Wives were called 'mother of' their first son, so Liza was 'Kama Stephen' and Rosemary was 'Kama Andrew'. I soon discovered that many Pokot children were called 'Coggis' after Peter, and it had become an established Pokot name. (In the years ahead there were not a few called 'Westa' after me). There was great sadness when it was announced that the Coxes would be leaving Amudat. Liza found the prospect of a move to Marsabit hard to accept, just as we had found our going to Amudat hard to accept. Liza was fluent in Pokot. Peter's heart and soul was with the Pokot people, and the hospital that he had established. It was indeed a difficult time for them, and their four children. But the medical advice was incontrovertible – Peter must leave Amudat for a healthier climate.

Peter lost no time in teaching me skills that I would need. Trachoma was rife – a form of severe conjunctivitis causing scarring of the eyelids, inversion of the eyelashes, and consequent abrasion and ulceration of the surface of the eye, leading finally to blindness. It was spread from person to person by flies. Many people were blind or partially sighted due to the scarring of trachoma. A simple operation to prevent this was to evert the eyelids, so that the lashes no longer rubbed – at the same time treating the underlying trachoma with eye ointment. This was one of my first lessons from Peter. (I later taught one of the dressers to do this sight-saving operation, and he did many hundreds most successfully). Hernias were not uncommon, and I learned to repair these using cheap nylon fishing line, which we bought by the reel down country. It was just as effective as surgical nylon, and a fraction of the price. Dentistry was a skill I had never practised until now (although I had been at the receiving end of my clergyman father's attempts at tooth extraction, as a child in Marsabit). Peter taught me how to give a mandibular block injection, to extract molar teeth. The removal of a rotten tooth from someone who had been in agony for months, and who might already have suffered attempted extractions by the local medicine man, using an arrowhead and a rock – to remove such a tooth painlessly and rapidly was one of the best ways of making friends and influencing people. Peter also brushed up my laboratory skills – how to recognise the amoebae of amoebic dysentery, and malaria parasites, and the parasites (Leishman-Donovan bodies) in the spleen fluid of patients with visceral leishmaniasis (kala-azar).

Someone I began to get to know during this time was Max. Max was a Texan – or a caricature of a Texan – a larger than life figure, and a Vietnam war veteran. He was a sergeant in the United States army, and he was based at Amudat Hospital. Peter explained. In Amudat and the surrounding area kala-azar was rife. As part of its Global Epidemiology programme the US army wanted to do some research into kala-azar – probably not so much for philanthropic reasons as to have some knowledge as to how the disease might better be diagnosed, treated and prevented if ever their soldiers were involved in such a theatre of war. Peter had been approached by Colonel Dale Wykoff of the US army, a pathologist and epidemiologist, who asked if a research programme could be based at Amudat, and done in cooperation with the hospital. In return the US army would provide the hospital with equipment and facilities, and at the end of the research would leave its supplies with the hospital. All this seemed a good idea. Sergeant Max Wynne, a laboratory technician, would be based in Amudat. Colonel Wykoff and a British entomologist, George Barnley, who was the third member of the research team, would be based at Makerere University in Kampala. Kala-azar was known to be spread by sandflies, which live in termite hills. The aims of the research were to study the biting habits of sandflies, and to devise a less invasive test for kala-azar than the current one of spleen puncture.

Some time before our arrival in Amudat Max had moved in, and built for himself a mud house. 'Built for himself' is not strictly accurate. Max did nothing for himself. He hired a mini army of local lads to be his vassals. He established over the next two years a little empire in which he ruled supreme. Max had a drooping moustache, a cowboy style hat, khaki bush jacket and sandals. He wore round his belt a variety of sheath knives and ammunition pouches. He had several rifles, for which he had somehow obtained a license. He tended to shoot anything that moved – birds, dik-dik, snakes, warthogs, hyenas – whether edible or not. He came close at times to shooting people. He built up a little village of mud houses for his retinue. He shouted and swore at his staff in his Texan drawl, and threatened or dismissed them at the slightest provocation. In other words, Max was a liability. The problem, as I soon realised, was that, because Max was based at the hospital, he was considered by the local population to be one of us. And yet in his behaviour and language he set an example that we did not wish to be associated with. Colonel Wykoff tried to rein in the worst excesses of his behaviour, but it was difficult to do that from two hundred and sixty miles away. To us missionaries Max was, of course, politeness itself. We were necessary to him. He and Dale Wykoff would bring us generous 'sweeteners' from Kampala (books, kitchenware) or haunches of game from hunting trips. It was a difficult relationship, and one that I struggled with over the next two years. Sadly, for reasons that will become apparent, there was very little useful outcome from their project.

While my time was taken up with the hospital, and with making the most of this overlap period with Peter, Rosemary was trying to adjust to life in the bush. Andrew toddled around the house and its environs, exploring and investigating. Rosemary's constant fear was that he would fall down the long-drop latrine, or swallow medicine that had been left lying around, or get bitten by a snake or stung by a scorpion, or just wander off into the bush and get lost or eaten by a lion. The possibilities were many. In fact no such disasters overtook him. One of the times that he, and we, enjoyed most was in an evening, when the heat of the day was over, and work was done (emergencies allowing). We would walk for about half a mile through the bush to the Kanyangereng riverbed. The walk in itself was enjoyable. The thorn bush was interspersed with the serrated tongues of aloes, and the sharp spikes of sansievra (a form of 'mother-in-law's tongue'). Desert roses, with their huge bulbous stems, were magnificent when in flower – a profusion of pink and white. Slender little dik-dik, always in couples, would often trot away from our path. There would be the footprints in the sandy soil of wild animals that had passed that way. And always there were colourful birds in profusion. But the riverbed was our chief delight. For much of the year the Kanyangereng was a broad swathe of sand, snaking through the bush, and lined on its banks by huge shady wild figs and other fruit-bearing trees and bushes – home to vervet monkeys, and many birds. The sand of the riverbed was a paradise for children. When, in the rainy season, the river was in spate it became a raging torrent, carrying all before it. But then for some weeks it would settle down to a gentle flow, and finally to pools of water. Many happy times were spent cooling off in the sandy pools of the Kanyangerang. It was restorative after a hot and busy day.

The due date for our baby's birth was drawing close. It was time to go down to the capital of Uganda, Kampala, a sprawling city set on seven hills. Max offered to take us in his Landrover the first one hundred and ten miles, to Mbale. From there we took a very crowded and uncomfortable *matatu* for the remaining one hundred and fifty miles. Friends of the Coxes, Dr Ralph and Enid Schram, had most kindly offered to accommodate us over the time of the birth. Ralph was Lecturer in Public Health in the Medical School at Makerere University. Their house was on the university compound on Makerere Hill. Their welcome and kindness to us was overwhelming. On 16 November 1967, right on cue, Rosemary went in to labour. She was admitted to Mengo Hospital, the CMS hospital on Namirembe Hill, and there Dr Hugh Oliver delivered her of a son, Paul Jonathan, ten pounds and two ounces. It was a memorable moment, and it felt significant to be in that historic place, just below Namirembe Cathedral, the birthplace of Christianity in Uganda. My boyhood missionary hero, Alexander Mackay, had trod this hill, Namirembe, the 'hill of peace'. And that great pioneer missionary doctor, Albert Cook, had founded the very place where we were, Mengo Hospital. Paul was born on holy ground.

The following days were not easy, either for Rosemary or me. Paul was, from the outset, a very hungry baby, and Rosemary did not have the milk. Then she got dysentery from some oranges that I had bought in the market. She had to remain in hospital for twelve days. Meanwhile I had the nightmare of trying to register Paul's birth. I traipsed from office to office, with little Andrew in pushchair or arms, being referred from one dilatory official to another. It took three days of queuing and waiting to get the required documents. An embarrassing episode marked the end of Rosemary's time in Mengo Hospital. We had understood from Peter Cox that we would be charged a reduced missionary rate (BCMS did not at that time pay for maternity costs). When the hospital bill was presented it was for £35, the full rate, and more money than we had in the world. As BCMS missionaries we did not qualify for the special CMS rate. I did not know what to do. I could not pay the bill. Ralph Schram got wind of our dilemma and insisted on paying the bill for us. When the time came to return to Amudat Ralph and Enid would not hear of us travelling by *matatu*, and took us back in their car.

Coping with a newborn baby, as well as a toddler, in our hot little guest house in Amudat was not at all easy. Night after night Paul screamed with colic – and the volume of his cries was commensurate with his size. Even the hyenas were outdone. Meanwhile at hospital I was again seeing disease in its grossest form – a child with her nose and centre of her face eaten away by cancrum oris; a man with his arm almost bitten off by a lion (Peter gave the arm a sharp tug to complete the amputation); a baby with third degree burns after falling into a fire in the village. A medical worry closer to home came when four-year-old Gordon Cox developed a high fever with an enormously enlarged spleen. Blood slides were negative for malaria, so we sedated him and did a spleen puncture, which proved to be strongly positive for kala-azar. I was given the unpleasant task of giving him ten painful daily injections of Pentostam. Fortunately he responded well – but it was another reminder that we were not living in a health resort.

We had barely settled again into life at Amudat when it was time to leave for a two-week Swahili language course in Nairobi. Once again Max came to our aid, taking us the first eighty miles to Kitale. From there we travelled by *matatu*. We broke our journey in Nakuru, staying with our bishop, the Right Reverend Neville Langford-Smith. He was a former CMS missionary, an Australian, and was the only remaining white bishop in Kenya. He had an ambivalent attitude to missionaries, especially BCMS ones, and liked to keep tight control of his huge diocese. He was known as 'an iron fist in a velvet glove'. Certainly on that occasion we experienced only the velvet – he and his wife were most hospitable. The following morning, when I took our suitcase to the door, I was confronted by the sight of the bishop's car reversing out of his garage, and little Andrew (who had somehow escaped from the house) standing immediately behind it. The car reversed into Andrew, knocking him down, and he fell behind the back wheel. I have never, before or since, shouted at a bishop as I shouted then. He heard me, and stopped just in time, and we were all shaken – and thankful to God that I had come to the door when I did.

Language School in Nairobi was a difficult and fairly unproductive time, especially for Rosemary. We were booked into the YWCA about a mile away. They did not realise that we had two children. We were in a very small room. Andrew had to sleep on a shelf in the cupboard, and Paul's carrycot occupied all the floor space. Each morning we had to walk to the language school, pushing the children and all the luggage for the day. The children were cared for at a language school nursery in a nearby garden. Andrew hated it, and cried whenever we left him. It was after several days, when Rosemary turned up unexpectedly, that we discovered that the nursery attendant was tethering him to a bench for the day, so that she did not have to keep running after him. It was during this time in Nairobi that Rosemary had a rare and brief telephone conversation with her parents – the cost of overseas calls was prohibitive, but, in Amudat, not possible at all.

We were back in Amudat in time for Christmas. The temperature on Christmas day was ninety-five degrees Fahrenheit. We had a service for the patients and their relatives in the open-sided wards of the hospital. It was a motley array of men in their cloth *shukas* and mud headdresses, carrying their spears and wooden stools; and women in skins and beads; and naked children with sticky fly-ringed eyes and runny noses. Many were hearing for the first time of a God who loved us so much that He sent His Son as a human baby, born as one of us. To them God, *Tororut*, is a remote and vengeful Being, who brings famine and sickness, and who must constantly be appeased with sacrifices of precious animals. The idea of a God who Himself made the only necessary sacrifice, once and for all, was Good News indeed. After the service came the distribution of presents. Each patient was given an extra portion of maize meal and an empty tin. The delight caused by the tins was amazing – to them very precious containers. Each child was given an orange, but they had to be shown how to peel it first, otherwise they ate it skin and all.

Soon after Christmas Rosemary became ill, with a high temperature. Malaria slides were negative. A patient was admitted to hospital with jaundice due to infectious hepatitis, and proceeded to lapse into a coma and die. Coinciding with that Rosemary developed jaundice – she too had infectious hepatitis. My immediate worry was whether the local strain of Hepatitis A was particularly virulent. Other patients in the hospital with hepatitis had died. Rosemary felt wretched, and was struggling to cope with the children. The Coxes had meanwhile gone on holiday. To our rescue from the mission at Nasokol came Alice Dukelow, who had been with Rosemary at Dalton House in Bristol. She took over the running of the home and care of the children. Dear Alice had a heart of gold, but was not very practical. The day came for a visit of the Flying Doctors from Nairobi – a Chinese surgeon, an Indian anaesthetist, a Kenyan nurse and a British pilot. They would need lunch. 'What shall I make them?' Alice asked Rosemary in her soft Irish brogue. 'How about cauliflower cheese? I think we have both. Do you know how to make the sauce?' asked Rosemary weakly. 'Sure I do!' replied Alice. At lunch I served our guests, and then Alice, who tucked in heartily. The guests I could see were rather tentative with their cauliflower cheese. The reason became clear when I started mine – Alice had made the cheese sauce with sugar. It was revoltingly sweet. Yet Alice was oblivious, clearly enjoying hers, and I could hardly apologise to our guests in front of her. Somehow we all ploughed our way through it, but I guess there was an interesting conversation on the flight back to Nairobi, between a Chinese, an Indian and a Kenyan about the strangeness of English (or perhaps I should say Irish) cuisine.

Rosemary was making little headway in the heat of Amudat, so it was agreed that she and the children would go up to the cool seven-thousand-foot heights of Nasokol, with Alice, and recuperate there. While there both Andrew and Paul developed hepatitis, and later our nurse Ruth Stranex also had to go out to Nasokol, deeply jaundiced. It was some time later that I discovered why so many patients in the hospital died from hepatitis. I noticed a gourd full of crushed red bark under the bed of a hepatitis patient who had suddenly deteriorated. On asking what it was I was told that this was their traditional treatment for hepatitis, and that everyone was given it, whether in hospital or not. Things began to add up in my mind. I banned the bark medicine for hospital patients, and from that time hepatitis patients began to make normal recoveries. Some of the Pokot traditional medicines were undoubtedly effective (such as aloe juice as an antiseptic), but this hepatitis 'treatment' was undoubtedly poisonous. Another traditional treatment that we discouraged was the dressing of leg ulcers with cow dung – a frequent source of tetanus. Bathing them, however, with urine was not discouraged – urine was no doubt more sterile than any water from waterholes.

The Coxes returned from their holiday, and began to pack for Marsabit. Fortunately our sea luggage, which had been redirected from Marsabit, finally caught up with us. As the Coxes packed so we unpacked. It was an embarrassing time. Their things were well worn and chipped, and pretty basic. Much of ours were as yet unused wedding presents, and looked decidedly posh. We realised that we had made a mistake in bringing a lot of it out. We had wanted to make our first proper home nice, but some of our things were just too nice for the situation. They made us look very affluent. We packed a lot up again, and sent it back to England. As the Coxes packed Peter announced that the Missionary Aviation Fellowship pilot who was to fly them to Marsabit (thus saving them a six-hundred-mile road journey) had told him that they could take six hundred pounds of luggage. I was astonished at the growing pile of carefully weighed items that were to go on the plane. 'Perhaps MAF have bigger planes than I realised!' I thought to myself.

On 2 February Paul was baptised in the little Amudat church by the Reverend Timothy Oluoch. Peter Cox was the only godparent able to be present. Two days later came the Coxes departure date. The MAF plane flew in – a rather small one! Somewhat smaller it seemed than the pile of waiting luggage – not to mention Peter and Liza, the four children, and the dog. The pilot was appalled at the sight. The total load, he explained, including the passengers, was six hundred pounds. There followed a rapid re-sorting, and Rosemary and I were left with a huge pile of stuff to 'please pack in something and send by road to Marsabit.' As it was the plane was loaded to capacity. The Amudat airstrip is just a clearing in the bush, fairly short, with (at that time) longish grass and the odd anthill. The pilot said he would like to make a trial take-off with one passenger short. Liza happily remained, chatting to her many friends – the whole of Amudat had turned out to see them off. She appeared not to give so much as a glance at the trial take-off, with all her precious family on board. 'Why can't I be so calm and confident?' thought Rosemary, whose heart would have been in her mouth in similar circumstances. The plane landed again, Liza tore herself from her farewells, climbed on board, and once again the little laden plane gathered speed down the airstrip, its engine roaring. Would they make it? Once in the past a similar plane, with the Cox family on board, had flipped over when trying to take off from Amudat airstrip. Fortunately nobody then was hurt (just the plane). This time they made it. They just skimmed the thornbush at the end of the strip. The red plane circled as it climbed against the magnificent backdrop of Kadam mountain, it flew back over the waving crowd, dipped its wing in salute, and headed east for Marsabit. And we were left standing in the hot sun, with mixed feelings – of loss, of envy, of responsibility. Doctorwise I was on my own, responsible for a busy hospital, for a scattered population, and, not least, for the health of my own family. May God help me!

The Landrover on the road to Amudat

The road to Amudat and Kadam mountain

Kadam mountain

Amudat town centre

Our home in the bush

The renovated house

Songa Karibu lighting the fire to heat our water

Andrew and Paul in their car

Setting off for work

Pokot lady with Paul

Ruth Stranex supervising the outpatient clinic

Lilian Singleton in the pharmacy

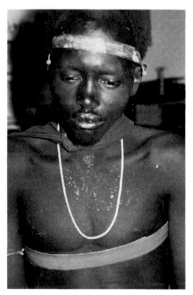

A patient with sansievra strips

Amudat hospital

Amudat hospital staff

Patient arriving by wheelbarrow

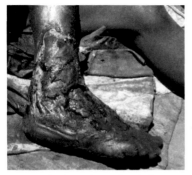

Wood ash on ulcerated snake bite

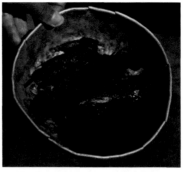

Traditional treatment for hepatitis

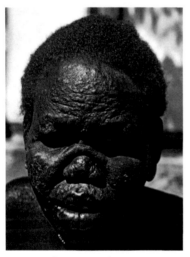

Lepromatous leprosy

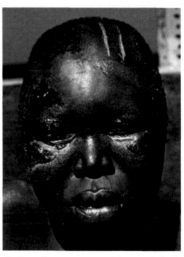

Lady with panga cuts and fractured skull

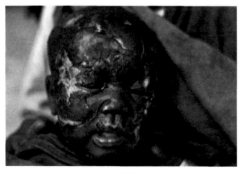

Baby with third-degree burns

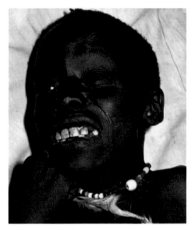

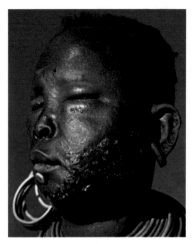

Child with tetanus.
Note goatskin strips from sacrifice

Anthrax

Examining for trachoma

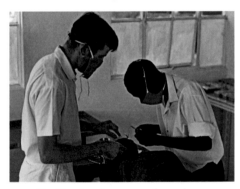

Teaching Joseph to operate for trachoma

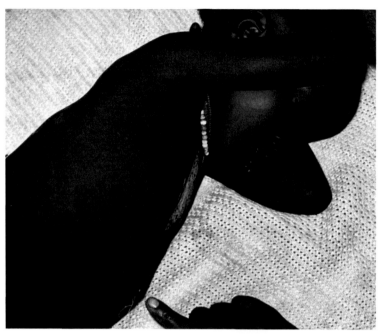

Speared child showing entry and exit wounds

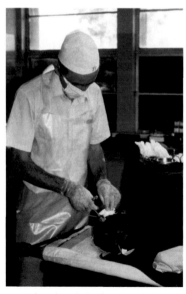

Making burr holes for a head injury

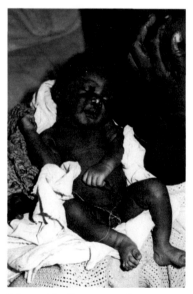

Baby resulting from extrauterine pregnancy

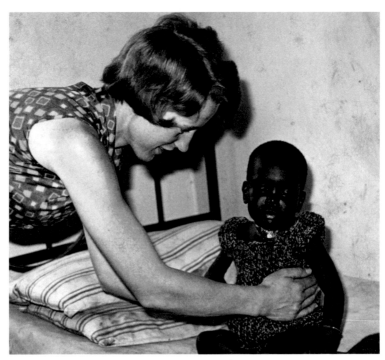

Rosemary giving physiotherapy after tracheotomy

Flying doctors evacuating a patient

Two cultures meet

My solar heater

Laying a water pipe

Starting the diesel engine

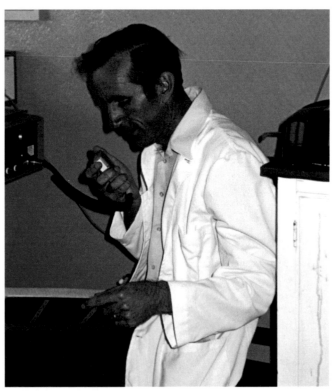

On the radio to Foundation Control

A Pokot man   Man with ostrich feather

Decorated warriors after a kill

Passing the time of day

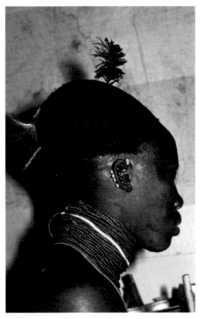

Unmarried man

Married man with Brasso snuffbox

Girl following circumcision ceremony

Denis Burkitt visits a manyatta

Bleeding a cow

A married woman

Pokot girls

Pool in a riverbed

Amudat church and congregation

Rosemary with her Sunday School

The rebuilt church

Blind Joshua Mlee

Justus Okiru

Wilson Akiru with his baby
following his wife's death

Stephen on a termite hill

Aloe   A desert rose

Crossing the Kanyangereng

Charles preparing to immunise on safari

Tooth extraction on safari

Bush clinic

Katabok dispensary

Idi Amin in Iriri

Chapter 8
A HOUSE TO A HOME

The rambling house in the bush, such as it was, was ours, and we could begin to turn it into our home. Our minds turned to such mundane but essential matters as where our food would come from. There was little to buy in the local shops, or *dukas*, which consisted of a dozen or so ramshackle buildings, mainly of corrugated iron, that lined either side of the dusty main road, near the hospital but a mile from our house. The main shop, the superstore, was owned by an Indian gentleman, Kanti Patel. Kanti stocked such items as maize meal, rice and sugar (all in sacks), bales of calico, nails, paraffin and beads. He would arrange to get almost anything one wished, but this would depend on his next trip down country. For our regular food supplies we had to look elsewhere. We adopted the arrangement that the Coxes had had, and which Ruth and Lilian used. We had a regular weekly order with a grocery in Kitale, eighty miles south. Once a week our standard box of food would (or should) arrive on the lorry of a Mr Kaka, as it made its weekly trip to Lodwar in the north. The system worked unless Kaka's lorry broke down, which it often did, and our perishables sat in the blazing sun for a day or two. The other problem was that our standing order of food was fixed, but our guests varied enormously in number, and were often unexpected. But we never went hungry, or failed to feed our visitors, although at times it was touch and go.

Because of the unreliability of our home water supply from the nearby borehole, and its unpleasant metallic taste, I decided, in due course, to lay a PVC water pipe from the hospital to our staff houses. The hospital had a four-hundred-foot borehole, with pleasant and ample water. This also meant that only one borehole pump would have to be maintained. Because of the rockiness of the ground we were able to dig only a shallow trench for the pipe through the bush to our houses. It was not long before Pokot herdsmen discovered that a bit of drilling with a sharp spear through the PVC pipe resulted in a very satisfactory fountain of water.

They could water their cattle and goats, have a wash themselves – and then walk away leaving our precious water spewing into the bush. I soon refined a method of repair, using a cotton bandage and Araldite. Our water pipe became very patched, I got frequently exasperated, and I had to recruit the support of the chief and elders of the tribe to dissuade the local people from such a tempting practice. For all of us – Pokot people, hospital, and ourselves – water was our most precious commodity. We never took it for granted.

Not long after the Coxes had departed our BCMS representative, Archdeacon Robert McKemey, and the Mission Treasurer, came on a pastoral visit to see how we were settling in. Without hesitation they agreed that the dilapidated wooden part of the house must be replaced. How it would be funded they were not sure – because it was actually a Government building, and a Government responsibility to replace it. But there was little hope of getting funding from the Government, so they told us to go ahead and find a builder, and they would take responsibility. It was an enormous relief to us, and plans were soon under way to put up a dexion (a sort of giant Meccano) and cement structure, and to link it with the existing bedrooms. In the end Oxfam funded the building, as part of their major contribution to the medical work at Amudat. An incident occurred shortly before the old wooden building was demolished. In what had been Peter Cox's study there was, pinned on the celotex wall, a map of Kenya. Peter had shown me how, if one ran one's hand over the map, there was a definite hot spot exactly under Marsabit. Peter had told me (in jest) that this was clear guidance that they should move to Marsabit. In fact the hot spot was the epicentre of a swarm of bees which had taken up residence between the outer wooden wall and the celotex lining. One day I had been on a fly-spraying expedition to the long-drop latrine, and as I returned I casually squirted the spray towards the entry to the bees' nest. The effect was instantaneous and terrifying. African bees are known for their aggression, and these bees demonstrated it. I fled into the house. It was only thanks to the proximity of the door, and the fact that all the windows were screened with mosquito netting, that I was not seriously stung. The furious bees massed at each window, trying to get in at me. A few did slip in through the door, and we had some painful stings. It was some time before we dared to leave the house. A Pokot man was very happy to rid us of the bees – he nonchalantly smoked them out, and retrieved handfuls of honey from our wall.

For Rosemary it was a major challenge to turn our bush house into a home. With ferns and begonias and bougainvilleas growing in kerosene tins on the verandah, and a lick of paint around the house, and the most basic of furnishings, it began to feel homely. We wanted to establish friendship with people from nearby Pokot villages, and to support them, so we decided to buy milk from them, rather than use powdered milk. Their milk had a smoky taste, due to the milk gourds being cleaned with hot ashes. But it soon began to have another odd flavour, and to curdle when heated. We discovered that our milk supplier was rinsing out her gourds with cow's urine. We opted after all for powdered milk.

Another local custom took some getting used to. A child is welcomed and blessed by spitting on it, or spitting into the hand, and smearing the child with saliva. When we first arrived back from Kampala with newborn Paul a succession of goatskin-clad, beaded ladies came to the house to see the white child – and to bless him in the traditional fashion. They meant well, and it would have been churlish to whisk him away, or express horror. But, with thoughts of prevalent tuberculosis in mind, it was at times like this that we had to trust in God's protection. Having recovered from infectious hepatitis both Rosemary and Andrew were ill for quite a long time with what must have been the 'Amudat virus' – the virus that led to Peter Cox's departure from Amudat. At times the worry of the family's health weighed heavily. And it was not only illness. Rosemary had the shock one day of finding little Paul suspended by the neck from his 'Bonny Bouncer', blue in the face. Somehow he had slipped out of the harness. With no car at the house, and no telephone, she ran the mile through the bush to the hospital, clutching Paul, distraught. He soon recovered – the run probably helped to revive him – but this sort of incident tested one's faith and resolve. There were times, when it was very hot, and life very busy, and everything seemed to be going wrong, and the children ill, that we wondered what we were doing there. And then we had to remember that mutual calling from God.

The challenge of running a one-doctor bush hospital like Amudat was that of having to be a jack-of-all-trades. A routine day's work could include clinics and ward rounds, surgical operations, laboratory tests, fixing a water pump, grinding the valves of a diesel engine, doing a post-mortem, going out in the Landrover on an emergency call, stock-taking, writing reports and begging letters, preaching – even, on occasion, treating a sick goat. It was the variety of work that made it so interesting. And it was the colleagues with whom I worked who made it all possible. By 1969 we were treating four thousand outpatients a month, and the wards were always full to bursting. At night it was physically impossible to move around the two wards because every square inch of floor space was occupied. We had a staff of two nurses (Lilian and Ruth) and six dressers. Our annual grant from the Uganda Government to run the hospital was £4,800. Of this £800 was allocated for all drugs and equipment. In other words we were running the hospital on a shoestring. Medications were used only when really necessary, and only the cheapest varieties. When Metronidazole first became available as a safe and very effective treatment for amoebic dysentery, I rashly asked the Flying Doctors to bring a tin of one hundred tablets. When I saw the bill it represented our total drugs budget for a whole month. The tin went back to Nairobi with the Flying Doctors.

Work sometimes called me much further afield. Supplies had to be collected from Entebbe and Kampala. And from time to time I had to attend meetings of the church's Provincial Medical Board in Kampala. It was at those committees that I met a tall and striking and warm hearted man, soon to be made bishop, and then Archbishop of Uganda – Janani Luwum. He chaired our meetings, wisely and gently.

One thing that Amudat did was to turn me into a good beggar. Clearly we needed better facilities, more ward space, an x-ray, more money for drugs. One possible source of help that immediately came to mind was Oxfam. Part of our problem was the demand on our resources by the twenty thousand Sudanese refugees who were camped just twenty miles away. Surely, I thought, Oxfam will respond to this need. I wrote a detailed application to the Uganda Representative for Oxfam. I made out, I thought, a very strong case. All this had to be typed out on a stencil with my ancient Remington typewriter, and then duplicated one page at a time, using an old hand-rolled duplicator. I would crouch over it on the floor, and end up covered with ink. It was a slow and messy business – but surely worth it. Or so I thought, until I had a firm rejection from Oxfam. 'It is not Oxfam's policy to get involved in the running of hospitals.' I was not prepared to take that reply as the final answer. I redirected my application to the East African Director of Oxfam, Malcolm Harper, and invited him to come and visit us. He did, and immediately I sensed a real interest and concern. It was the beginning not only of substantial help from Oxfam over a number of years, but also of a good friendship. Malcolm always said that Oxfam liked to give money to Amudat Hospital because they knew that every shilling would be spent on what it was given for. Oxfam funded a new TB ward, a maternity ward, an x-ray building (the German charity Bread for the World later donated an x-ray machine), and they gave us funds which enabled us to treat better the many cases of brucellosis. The US army research project built a new laboratory, which in due course they left us. In a fairly short space of time Amudat Hospital had doubled in size. The new building was officially opened by Malcolm Harper on 7 March 1969. He ceremonially planted a flamboyant tree to mark the occasion – and it promptly died from a surfeit of goat manure. We hoped that there was no symbolic significance in that.

Some of the medical conditions we had to deal with were extreme. Often patients survived and recovered against all the medical odds. I put this down to two things – the innate toughness of the people (after all, only the strongest survived childhood) and to the prayer with which our work was surrounded. Each new day began with prayers, for all the hospital staff. Most of them were committed Christians. We often began an operation with prayer. We were always conscious of our need of God's help. After daily prayers there would be a medical lecture for the dressers, and every Saturday morning a test. We only taught them those things that were relevant to Amudat. They needed to be able to diagnose and treat all the prevalent tropical illnesses. But such conditions as coronary heart disease and hypertension were largely irrelevant, and we did not waste time on them. The dressers, former herd boys, who had had just a few years of Primary School education, became experts in their field. They learnt to make proper diagnoses, not guesses, and to give appropriate treatment – not the blunderbuss cocktail of chloroquine, penicillin injection and aspirin given randomly in many Government dispensaries. We encouraged them to specialise – one in laboratory work, one in health education, one in eye operations for trachoma, one as the operating theatre assistant. And day by day they did the bulk of the work of seeing outpatients, under the skilful supervision of Lilian or Ruth.

Many of our cases were of trauma. The tribe to the northwest, the Karamojong, and the Turkana in Kenya, to the northeast, made frequent cattle raids into Pokot territory – and the Pokot did likewise in return. Cattle were the wealth, the currency, the status symbol, of all these tribes. Brides had to be paid for with cattle, and the quickest way to raise a bride-price was by a cattle raid. These raids led to many deaths, and to horrific spear wounds (nowadays Kalashnikov rifles have replaced spears). One of the earliest cases I had to deal with was of a six-year-old Pokot boy. He was sitting on an anthill near to his home village, forty miles from Amudat, minding the goats. Karamojong raiders crept up behind him, and speared him. The spear entered below his right shoulder blade, and came out of his left flank. He was left for dead. But he was not dead. He was carried the forty miles to the hospital. The spear had clearly gone through his right lung, and must have missed his heart by millimetres. Open chest surgery was not an option for us, so I put in a chest drain, stitched the wounds, put him on antibiotics, and Rosemary gave him daily physiotherapy to re-expand his collapsed lung. Two weeks later he walked home, fit and well.

Another patient had been speared in the abdomen. He arrived at hospital with his bowel hanging out of his abdomen. We had no blood bank – our blood bank was walking around in the form of relatives and friends (and, in extreme emergencies, hospital staff). We had to find a few willing friends of the correct blood group, and cross-match blood. Then came the anaesthetic – always a spinal if operating 'below the belt', otherwise an ether/air mixture. Then, in this case, an exploration to assess damage done. His bowel had been perforated in a number of places, and a very taxing (for me) operation followed, that involved resecting sections of bowel, and rejoining them with anastomoses. The encouraging thing was that he survived. It always gave a tremendous feeling of satisfaction that, by being there and doing one's best, one had made a difference.

One of the operations in most demand, and for which Amudat got a reputation, was that of repair of prolapse of the uterus. But this was repair with a difference. Pokot women deliver their babies in the squatting position, and they are encouraged by the village 'midwives' to push from the onset of labour. To add to all this downward pressure the 'midwives' squat behind the mother and, wrapping their arms around the woman's abdomen, press on the uterus. Two other factors play a part. Very generous and mutilating incisions are made in the perineum, to compensate for tight circumcision scars and to aid the baby's exit. And Pokot women generally have wide pelvises, which offer little resistance to the progress of labour. All this leads to the frequent occurrence of total prolapse (procidentia) of the uterus in young women, often after just one labour. And they come to hospital, not to have a hysterectomy – that is the last thing they want. They come to be 'put back' so that they can have more children. Now that is a surgical challenge. Peter Cox and I jointly wrote an article, published in the East African Medical Journal, on 'Prolapse in Pokot Women'.

A small girl was brought one night with severe breathing difficulty (stridor) caused by swelling of the epiglottis. A strip of goatskin was tied around her chest, and her body smeared with some concoction of herbs – signs that a goat had been sacrificed and village remedies tried. She was moribund, and taking the odd gasp with extreme difficulty. She was within minutes of death. I did an emergency tracheotomy (a first for me), and the relief was dramatic. Rosemary's physiotherapy skills were again called for, and after a few days the tracheotomy tube came out, and she went home a happy, healthy child, with grateful parents. The gratitude of some patients was more than generous. An elderly man came in with acute retention of urine. He was in severe pain, and convinced that he was dying. A catheter brought instant relief. He remained in hospital for some weeks while we treated his underlying problem, and also the recurrent infections caused by his inclination to poke grass stalks up his catheter 'to clear it'. When he finally went home, catheter-free and well, he was so grateful that he offered me one of his daughters in marriage. I said I would need to discuss it first with my wife, but thanked him for the kind thought.

A common problem that we faced was that of severe burns. In the centre of each hut in a *manyatta* there would be a fire, for cooking by day and for warmth at night. In the absence of matches fire was precious, and would never be let out. If the village moved to new grazing grounds, the fire would go too, as burning embers in a container. These permanent fires in each hut were therefore a risk, particularly to children and to people with epilepsy. Epilepsy was quite common, due often to birth injuries. An epileptic person, having a fit in their hut, might be severely burned by the time they recovered consciousness. Skin-grafting of burns was one of our commoner operations. A patient with epilepsy arrived at the hospital one day, his right arm covered in a cloth. I was shocked, on removing the cloth, to find that the whole of his arm, from shoulder down, was just skeleton. The bones were bare. Just here and there a bloated maggot was finishing off the odd scrap of tissue. He had had a fit and fallen in the fire several weeks previously, and had obviously cooked the arm thoroughly. Maggots had done the rest. I offered to amputate ('disarticulate' is probably a more appropriate word) the arm. He was appalled! He wanted it mended, put back like it was. When I explained that that was just not possible he said he would go home as he was, and try the village medicine man again. What that man really needed was anticonvulsant treatment to ensure that he had no more fits. But treatment for chronic conditions like epilepsy (and tuberculosis) was a real problem. People often lived many days walk from the hospital. And their villages moved according to the grazing and water sources. They could not come back regularly to get medications. Yet if we gave them a big stock to take away with them there was a high probability that they would take them all in one go, in an attempt to get cured once and for all, or would sell them to other people. The concept of long-term, preventative medicine was not readily understood. If you ran out of tablets, and your problem recurred, then it was clearly a useless medicine.

Not all our surgery was dramatic – in fact most consisted of routine eye operations, hernia repairs and skin grafts. But one never knew what might come next. A pregnant lady was brought in, carried on a litter made from branches. She had been in labour for four days, but making no progress. She was weak and dehydrated. The baby was lying crossways (transverse lie) so there was no possibility of a normal delivery. She needed an urgent caesarian section. I made the abdominal incision (which of course is normally followed by the incision into the uterus). But as I opened the abdomen I experienced a surreal moment, when I wondered if I was dreaming. Because lying there was a large, healthy baby. But surely, I thought, I had not yet opened the uterus. Nor had I. This was a rare case of a pregnancy developing outside the uterus. The placenta was attached to the outside of the uterus – to one of the tubes and broad ligaments. The baby had managed to obtain all its nourishment, and grow to eight pounds in weight, through this bizarre attachment. Fortunately I was able to remove the placenta, and mother and baby did well. If life had not been so busy I would have written up this case for a medical journal. It was another of those humbling occasions when one realised that if we had not been there that mother and baby would both have died. Our being there, for them, had made all the difference, and made it so worthwhile.

Chapter 9
THE POKOT PEOPLE

Amudat Hospital was there primarily to serve the Pokot people, although our clients also represented many other neighbouring tribes. Patients came from far and wide, mostly on foot, but also by lorry, even by bus (during those short intervals when a spasmodic bus service ran from the nearest Ugandan towns of Moroto and Mbale, eighty and one-hundred-and-ten miles away respectively). Patients who could not walk were sometimes carried to hospital, often for many miles, on home-made litters constructed from branches. The discomfort for those in pain can be imagined, but they rarely complained. Occasionally patients were even brought by wheelbarrow. The Pokot were, by and large, living their traditional way of life, in scattered *manyattas* consisting of huts made from stick frames covered by skins or grass. Here a man and his several wives and dependants would live. The *manyatta* was surrounded by a thorn bush enclosure, to keep out wild animals, and within that barricade a further enclosure housed the precious cattle and goats at night. Their life-style was nomadic – when pasture for grazing in an area was exhausted the people of that *manyatta* would literally up-sticks and move on to new grazing grounds. Sources of water were also important. These might be pools in a dry riverbed, or a borehole. Sometimes, because of grazing, the *manyatta* would be situated miles from the water source, and one of the daily tasks of the women and children would be to fetch gourds of water for the village. It was also the work of the women to collect firewood, repair the huts, cook the food, and do all the daily chores. Children might help them, or herd the goats in the vicinity of the *manyatta*. It was the job of the men to herd the cattle, and to protect them from cattle raiders from neighbouring tribes. Every man carried his spear, and a small wooden stool – his seat by day and pillow at night.

The land does not lend itself to agriculture – it is too dry and stony, and the climate too hot. A little millet or sorghum was grown, usually near riverbeds. But the staple diet of the Pokot was the meat of their goats and cattle, together with milk for the women and children, and blood mixed with milk for the men. As their cattle were their wealth and their bank balance they were not readily killed for eating. But opportunities for a meat feast arose whenever a sacrifice was made to *Tororut*, in the event of sickness, or drought, or other disaster, or at a celebration. The staple drink of blood and milk for the men did not involve the killing of a cow. A ligature would be put around the cow's neck to engorge the jugular vein. A specially prepared arrow, with short tip, would then be fired from a few inches away into the vein. The spurt of blood would be collected in a gourd – perhaps one or two pints. A slap of mud over the vein stopped the bleeding. The blood was stirred with a stick to encourage clotting and the separation of the fibrin (which was eaten). The cow would then be milked, and the milk added to the blood, providing a smooth, nutritious, pink yoghurt-like drink. The initial taste was the sweet taste of milk fresh from the cow; the lingering taste was the salty taste of blood. Pokot men would particularly partake of a gourd of blood and milk before setting off on a cattle raid – which might involve a run of thirty miles or more into neighbouring territory, a fight, and then (if successful) a run back with the stolen cattle. There would be no time for picnics and drinks – the blood and milk had to set them up for a long run. It also, unfortunately, often gave them brucellosis or tuberculosis, both prevalent in their cattle.

I noticed in the men's ward one day three young Pokot warriors, wearing the usual *shuka* knotted at the shoulder and with the customary decorated mud headdresses. But in addition they had thongs of white goatskin tied around each wrist and ankle, and their faces and chests were decorated with stripes of white pigment. I asked one of the dressers who they were, and why they were decorated like this, and for what reason they had been admitted to hospital. The dresser looked rather sheepish. And then the story emerged. They were three warriors who had been on a cattle raid, during the course of which they had each killed a man. They had blooded their spears. This, in tribal terms, was a matter of great honour. But it also meant that they were ceremonially 'unclean'. In Old Testament fashion they each had to sacrifice a pure white goat to atone for their blood-letting. Strips of the goat's hide were then tied to their limbs, and their bodies decorated with pigment. They were then, according to custom, banished from their home villages for a month (as measured by the moon), and were allowed no contact with their girlfriends or wives. At the end of the month their right shoulders and upper arms would be scarified with an arrow head, with scores of small cuts, and an irritant plant sap rubbed into the wounds to ensure the formation of good keloid scars. These scars would, for the rest of their lives, mark them out as heroes. If they were ever to kill another person, their left shoulders and upper arms would be similarly scarified. So these three men were going through a tribal ritual. Being, however, men of resourcefulness, they had decided that, rather than sleep out in the bush for a month, they would conjure up an illness and get themselves admitted to the hospital for a period of free board and lodging.

To the Pokot our western medicine was as strange and irrational as many of their treatments were to us. Their trust had to be won. Peter Cox had done a good job over the years in winning the confidence of the people. But it was selective confidence. They trusted obviously successful treatments, such as antibiotics and hernia repairs. The more painful and unpleasant a treatment the greater their trust in it – so an injection was infinitely preferable to a tablet. And a quinine tablet beat a paracetamol hands down. But when the results were less obvious there was still a huge margin of distrust. Preventative treatments, such as those for epilepsy; or long-term treatments, when there was no immediate result, such as those for tuberculosis or leprosy, were regarded with great suspicion. Immunisations also came into this category. The sticking of needles into their children showed no obvious advantage. It took us years to demonstrate that when, for instance, a lethal measles epidemic struck, the immunised children kept well. What we had promised would happen happened. Intravenous drips were also regarded with great suspicion. On many an occasion when we had put up a drip on a child with, for example, meningitis, we would find the drip swinging, and the mother and child gone. It was often very frustrating, and time and again the patient disappeared just as they were beginning to respond to treatment. Sometimes the reason for their disappearance was not so much a distrust of our treatment, but a desire to carry out traditional treatment in parallel. A child with burns that I had skin grafted, and who was swathed in dressings, would disappear from the ward, and not infrequently we would find the family in a nearby riverbed, all the dressings removed and the child wrapped in the entrails of a sacrificed goat. They wanted to appease *Tororut*, not to displease the doctor. There was this spiritual element to so many of their traditional treatments. We had no wish to undermine their own culture, but the liberating message of the Christian Gospel was particularly relevant to this fear of God.

We could have spent all our time at Amudat Hospital, waiting for patients to come to us. But we needed to be proactive – to make regular monthly safaris to outlying villages, and stay for two or three days, and win the friendship and trust of the people. Sometimes Ruth or Lilian would go with a hospital dresser. Sometimes I went. And when I went sometimes the family came with me. But this was not luxury camping. This was camping at its rawest. We would drive twenty or thirty miles into the range of rugged hills, the Karapokot Hills, to the east of Amudat. These hills stretched for sixty miles from north to south, along the Uganda/Kenya border. We would head for little centres, such as Alale, Kauriong and Kasei. Or sometimes we went to Katabok, at the foot of Kadam mountain. The tracks to these places were extremely rough, and required four-wheel drive and low ratio for most of the journey. There were steep riverbeds to cross, and gullies and rocks to negotiate. It was slow going, and hard on the Landrover. Often the track had to be patched up before we could pass. Some of these outposts had a small primary school, in which case we would pitch our tents next to the corrugated iron schoolroom, and set up clinic. The news would soon spread to neighbouring *manyattas* that we were there, and people would begin to arrive from the hills and valleys around. Everybody would claim to be ill. Nobody wanted to miss out on the opportunity for some medicine. Some would join the queue twice in the hope of getting another dose of something – anything would do!

Always we gave priority to immunisation. So many of the killing and disabling illnesses were entirely preventable – measles, tetanus, poliomyelitis, tuberculosis, whooping cough and smallpox (the last being finally eradicated from the world soon after that, thanks to effective immunisation). On each occasion increasing numbers of mothers would agree to let us immunise their children, and each time it was a step forward. At some stage in the day we would break off and have a very informal service – the dresser might teach them a Christian song in Pokot, and then tell them what his faith in Jesus meant to him. I might give a very simple explanation of the Christian message. Then it would be back to work. By evening, and before the swift fall of darkness, people would begin to drift off home to their *manyattas*. We would have a simple supper round the camp fire, and marvel at the panoply of stars, so bright and clear in the dark, unpolluted night sky. We would lie on our backs and see who was first to spot a meteorite shooting through the sky. It was at times like this that we really got to know our dressers, and their background stories, and their hopes and aspirations. We exchanged tales and jokes. We prayed together. Then to bed, serenaded by the African night sounds. There would often be distant rhythmic singing from a *manyatta*, the words of the songs probably recounting the events of the day – the day when the doctor came.

On one safari, at Kasei, in the hills, a lady asked me to visit her mother who had a bad leg. 'How far?' I asked. 'Oh, only just over the hill. Not far,' she said. Two and a half hours and seven strenuous miles later we reached her mother's village. The old lady was seized up with arthritis, and could hardly move. 'All I want is life!' she said. We had so little to offer her medically, apart from some temporary painkillers. The dresser, Andrew, spoke briefly to her about the new life that God offers in Jesus, and which continues through illness and beyond death. The old lady really appreciated that we had gone – that we had bothered. Medically it had been a wasted trip, and yet it is never a waste to bother. It was on that safari that the teacher in the little primary school gave us a parting gift of a haunch of meat – beef, we assumed. This was a rare treat, and we were most grateful, and looked forward to enjoying it when we got back to Amudat. Just before we left I happened to pass his tin house, and glanced in. There, sitting on a tray in the middle of his table, was the head of a donkey. For some reason our appetites dissipated! We gave the 'beef' away to a grateful recipient once we got back to Amudat.

Travel to remote villages had its hazards, but so too did travel on main roads. We were driving to Mbale, the main Ugandan town to our southwest, to collect petrol, salary money and other supplies. My sister, Marilyn, was visiting us from England, and Rosemary and the children were with us. As we neared a small settlement, Namalu, we saw ahead a column of people, walking in single file. As we drew closer we noticed that they were all tied round the neck to a long rope – and that a considerable length of spare rope still trailed at the rear of the column. They were being marshalled by a very officious looking man with a gun. He flagged us down, stuck his very alcoholic-smelling face through my window, and shouted 'Wapi codi?' Fortunately I understood what he meant – a visitor would not have done so. He wanted to see my poll tax receipt, which, it just so happened, I had sent off to our Mission Treasurer in order to get a refund. When I explained my problem, and the drunk official saw that I was not going to produce my 'codi', he wrenched open the car door, and began to drag me out. Clearly I was going to be the next victim on his rope of 'codi' dodgers. In fact we might all end up on his rope. Fortuitously my seat belt prevented him from hauling me out. I put the car in gear and drove off. He ran with the car for a bit, but then had to let go, and my last view of him in the rear mirror was of him trying to get his gun off his shoulder.

I had one or two brushes with officialdom in court. From time to time I was called to give medical evidence in court cases. We had not been in Amudat long, and I was busy at work in the hospital, wearing my usual shorts and open-necked shirt, when a policeman arrived to summon me immediately to give evidence in court, taking place in a nearby schoolroom. I went as ordered. The schoolroom was built of corrugated iron, rather dilapidated and hot as an oven. The magistrate was seated at a rickety wooden table; the ragged individual whom I assumed to be the accused stood behind a school desk. There was a motley array of spectators sitting on a bench at the back of the room. I was told to take the witness stand, was sworn in – and then the magistrate began a furious tirade. At first I thought it was directed at the accused, but then I realised it was at me. 'How dare you insult my court? How dare you?' he shouted. I must have looked rather nonplussed. 'Where is your tie? Why are you not properly dressed?' I was given no opportunity to explain that I had had no warning of my summons to court; or that any tie I possessed was still on a ship somewhere between Mombasa and England; or that I had certainly intended no insult. He ordered me out of court, and gave me twenty minutes to return properly dressed. I returned to the house, was loaned by Liza a gaudy tie of Peter's, had to accept that I had no long trousers or jacket (still on the ship), and returned to court. The tie did the trick. I was now acceptable to give evidence – though probably still borderline. Here in remote Uganda, in oppressive heat, in a tumbledown schoolroom, with the accused and spectators wearing rags or next to nothing, I had to wear a tie, in order to satisfy the self-importance of the magistrate. It was interesting how different his attitude was the next time I met him – when he had driven eighty miles to get treatment from me.

The Amudat police inspector (a down-country Ugandan) called at hospital one day to ask if we had admitted a man who had been knocked down by a Landrover. We had not. He said that the Pokot who were with the man, and who had reported the incident, were ignorant people, who could not give the number of the vehicle, or even describe it. How then, I wondered, did the police inspector know that the vehicle had been a Landrover? After he had gone I discussed the matter with the staff, and we all agreed that we had seen only three vehicles that day travelling on that road, and all three had been police Landrovers, and all driving very fast. We heard and thought no more about the incident until two weeks later, when a CID officer asked me to go with him to view a body near the roadside, about ten miles away, and to establish the cause of death. There, under a bush, was a bloodstained cloth, some beads, a jaw bone and three chewed ribs. And standing beside them a very distraught elderly Pokot man. 'Now they have brought you!' he cried out to me. 'I found my son's body soon after he was killed. I reported to the police then, and they would not bring you. Then his body was whole. Now the hyenas have eaten him. And *now* they bring you!'

The CID officer was clearly angry with the man for what he was saying. I turned to the policeman and asked him, 'How do you expect me to establish a cause of death from these remains?' It seemed very clear to me that that was precisely why they had delayed bringing me until now. They did not want a cause of death to be established – because it had involved a police Landrover, driving very fast, two weeks earlier. At times like that how I wished I had forensic experience, and the power to examine all local police Landrovers for dents and damage. Report it, maybe, to the Head of Department? But I was talking to him! Corruption will be the death of Africa.

Chapter 10
A SEEDLING CHURCH

The Christian Church in Amudat grew out of the medical work. The approach of the Coxes, and Lilian and Ruth, and other mission partners in Amudat had, from the start, been holistic – to care for body, mind and soul. The Pokot people had enormous health needs. Most would agree that those should be met. But some would say 'Leave it at that! Don't interfere with their beliefs and traditions. Don't try to impose a 'western' belief system on them. Don't try to convert them to Christianity.' The problem with that viewpoint is threefold – firstly their health needs, spiritual beliefs and culture were closely interwoven and inseparable; secondly, Christianity is no more a western belief system than Jesus was a westerner; thirdly, as Christians we have a commission, a duty, laid on us by Jesus Himself to share the Good News with all the world. A non-Christian will not accept the last point, but the first two are unarguable. The Pokot have a holistic view of life. They believe in the Supreme Being, *Tororut*, and they see every event of life – whether birth, death, sickness, drought, rain, famine or disaster – as being inextricably linked with the spiritual. Their customs, culture and whole belief system involves the physical and the spiritual. In fact they would have been most surprised if we had come just to treat their bodies, and had ignored their spiritual needs. The policy of our Mission, BCMS, was to share unapologetically the Good News of Jesus Christ, at the same time caring for medical and social needs to the best of our ability. In other words, to care for the whole person. It was not our policy to denigrate or destroy the many good aspects of tribal culture – the strong family structure; the way of life in which everybody made their contribution; the strong tribal loyalty. Nor was it our policy to encourage naked men to wear trousers, or women in skins to wear dresses – although from the point of view of hygiene dresses did have an advantage over goat skins. Ironically it was the African Government of Uganda which ruled that western type clothes must be worn. It was they who felt ashamed of, even sometimes despised, their 'naked' countrymen in Pokot and Karamoja. It was (in due course) General Amin's trigger-happy soldiers who shot dead anybody seen naked or in skins. It was not missionaries who changed all that – although it is missionaries whom anthropologists love to blame.

Over the years, from when Peter Cox first arrived in Amudat in 1957, small numbers of people began to come to faith in Jesus Christ, and the seeds of a Church were sown. For each individual the experience of personal faith was hugely liberating and transforming. The concept that *Tororut* is a God of love; a God who knows and cares for each individual; a God who came among us, and died for us, and offers a whole new quality of life here and now, and life beyond death; a God who forgives, and renews, and offers new starts, and joy and hope. All this replaced the cloud of fear and hopelessness under which they had lived. It was not a case of doing away with their God, but of bringing new insight and understanding about him. And all this is not the starry-eyed wishful thinking of a missionary. It is the real experience of many Pokot friends we have known. It is their own testimony.

In time the little mud church was built, and a Christian community grew up. It was an Anglican church by denomination, because BCMS is an Anglican missionary society. Our vicar, the Reverend Timothy Oluoch, was Anglican. But the label was unimportant – except in so far as it was helpful for the little Church to belong to a wider Christian organisation. The Sunday services were basically Anglican in form. It was ironical that we missionaries would have liked much more local culture in the services – drums, and Pokot tunes, and informality. But for the local Christians some of these things were too close to a life and to beliefs from which they had moved on. To them Anglican worship was new and exciting. Christian worship was not just confined to Sunday services, but was integrated into all that we did. We had a daily ward service in the hospital, we shared the Christian message when out on safari, there were fellowship meetings for Christians in the week, faith often came up in conversation with people. Rosemary helped to run a thriving Sunday School, and she had a little bookstall on a rocky outcrop outside church each Sunday. Most Sundays someone (often Rosemary) would visit Amudat's little prison, and hold a service there. On one occasion I was speaking in the prison when a cow chose to give birth just outside the prison's barbed wire fence. There was a terrific hullabaloo of mooing and moaning, which quite distracted us all, and my talk had to be interrupted until the birth was safely over. In one way and another the foundations were being laid for – or, perhaps, birth being given to – what is now a thriving church.

A factor that complicated Christian witness in Amudat (as in most of Africa) was the presence of two rival versions of Christianity – the Protestants (us) and the Roman Catholics. Catholic missionaries belonging to the order of the Verona Fathers arrived in Amudat soon after Uganda's independence, and established a mission about half a mile from the hospital and Anglican church. They did not see the Protestant version of the faith as being valid, and set out to convert or proselytise as many people as possible. Their catechists were even paid a bonus for each convert baptised into the Roman Catholic church. The Verona Fathers were well resourced, and able to build a far superior church and school to ours. They were also in a position to recruit 'rice Christians' by their generous hand-outs. Time showed that such converts have little substance. Such rivalry is sad, and surely contrary to Jesus' prayer that His people would be one. On a personal level we established good relationships with the Fathers (as the Coxes had done before us). Father Raphael was a cheerful, avuncular Italian, and his colleague, Father Petri, a most friendly, gentle person. From time to time we had a meal together, and discussed the faith, and found that we had much in common. It was so sad that their rules forbade us to share communion with them, and that they considered 'our' Christians to be invalid, both in doctrine and baptism. An occasion that left me feeling very uncomfortable was when one of the Catholic priests (not Raphael or Petrie) confidentially brought a teenage schoolgirl to me and asked me to carry out an abortion on her. I was amazed to be asked such a thing by a priest, and explained that it was against my Christian principles, but that I would help her in any way I could with the pregnancy. The priest was very persistent, and it eventually, and inevitably, emerged that he was the father. The colour of the baby would, in due course, make that very obvious. I arranged for the girl to be cared for at a home down country, and the priest soon disappeared back to his country of origin. To me it underlined the problem of a celibate priesthood. It was a very lonely life for these Catholic priests. All credit to those who remain true to their vows – and all credit, too, to that noble army of single lady missionaries, who have contributed so much, so selflessly, to the cause of mission. I do not know how I would have survived the loneliness and rigours of Amudat without Rosemary and the family.

Very soon after our arrival in Amudat I was asked to preach at the Sunday morning service. I did so in English, and was translated into Kiswahili (for down country folk – police etc) and Pokot (for the locals). It was not long before I was challenged by the Reverend Timothy to preach in Kiswahili. It was this challenge, and the preparing of sermons in Kiswahili, that did far more for my language skills than any amount of study or Language School. Whether I always said in my sermons what I intended to say is of course another matter. I can probably be held personally responsible for any strange doctrines that may be going around Amudat to this day. On one occasion a visiting English preacher spoke about the nature of Jesus, and His being 'wholly' man and 'wholly' God. Throughout the sermon his translator used the word 'mtakatifu', or 'holy', which, though true, somewhat missed the point of the sermon. Translation, whether in church or in the hospital, sometimes ended up like a game of Chinese whispers.

Our bishop, Neville Langford-Smith, became aware that I was regularly leading services and preaching. According to Anglican protocol this was strictly irregular. I had not been licensed to do so. But he knew well that, in our remote situation, anything he said would make little difference. It was easier to 'go with the flow'. No doubt taking into account my six months theological training at Tyndale Hall he decided to make me a Licensed Lay Reader. On 5 February 1969, out of the blue, a most impressive document, complete with Episcopal seal, arrived in the post. It began with stirring words, along the lines of: 'We Neville, by the hand of God, in the year of our Lord . . .' and proceeded to tell me that I was now a Lay Reader in the Anglican Church and could legally do what I was doing already. Being something of a rebel I thought it was all rather amusing. The document became known in the family as the 'We

Neville' document. I filed it, and forgot about it. I never wore robes, or obtained a Reader's scarf – it never crossed my mind to do so. Ten years later, at Malvern Priory, that document proved to be very useful in saving me from a long and demanding Readers' training course. I whispered a rather belated 'Thank you!' to Bishop Neville.

Sunday services in Amudat, though often long, hot and tedious, were never conventional. There would be frequent hawking and spitting in the congregation. A naked warrior might suddenly arrive and greet the congregation. Proceedings would stop as greetings were reciprocated, and he settled himself onto a bench. On one occasion I had thrown out a torn but colourful pair of pyjamas – a relic of our honeymoon. They were retrieved by Songa Karibu, our hot water man, who bore them proudly home. Next Sunday there stood Songa in church, just in front of us, resplendent in my pyjamas, the rent across the trousers tacked colourfully together with bright cotton. Another memorable service was one of baptisms, including that of the baby of Samson and Mary – an important occasion, clearly calling for the very best in headwear. Mary was wearing a colourful plastic shower cap, that Ruth had discarded. It rose from her head in layer upon layer of resplendent frills. Appropriately a heavy shower of rain began to drum on the leaky tin church roof, drowning out at times all sound of the service. That baptism service was conducted by our rather parsonical Archdeacon Mukula, who was visiting Amudat. Perhaps due to the noise of the rain he misheard the name 'Geraldina' of one baby, and baptised her 'Jellybeana'. The Websters could be seen apparently in fervent prayer, heads bowed, shoulders shaking convulsively, and tears streaming down our faces.

Some of our Amudat friends were remarkable people, with vibrant faith. Solomon Mworor was headmaster of the Primary School. He married Margaret, daughter of the tribal chief, Lopongo. It was an important wedding. Solomon and Margaret asked us to decorate the church for the wedding. How do you decorate a church in the middle of a semi-desert? Ingenuity was called for. We cut a large branch from a thorn tree, and on to each three inch thorn we threaded a frangipani flower. The effect and the scent were beautiful. Solomon's mother came to the wedding adorned in traditional Pokot dress – with numerous necklaces and bangles of copper and beads. It was a big tribal, as well as Christian, occasion. And it was a wonderful witness to the importance and sanctity of Christian marriage. Present at that wedding was Solomon's teenage brother, Stephen Kiwasis, then a schoolboy. Stephen became a Christian around that time. Now he is Bishop of Kitale, responsible for the multiplying Anglican churches throughout Pokot country.

Samson Adio was short and jovial, enthusiasm personified. He became our hospital Health Worker, with the ability to convey to patients, in an understandable and practical way, simple hygiene measures – the danger of flies, the importance of washing hands and face, how to prevent burns in the hut by simply covering the open fire with a flat stone, and so on. He was also a most effective evangelist. Samson married young Mary Chemosop, who became Ruth's helper in running a hostel for girls. We had high hopes for them. Sadly, in time, Samson succumbed to drink, lost his faith, and the marriage broke up. Mary continues to be a leading light in the community.

John Makal was a young schoolboy whom we recruited as a dresser. He married another Mary. John grew in faith during his time as a dresser, and in due course left Amudat to train for the Church Army. Years later he was ordained into the Anglican Church. He has been vicar to a burgeoning parish in the Karapokot hills, with new churches springing up all over the place. He has done, and is doing, great work for God.

Before we came to Amudat a father had brought his young son to the hospital. He was called Mlee, or 'Bag' – probably because he had been born in a caul. His father thought Mlee was going blind. He was right – he was going blind from juvenile macular degeneration, an untreatable condition. When this was explained to the father he abandoned Mlee at the hospital. After all, how could a blind child possibly cope with life in the *manyatta*? He would be a liability. In due course Mlee went to the Primary School. As his vision deteriorated so his faith in Jesus began to blossom. He asked to be baptised, and was called Joshua. For a while he helped in the hospital, and then it was arranged for him to go to the superb Salvation Army School for the Blind at Thika, in Kenya. By now Joshua was totally blind. He learned Braille, and various practical skills. And his faith continued to grow. His one aim was to return to his own people, and to help other blind people to make a go of life. Joshua had the most lovely wall-to-wall smile, with flashing white teeth. He loved to share his faith with anyone who would listen. One of his favourite quotes was from the story in the Gospels (John 9:25) of the blind man healed by Jesus. The man, when challenged by the sceptical religious leaders of the day, said, 'One thing I know – once I was blind, but now I can see!' 'This is true for me too,' Joshua would add, beaming. 'But you can't see! Once you could see, but now you are blind!' his listeners would protest. And Joshua would say: 'My eyes may be blind. But once my heart was blind. I did not know Jesus. Now I know Him, and in my heart I can see! That is the one thing I know!'

Chapter 11
VISITORS

Amudat is remote and isolated, and yet we found ourselves hosts to an enormous numbers of visitors. The reason was that its isolation is enough to be exciting, romantic, 'the real Africa'; and yet it is accessible by any reasonably sturdy motor vehicle. A further factor that added to our number of guests was the Kanyangereng river. Lying immediately north of the shops, the riverbed bisects the main road leading to Lodwar and to the western shores of Lake Turkana. Lake Turkana was a popular holiday venue for adventurous Europeans. Its wildness and remoteness and mystery attracted those with a bent for exploration – especially teachers on holiday. But when the Kanyangereng was in spate it was not crossable, and the road to Lake Turkana was closed. (My father had discovered this many years before, when on safari in the area with the then bishop. Their car came to a full stop mid-stream. My father climbed out to assess the situation, stepped off the rough causeway, and disappeared under the muddy water. The bishop was highly amused, and asked him to do it again for a photograph.) In my father's time there was nothing to do but to wait on the riverbank until the water subsided – which could be several days. In our time, however, if a carload of Europeans found their way blocked by the swollen river the local people would direct them to our house for accommodation. Africans are, by nature, very generous and hospitable, and just as they would expect to look after their own in a crisis, so they assumed that we would wish to take care of any *Wazungu* in need.

Our visitors' book reveals that, during our six years in Amudat, we had, on average, more than one visitor on every day and night of those six years. They were mainly of four categories – people stranded by the river, or just wanting to break their journey; friends or missionary colleagues having a break; medical visitors who had come in a professional capacity; and medical students from Britain, staying with us for their Elective Periods. We did not often have the home to ourselves and treasured those times when we did.

The Kanyangereng sometimes brought us visitors in bulk. On one occasion I was called from the hospital to help some *Wazungu* who were stranded. I found a convoy of four carloads of teachers and their families, on their way to Lake Turkana. There were twenty one of them in all, including children. They were not sure whether to attempt to cross the swollen river. I strongly advised them against any such thing – even a Landrover would have been swept away. I invited them to stay with us until such time as the river subsided. I told them how to find our house, and hoped to get there first to warn Rosemary. But I got delayed, and arrived at the house just in time to see Rosemary and one of the wives falling into one another's arms with shrieks of delight. They had been together at St Catherine's School, Bramley, eleven years previously. That was one of those occasions when we had plenty of guests but very little food in the house. They contributed some, but we were still short, and we had no idea how long they would be with us. As we were contemplating this dilemma a truck drew up at the house. It was the builder, Bert Allen, who was working on the hospital extensions. He had just arrived from his home at Tororo, and had brought us a load of fresh vegetables, fruit and meat. 'I thought you might find them useful,' he said. We did! Every corner of the house was occupied that night. Two days later the river had subsided sufficiently for me to tow their cars through with the Landrover.

This was by no means the only time our needs were met at the last minute. On one occasion visitors stayed longer than expected, and the cupboard was literally bare. We had no idea what we would eat at the next meal. Again, a car drew up. It was a friend from down country with a box full of fresh provisions. Time and again we experienced the faithfulness of God through the generosity of people.

One of the great privileges of living in Amudat was the contact that it brought with many outstanding medical specialists. Some came on visits with the flying doctors. Some drove up, and stayed. There was a great fund of goodwill in the upper echelons of medicine in Kampala and Nairobi to help, support and encourage our work in Amudat. This was largely due to good relationships built up by Peter Cox over the years. Particularly supportive were Michael Hutt, the Professor of Pathology at Makerere (who had taught me as a student at St Thomas's), Denis Birkitt (of the Medical Research Council) and Ralph Schram (with whom we stayed in Kampala at the time of Paul's birth). In due course, when we returned to England, I had to detail for the medical powers-that-be such medical teaching that I had had during my time in East Africa. I was able to provide two A4 pages of names of medical specialists of consultant level, many of them of world renown, who had actually stayed with us. I had done ward rounds with, operated with, and sat under the stars and discussed medicine with, some of the very best. It was a time when Makerere and Nairobi medical schools were in their heyday.

One of our greatest joys over the years was that of having medical students come to stay for their Electives, often for two months. We forged many lasting friendships in this way. A number were from St Thomas's, and were members of the Christian Union. They knew about our work, and prayed regularly for us. It was especially good, for us and for them, when they could come and be a part of it. We also had applications from further afield. Paul and Sophie were a delightful American couple, Pentecostals and newly married. They came from a city background. Sophie offered to help in any way, and Rosemary asked her if she would shell the peas for supper. Sophie looked puzzled, and asked what to do. She had never seen peas in anything other than a frozen pack. It was a long way to come to discover peapods. Paul and Sophie were desperately keen to hear a lion while with us, and we assured them that they would. But for some reason the lions went quiet throughout their time. Their last night came, and I did not wish them to leave disappointed. When they had gone to bed in the little guesthouse I crept out with our battery operated record player, and a record of animal sounds. I placed it under their window, put on the lion-grunting section, and crept away. Two wide-eyed faces appeared at the window, straining to see the lion. 'Oh Paul!' 'Oh Sophie!' Their voices trembled with excitement. Unfortunately the moon was full, and as their eyes adjusted Paul let out a reverberating 'Oh no!'

On another occasion I went through the same procedure for another couple, who were staying in Ruth's little house, about two hundred yards from ours through the bush. I sat, with the record player, in a gulley just below Ruth's house. As the grunting and roaring of my record got going

I was horrified to hear a real lion replying from a bit further down the valley. My 'lion' had obviously encroached on another's territory. I picked up the record player, still playing, and headed for the safety of Ruth's house – and met head on our intrepid friend who was coming the other way, in the darkness, to get a better view of the lion.

Before we arrived in Amudat, or knew that we would be going there, Peter Cox had made an arrangement for a medical student and his wife from New York to come to Amudat for two months. I inherited that arrangement. I will call them Bob and Annie. Bob was a final year medical student. Annie was already a qualified doctor. On the day that they were due to arrive Father Petrie shot a warthog – 'He looks just like the devil himself!' he assured me, but whether he knew that from personal experience he did not say. Father Petrie gave us a leg of the warthog, a rare treat – and such an appropriate way to welcome our new American guests. They arrived in a car that they had bought in Kampala (all the hospitality money that they were supposed to pay us had gone towards its cost – they would pay us when they eventually sold the car, they assured us). Things seemed to start reasonably well, and Bob tucked into his warthog. 'This is sure nice turkey you've got here!' he said. 'Actually it's not turkey, it's warthog,' Rosemary explained cheerfully. 'Oh!' he said, and pushed his unfinished plate away. In our naivety the penny did not drop. I assumed that maybe they were anti-hunting. The next day we had pork sausages – for the sake of convenience, and ease of transport, a regular part of our food order from Kitale consisted of sausages. This time both Bob and Annie pushed their plates away. Still we did not register. But the damage was done. It was not until several days had passed that we realised that they were Jews, and Orthodox Jews at that, who ate only kosher food. They had not forewarned us – or maybe Peter Cox forgot to tell us. On that first day they apparently went to see their fellow American, Max, and told him that we had deliberately set out to insult and humiliate them on their very first evening with us, by giving them pig. Max, instead of telling us, decided to clear out of Amudat for the next two months. 'Oh! Oh!' he told us in his drawl, weeks later, 'I sensed trouble ahead!' We were indeed naïve. Apparently Bob and Annie's surname was a give-away – a common Jewish surname in New York. We did not know that. Nor did we know that their medical school in New York is for Jewish students. Max knew, and he assumed that we did too. Our relationship with Bob and Annie had got off to a bad start, and went downhill from there.

On their first day with us Bob and Annie came to hospital for the daily ward round. As was our practice, the wards had just been washed down with Lysol. Annie's eyes began to stream. She was allergic to Lysol. She said she would have to return to the house. I offered to drive her home, but she insisted that she would walk. I pointed out the short cut to her. 'Walk to that thorn tree. Just beyond it you will come to a road. Turn left up the road and you will come to our house.' The heat of the day was building up. Little gusts of hot wind were stirring up the dust. Annie's face was already red and sweaty. But she set off for home, while Bob and I continued the ward round. Nearly three hours later a beetroot red, distressed Annie staggered into the hospital. She had been lost in the bush. 'How?' I asked. 'Where could you possibly have gone wrong?' Annie had come to the road that I had mentioned. But to her a 'road' implied breadth, kerbstones, even tarmac, maybe street lights! My 'road' was just a track. So she had ignored that, crossed over, and continued through the bush until she eventually reached the banks of the dry Kanyangereng riverbed. Now here was something more like a road, she thought – wide, smooth, lined by trees. She turned left up the riverbed, and followed it for about two miles before realising that she must have gone wrong. Fortunately she was able to retrace her steps to the hospital. It brought home to me how wide was the culture gap between New York and Amudat.

Throughout their two months with us Bob and Annie found it impossible to bridge that culture gap. They insisted on prescribing very expensive antibiotics for relatively simple infections – because that was 'the right thing to do' according to American protocol. The fact that we were running a hospital for a year on a budget that would have barely lasted seconds in New York just did not register with them. When on safari in the remotest part of the Karapokot hills Annie asked why, in order to prevent brucellosis, we did not tell the people to buy tetrapak milk. It was as though they came from another planet. Everything I did was questioned and criticised. It was a most stressful two months. Their duplicity with money annoyed me. Bob would barter for Pokot spears and stools, and would knock the prices down to ridiculously low levels, because people were so desperate for some cash. They had already told us that they could not pay us anything for their keep until they sold their car. We were struggling financially, and were having to spend more out on food because of their dietary requirements. And yet this supposedly penniless couple bought, with cash, two expensive paintings from a passing artist – costing more than they owed us for the whole of their stay. So they had had the money all along! When they did finally pay us they deducted from the twenty-shillings-(£1)-a-day hospitality charge the cost of luxury items, such as prawns, that they had themselves bought to supplement the 'awful' diet we provided. Needless to say, the report I had to submit to the dean of his medical school about Bob's time with us was not altogether complimentary. Bob was furious, and in return submitted a report about me, which he thoughtfully copied to me. I was 'anti-Semitic, racist, arrogant, incompetent' and much more besides. We were glad when that episode of life was over. Fortunately the majority of our visitors were interesting, delightful people, who enriched our lives, and with whom it was a privilege to share our home.

Chapter 12
TWO TRAGEDIES

Under the direction of Max, the US army kala-azaar research project limped along throughout 1968. It was not very clear what exactly their methods and objectives were. Max seemed to spend far more time hunting, or extending his little empire of mud huts and vassals, than he did in any serious research. Whenever Colonel Dale Wykoff came on one of his rare visits the main objective seemed to be to hunt. One could not help feeling that to them it was all a bit of a game – the big boys at play in the bush, by courtesy of the US army. To hear Max talk of his exploits in Vietnam made that terrible war also sound like something of a game. We did two medical safaris together, to find, diagnose and treat patients with kala-azaar. I carried out spleen punctures on likely cases, in the bush, under the trees – not as risky a procedure as it may sound, as the Pokot all had quite firm, fibrous spleens from recurrent malaria. We microscopically examined spleen fluid on the spot to confirm the diagnosis, and Max took blood samples. This was all useful cooperation, and it benefited the patients. But our working together like this happened all too rarely.

An aspect of the research that did concern me was that of capturing and identifying biting sandflies. Sandflies are very small insects – smaller than mosquitoes – which carry the protozoa that cause kala-azaar. One of their favourite daytime habitats is inside the cool tunnels of termite hills. At dusk they emerge to find and feed on the blood of any warm-blooded creature in the vicinity. It is the females which bite. The aim of the research project was to identify which sandflies bit, and how many were carrying the kala-azaar protozoa. In order to do this Max hired lads to sit on anthills in the evening time and to look out for any sandflies that bit them. They then sucked the biting flies with a pipette into a test tube. The test tubes were carefully marked with the date and site of the anthill. Hundreds of specimens were thus collected over a period of time. My concern was that these lads were being deliberately exposed to the risk of getting kala-azaar – a serious and debilitating illness, with an unpleasant treatment that did not always work. The ethics of it disturbed me.

In early January 1969 the British entomologist involved in the project, George Barnley, came up to Amudat with his wife and young daughter with the object of picking up all the sandfly samples – boxes and boxes of test tubes, awaiting further examination and identification. They stayed overnight and set off back to Kampala with their precious cargo the next day. Later that day we received the tragic news, by our Flying Doctor radio, that their Landrover had overturned on a bend. Mrs Barnley had been killed, and George and his daughter injured. Max, who was away north at Moroto, had been ordered by Colonel Wykoff to proceed immediately to Mbale to collect the body of Mrs Barnley, and to take her to Kampala. We were all greatly upset by Mrs Barnley's death. We also discovered that the many specimens of sandfly had been smashed in the crash, and months of research work had been destroyed. In the circumstances this loss seemed relatively trivial.

That night, at about 10 p.m., as was our routine at bedtime, I set off along the path, through the bush that surrounded our house, to our little generator house, to turn off the lights. Suddenly I was startled by a crashing in the bushes to one side, and a wild looking Max appeared through the inky darkness, his rifle at the ready. 'Max, don't shoot! It's me!' I shouted. It transpired that Max, very distressed at the news of Mrs Barnley's death, had set off, as instructed, to collect her body. But he needed to come via Amudat to get some clothing. He turned up, unexpected by his gang of employees. They were under orders never to leave his compound at night, and never to entertain others on his premises. In both respects they had taken advantage of his absence to disobey his orders. Max arrived back after dark to find half his men missing, and strangers sleeping on the compound. He went wild with anger, grabbed his rifle, the strangers fled, terrified and naked, into the bush, and Max chased them. He thought that I, on my way to turn off the generator, was one of them, and I came close to being shot. Max set off again that night to Mbale and Kampala on his distressing mission.

Three days later it was siesta time. The heat of the day was at its peak. The glare of the sun, as it shimmered over the bare, burnt acacia scrubland, was painful to the eyes. The birds, even the flies, were resting up in whatever shade they could find, and the world was silent. Rosemary and I had collapsed, as was our custom after lunch, onto the bed in the relative cool of our bedroom. How thankful we felt for the spreading fig tree that shaded that end of the house. I was trying to keep awake, and to concentrate on a book, but torpor was getting the better of me. Suddenly and startlingly the stillness was broken by a breathless, terrified youth, who burst up to our door, panting 'Doctor! Doctor! You must come at once! Max is going to shoot us!' I hurried with him to Max's compound. There to my astonishment I found that Max had trussed up several of his lads – hands and feet tied together behind them, so that they were bent back double, and quite helpless. He had placed one of them on a table, with a loaded rifle pointing at his head. 'Max!' I shouted. 'What do you think you are doing?' 'I'm just interrogating them, Dave!' he drawled 'They disobeyed my orders the other night, and I caught them red-handed! They are a bunch of thieves!' I was appalled. No doubt Max imagined in his fevered mind that he was back in Viet Nam, interrogating Viet Cong. 'You have no right to take the law into your hands, Max!' I protested. 'If you have anything to accuse them of then tell the Police!' 'O.K. Dave! I'll do it your way,' he said, as I began to untie his victims. We went together to the Police, to ensure things were done properly. Five days later, when Max had gone off to Kampala again, I discovered that two of his lads were languishing in prison – Max had apparently insisted that the police lock them up. Uncharged, untried, unconvicted they were nevertheless in prison, in effect at Max's pleasure. I negotiated their release, and the matter was never mentioned again by Max.

Just as 1968 had been a year of culture shock, adjustment and illness, so 1969 seemed to be the year of tragedies. Six years previously, at the St Thomas's Hospital Christian Union Houseparty at which Peter Cox spoke, and when Rosemary and I both felt, quite independently, God's call to missionary work, a third person present had also felt God's prompting. Janet Fenwick had recently qualified as a Nightingale (a St Thomas's nurse). 'Qualified' is an understatement – Jan had won the Gold Medal. She was at a crossroads in her life, and at that houseparty Peter Cox persuaded her to join him in Amudat for a year, while Lilian

Singleton took home leave. Towards the end of Jan's year in Amudat Dr Graham Fraser arrived to do a locum. He and Jan only overlapped by three weeks, and so did not have long to get to know one another, but it was apparently long enough. Correspondence followed, when Jan returned to England. It is said that when Graham flew in to Heathrow to see his beloved once again he was wearing one brown shoe and one black – surely the sign of a man very much in love! They returned to Kenya, got married, and initially went to Marsabit, and then to Kapenguria hospital, just sixty miles south of Amudat, and over the Kenya border. They were our nearest medical neighbours.

Graham Fraser, Peter Cox, Maurice Heyman, Peter Green and I were all part of what was called The Northern Frontier Medical Mission (NFMM). This was really the brainchild of Peter Cox and Bishop Neville. Scattered across the vast northern districts of Kenya were Government District Hospitals – notably Marsabit, Moyale, Maralal and Kapenguria. Although strictly in Uganda, Amudat was included in the scheme. The Kenya Government found it difficult to staff these isolated hospitals with Kenyan doctors. A posting to any one of them was sometimes considered (and occasionally probably was) a punishment. A Government doctor so posted was quite likely to resign, and go instead into private practice in one of the towns. Missionary agencies, especially BCMS, had doctors available keen to work in these remote parts, but the policy of the Society was not, itself, to run hospitals. The NFMM was a scheme to match these needs – the Mission would second its doctors to the Kenya Government, to work as Medical Officers of Health, based at Government hospitals. They would be answerable to the Government, and have proper contracts, but it would also be recognised that they were members of a Mission. For a number of years the scheme worked well, and to everybody's benefit. Graham Fraser had come to Kapenguria as the MOH for that district.

In July 1969 Graham and Jan paid us a visit in Amudat. It was their first time to return since they originally met there. It was a very brief visit, but we got on so well, and we urged them to come again, and stay longer. I appreciated being able to share with Graham our mutual challenges and problems, in running one-doctor hospitals. They came again, for a long weekend in the October, with their two small children – Quentin, a toddler, and Simon, a baby. Graham and I had a long discussion under the terminalia trees outside our house, learning from one another. I loved his gentle nature, and his thorough approach to medicine. Running a hospital single-handed is a lonely job, and to share with a like-minded colleague was a blessing to us both. Graham was finding his work at Kapenguria a great relief after Marsabit. There he and Jan had had to contend with many stresses and problems, in particular the constant danger when travelling from active *shifta* (bandits). We looked forward to many more get-togethers, and arranged to visit them in Kapenguria two months later.

The day after leaving us Graham had to drive down to Nakuru for a Board meeting of the NFMM. On his way back, as he was nearing Kitale, and just thirty miles from home, his car's front tyre burst. The car swerved, hit a concrete culvert, and Graham was thrown headfirst through the windscreen. (The car had been booked to have seat belts fitted the very next day.) Graham was critically injured. He was taken to Kitale hospital. Jan got the news in Kapenguria, and rushed to be with him, arriving shortly before he died. It was stunning, heart-breaking news. We wept for Jan and her two small children. The funeral was in Kitale two days later. Crowds came to it. The Reverend (later Bishop) Howell Davies preached – 'He walked with God, and God took him.' Why God took him, such a good man, in the prime of life, is the sort of question one cannot answer. In human terms it was a tragedy; in God's terms a mystery. Jan had to return to England with the children, and that chapter of her life, so full of promise, was closed. Through her continuing work with BCMS (later Crosslinks) and All Nations College, and later a peripatetic teaching ministry, she and her second husband, Roy Stafford, have contributed enormously to Mission.

Chapter 13
RECONCILIATION

Tensions with Rosemary's parents – her mother in particular – had been running high when Rosemary and I made our sudden departure from England in October 1967. They could not understand our motivation. They thought us irresponsible, and inconsiderate of their feelings. I was the black sheep, the one who was taking their precious daughter, together with grandchildren born and unborn, to the remotest ends of the earth. I was *persona non grata*. And I could understand why. Our thinking was on a different wavelength. As a leaving present we gave them a framed photograph of ourselves. Rosemary's mother hung this on the living room wall, but with a postcard stuck over my face. Visitors asked her what the postcard was doing. 'I never want to see his face again!' she would reply. It took our friend, Jennifer Sears, the curate's wife, to insist that she remove the card. But such was her bitterness. She began to make very angry phone calls to our Mission Headquarters in London – something we did not hear about until much later. Letters to Amudat were always addressed to Rosemary only – it was as though I did not exist.

Before we ever left England one of Rosemary's mother's ploys was to tell her that her father was a sick man, and she would never see him again. After we arrived in Amudat we began to get messages, through our daily radio link-up with the Flying Doctor Service in Nairobi, that Rosemary's father was ill, and that she had better come home. We did not know whether to believe the messages or not. Fortunately by then Rosemary's godfather had taken up a retirement job, lecturing in Nairobi. He agreed to check out the truth of any such messages with Rosemary's brother, Hugh, in England. Stanley Savage would ring Hugh for us, and inevitably the message came back, via the Flying Doctor radio, that there was no life-threatening illness.

'Amudat calling Foundation Control! Amudat calling Foundation Control! Do you read? Over.' It was 27 November 1969, and I was making my daily 2 p.m. radio call to the Flying Doctor Service. They had a message for us that Rosemary's father was gravely ill, and would she come home. The Flying Doctors rang Stanley Savage for us, and he rang Hugh in England, and the message came back the next morning that this time it was genuine. Rosemary's father had just been diagnosed as having liver cancer, and was not expected to live more than three weeks. Significantly the message also said that there was money available for us all to fly home. I did not know if they genuinely wanted me to go, or if they feared that Rosemary would not go without me. We prayed about it, and had the strong conviction that, difficult as it was to leave the hospital, we should all go, and go immediately. It was a Friday. Ruth was away and due back that night. (Lilian was on leave.) I called the hospital staff together, and explained the situation, and that we were leaving that very evening. I said I would try to find a locum doctor in Kampala. We left a note for Ruth, packed the car, and set off for Kampala. We had sent a message to Stanley Savage in Nairobi that we would take the Kampala route, rather than Nairobi, because I needed to get tax clearance in order to leave Uganda.

Forty miles down the road we met a Landrover heading towards Amudat. As we passed we recognised an old St Thomas's colleague, Dr Frank Guinness and family, from Ngora. Both vehicles shuddered to a stop on the corrugated road. 'Frank, where are you going?' I asked. 'We are on our way to visit you, and stay for a bit if we may!' I explained our circumstances, and Frank willingly offered to stay in our house and keep an eye on the hospital. So within two hours of our leaving, the hospital had its locum doctor. That night Frank had to do an emergency caesarian section. We continued on our way to Kampala, and arrived at our friends, the Schrams, late that night. We explained that we wanted to get to England as soon as possible – even to fly the next day, Saturday. Ralph was very dubious. There were three problems, he explained. First, I would need tax clearance, and our Mission Representative, who could supply the necessary letter of guarantee, was away on safari, and unable to be contacted. Second, in order to fly, baby Paul would need a yellow fever injection (we and Andrew had had them in England). Yellow fever injections were only given on weekdays, by appointment, in batches of ten (the contents of a vial). Third, we would be extremely unlikely to get seats on Saturday night's plane to London. It was the most popular flight of the week, and always fully booked well in advance. Ralph advised us not to expect to fly at least until the following week. In fact, he said, tax clearance, even with the necessary letter, could take many days. Without a letter – who knows? I said to Rosemary that we must be realistic. She told me that we had prayed about it, and would be flying the next day.

It was with trepidation that we set off for the city centre on the Saturday morning. We agreed that I would go to the tax office, and plead my case. Meanwhile Rosemary would go to the Immunisation centre, and plead Paul's case. At the tax office I had a rude reception by an officious young man. I asked for tax clearance, but he gave me no opportunity to plead my cause. 'Give me your passport!' he ordered. I did so, and he went off to an inner office, no doubt to find my tax file, and check up on me. After about ten minutes he returned, slapped my passport on the desk, and said curtly 'You go!'

'Where do I have to go?' I asked submissively – I was used to being sent from one office to another, and excessive politeness was the best weapon.

'You go! Just go!' he ordered. Somewhat puzzled I took my passport, went round the corner, and opened it. There, freshly stamped, was 'Tax Clearance'! I could not believe my eyes. It was months later that I discovered that my tax file had been mislaid, and it was obviously easier for the man to give me clearance than to search for it. I hurried to join Rosemary at the Immunisation centre. She had explained our predicament of needing just one injection for Paul. The receptionist explained that that was not possible to give just one injection, let alone on a Saturday, but said she would speak to the doctor. Just then an Indian gentleman came in – he needed nine urgent Yellow Fever injections for his family. Nine plus one equals ten, the contents of one vial. The doctor immunised Paul on the spot. Two problems down, one to go! Rosemary's confidence in prayer seemed to be being vindicated.

We hurried round to the East African Airways office. 'Do you by any chance have seats for two adults and two children on tonight's flight to London?' I asked. But the answer was no, and that there was already a waiting list. 'Could you add our names to the list – just in case?' I asked.

Somewhat reluctantly he agreed to do so. I gave our names.

He repeated them, surprised. 'Dr and Mrs Webster and two children? But you are already booked,' he said.

'But how?' I asked.

'We haven't been here until now.'

'A Mr Savage in Nairobi rang through and booked you,' he said.

Stanley Savage, not realising the problems of tax clearance and yellow fever immunisation, had felt it right to book us. We were on our way! Ralph and Enid Schram were absolutely astonished, and said that we had broken all records. That night Prof Michael and Elizabeth Hutt took us to Entebbe Airport. There was a further little miracle at the airport when Paul, drinking orange juice from a wine glass, bit a piece of glass off and swallowed it. He had no ill effects whatever.

We were at Rosemary's parents home in Ashtead, Surrey, by 10 a.m. on the Sunday morning. It was less than forty-eight hours since we had made the decision to leave Amudat. Father, we were greatly relieved to find, was still alive, though very weak. His illness had progressed much faster than had been expected. He was especially thrilled to see Rosemary and the children. On the Monday we had a precious time with him. Andrew sang him his full repertoire, of 'Jesus loves me' 'Jesus friend of little children' and 'Twinkle twinkle little star.' He said his prayers with Grandpa. On the Tuesday he was very weak, and hardly able to talk, but as Rosemary and I were sitting with him he suddenly began to say the Lord's Prayer, his voice gathering strength. Then he added, 'Make them happy and keep them safe. Make them happy, happy always. Guard them from all perils and dangers. Look after them. I love them so much!' It was a very moving moment, a patriarch blessing his family. Later Mother asked him if he would like me to say a prayer, then added 'Or don't you want to be bothered?'

'But I do want to be bothered!' he said. He asked for Rosemary in the night, and next morning kissed Andrew, and asked to kiss Rosemary several times. Then he slipped peacefully away.

If arrangements in Kampala had not gone as they did, if our prayers had not been answered, we would not have got back to England in time. As it was we had a most healing time. Never before had we been able to pray with Rosemary's parents. The very fact that I had gone back, and had given them priority over the hospital, meant the world to them. My relationship with Rosemary's mother did a U-turn, and from then onwards we got on so well. She became very proud of what we were doing in Uganda – and she even became proud of her son-in-law. The postcard never went back over my face.

Chapter 14
RAIN

Our intention was to return to Uganda as soon as Rosemary's father's funeral was over, but I got a very nasty dose of flu, and then Rosemary followed suit. We spent Christmas in bed. Meanwhile in Uganda there was an assassination attempt on President Milton Obote. He was shot and wounded in the mouth. Tensions in Uganda were running high. We flew back on 4 January 1970. On this occasion our leaving of Rosemary's mother was so different from our initial departure in 1967 – our relationship had been healed. We did not quite know what to expect in Uganda, but the only outward sign of tension was the presence of numerous roadblocks. Between Kampala and Amudat we passed through seven. At only one of them were we searched – the soldier found the spring balance we used to weigh luggage, and wanted us to weigh him at the roadside. We suggested that he was a little too heavy to suspend. We found all well at Amudat. Two British medical students had been helping out since Dr Frank Guiness left. Ruth and the dressers had everything under efficient control.

We returned to a very busy time, both in hospital and at home. 1970 was a year of exceptionally heavy rain during the middle part of the year. The Kanyangereng was in spate much more often than usual, and this had the inevitable consequence for us – visitors. We also had an unusual number of medical visitors. During one three-week-period no fewer than fifty six people stayed with us, most of them for more than one night. It made life interesting, but tiring for Rosemary, who felt she was running a Guest House. This particularly busy time unfortunately coincided with the borehole pump breaking down (yet again), and we had no water in the house other than what we carried in cans from another borehole. I was called not infrequently to tow vehicles through the Kanyangereng when the water had subsided sufficiently; or to tow out vehicles that had come to rest in the flood. Some of our downcountry, expatriate guests really had little idea about how to cross flooded rivers. They drove in without testing the depth, and thought that speed would carry them through. Instead the bow wave flooded their engines.

On one occasion a car had come to a full stop midstream. A group of local youths were trying to take advantage of the Mzungu by quoting an astronomical price to push him out. He was in a difficult bargaining position – his family, including small children, were all in the car and the engine was thoroughly flooded. Fortunately I heard about the situation, and went down to the river. Like a latter-day Moses I waded into the flood, turned to those on the riverbank, and made an impassioned plea in Swahili to their better instincts. It must have been quite a moving speech because at first one, then another, leapt into the river to lend a hand. Soon a happy, cheering, singing crowd was pushing the car through, and the ringleaders of the scam had slunk away. I waved the family off on their way to Lodwar, waded back through the river, and had just reached the bank when a shout went up from the crowd. There was a roaring sound, and round the bend in the river came a tidal wave of water, about four feet high, swift, frothing, bearing a jostling jumble of tree trunks, and sweeping all before it. If it had been seconds earlier I would have been swept away. If it had been minutes earlier the car, and the family in it, would have been carried off and they would almost certainly have drowned. The Kanyangereng was not a river to be messed with. Its waters came from Kadam mountain, and heavy rain in the mountain could cause it to come down in spate, very suddenly, and very dangerously. During that rainy season several Pokot were swept away and drowned as they tried to cross the river.

The Kanyangereng was not the only river to add interest to life. Ten miles south of Amudat was the Alakas. This was different in that it was a long stretch of low-lying land which was prone to flooding, but never more than about three feet deep. Usually with the Landrover we could tow cars through. Bishop Neville Langford-Smith was due on an episcopal visit, bringing his wife and the diocesan treasurer and wife. The Alakas was in flood, so I drove out in the Landrover to meet him and tow him through. (Being Australian he was the proud owner of a Holden, the very car which nearly ran over Andrew in Nakuru).

I awaited his arrival on the Amudat side of the flood, intending to cross over when he came. In due course the Holden appeared on the far side in a cloud of dust. As he neared the Alakas to my astonishment the bishop showed no sign whatever of slowing down. I knew the water was far too deep for even a Holden to get through. I raised my hand to halt him, but perhaps he took the signal to be a reverential salute. Certainly it did not stop him. The Holden plunged in, raising an enormous bow wave, and juddered to a stop midstream, the water half way up its doors. The diocesan treasurer, a helpful man, started to open his door to get out to push. The bishop issued an immediate episcopal edict to keep the doors shut, and not let the water in. I waded in with a rope and had to submerge myself under the muddy water in an attempt to find some structure under the car to which I could attach the towrope – the makers of Holdens did not appear to have considered the need for towing. Meanwhile the episcopal party watched my diving attempts with interest from their dry cocoon. The treasurer was most embarrassed and sympathetic as I eventually emerged, soaked from head to foot in thick red mud and water.

For most of the year our house and garden were like a small oasis in a shimmering desert of dry, leafless thornscrub. But then at last the oppressive heat would begin to build up, and heavy black clouds gathered over Kadam, and the thunder rumbled over the bush, and huge raindrops began to slap the dusty ground. The longed for rains had come. Small dry gullies turned into streams; streams met up to form rushing torrents of earth-red water; and these poured into the Kanyangereng, adding to its swollen flood. Part of our garden became a river. The longdrop latrine, perched on its rocky prominence, became an island, approached by a causeway. The birds in our wild fig tree sang for joy. The air smelt fresh and cool. Within days the landscape was transformed as dramatically as the change from winter to spring. Stick-dry bushes, brown and apparently lifeless, burst into fresh, green leaf. Beautiful pink lilies appeared out of the bare earth, and shoots of tender grass. Purple convolvulus twined itself into the thorn bush, and the fragrant scent of acacia flowers filled the air. In the words of the Song of Songs:

> The flowers appear on the earth,
>
> The time of singing has come,
>
> And the voice of the turtle dove is heard in our land.
>
> (Song of Songs 2:12)

I took advantage of the rain to try to improve the environs of the hospital. In front of the hospital buildings was bare earth. Vehicles swept up to the verandah, enveloping wards and patients in clouds of choking dust. In the heat swirling dust devils danced and raced across the land. We needed some ground cover around the hospital. The dressers became really enthusiastic about it. We wired off an area (to keep goats and cattle off) and planted a variety of hardy grass. We also planted cassia trees for shade. Soon we had a lawn of sorts established in front of the hospital. I even acquired a small lawnmower – the first ever seen in Amudat. Our Pokot patients appreciated the cool and the green, but did think it very odd that we went to such trouble to grow grass, only to cut it down with a machine. Surely, they thought, grass is for feeding cattle and goats. On more than one occasion goats were sneakily let into our enclosure to feed on the lawn. If that had happened too often they would have destroyed both grass and trees. Goats are the world's worst creators of desert.

A side-effect of rain was the appearance of more snakes – flushed out of the ground by the water. On at least two occasions large cobras were found in the wards. One, a six-foot Egyptian cobra, slithered through the women's ward, to the great consternation of the patients, and then disappeared down an anthill just behind the ward. We dug it out, anaesthetised it with chloroform on the end of a long pole, and then it (or its head) joined my collection of snakes. Snakes came into our house. I collected three specimens of one variety. One of them I trod on in my bare feet, in the dark, in our bedroom. Another was entwined around a curtain rail – I wondered why the curtain would not draw. The third we found wrapped around a houseplant, in the process of swallowing our pet chameleon. (Attempts to resuscitate the chameleon, which had turned dark black, failed). In due course my snake collection was taken by a passing herpetologist from London's Natural History Museum. The three specimens found in our house were identified as a new species, and were named after Amudat.

Andrew was now four years old, and Paul three. They loved the free, outdoor life, and entertained themselves with simple pleasures. I built a shaded sandpit, and made a static car out of an old wooden crate. This was superseded by a real pedal car, donated by grandma, and called 'Lucky Boy' by Andrew. They had a number of Pokot friends with whom they played. Always there were hazards. Paul was stung on the hand by a scorpion, a very painful experience. They both had tumbu (mango) flies. These are flies which lay their eggs on damp clothing, such as that drying on the washing line. When the clothing is next worn a small larva emerges from the egg, and burrows into the skin. Here it grows, causing a reaction around it that resembles a boil. It is distinguished from a boil by close inspection – in the centre of the 'boil' a moving tail can be seen. With firm pressure out pops a fat, wriggling maggot.

Ruth Stranex had by now established a hostel for girls, where girls from remote *manyattas* could live and be cared for while attending the local primary school. Until then education, such as there was, was almost entirely the preserve of boys. Each week Rosemary held a sewing class for Ruth's girls, teaching them skills that would stand them in good stead for the future. The girls loved to come to our house, and to sit chatting and sewing on the verandah, and to make a fuss of Andrew and Paul.

We began to face the question of schooling for the boys. We would soon begin to teach them ourselves, but by the age of six they would need something more professional. We made a visit to St Andrew's School, Turi – a boarding school in the highlands of Kenya with a strong Christian ethos, where many missionaries sent their children. We were very impressed by the happy, family atmosphere of the school, and put the boys' names down for it, but we nevertheless dreaded the day when they would have to go away. I had such strong unhappy memories of boarding school in Nairobi. But that was a worry for the future. For now, though very busy, we were enjoying our life and home in Amudat. We had got over the initial culture shock. We had made our home in the bush. We had seen the hospital grow. We had wonderful colleagues. We had come to love the people, and to make many friends. We knew we were where God wanted us to be, and that our coming to Amudat had not, after all, been a divine mess up.

Chapter 15
BUILDING THE CHURCH

To our western eyes Christchurch Amudat was quaint. Its low, open-sided mud walls, and rough terminalia tree trunk posts holding up a rather tatty red corrugated iron roof, its seating made from rough planks balanced on tree trunks – all seemed appropriate for the setting. Peter Cox had had a hand in building it, and it was Peter's sort of church. To our eyes it was fine. But in the eyes of the Reverend Timothy Oluoch and the church council it was not fine. In fact it was rather a disgrace. They wanted something better for God than a mud-walled shed. In fact, given the choice, they would probably have imported a Norman abbey, complete with pillars and stained glass windows. But there being no abbeys available a compromise had to be reached. For a long time church council meetings were taken up with discussions about rebuilding the church. Daudi Chebtwey, lay reader and shopkeeper, a humble, gentle man, offered to be the supervisor of works. We agreed on a plan. I was anxious to preserve some degree of open-sidedness, both for ventilation and light. Our African brethren were more in favour of it being closed in – windows play little part in most traditional African houses. Again compromise was called for. The new walls were to be of concrete blocks, which we would make ourselves. The new church would be built around the old one, so that it could continue to be used throughout the time of building. We began with trips to the river bed to collect sand, and then the work of making blocks began – after work, on Saturdays, whenever free, members of the church made blocks. The walls began to rise. There was a rather tense time when the walls were clearly rising higher than had been agreed, and no window spaces were being left – Reverend Timothy was having his own way. We could see the building ending up more like a warehouse than a church. But good sense prevailed, some layers of blocks were removed, and everyone agreed that light and air were essential. It was a proud day when the new church was finished, and furnished with proper benches. The exercise had cost the local Christian community a lot in both money and sweat. It was a building far superior to their own homes, which were for the most part mud huts. And this is what they wanted it to be. After all, the monks and people who built our beautiful cathedrals and abbeys wanted only the best for God. To the Christians of Amudat their concrete block church was the best they could offer.

Far more important to all of us than the church building was the living Church, the Christian community. Here there were encouragements and disappointments, steps forwards and steps backwards. There was often an eagerness to accept the Christian Gospel, but it then proved difficult to live out. There was the tension between traditional customs and the new faith. In many respects the two were entirely compatible, but in other respects not. Marriage was a case in point. For the Christian man to have just one wife, and for the couple to remain committed and faithful to one another, was a new concept. In tribal tradition a man could have as many wives as he could afford, and he would certainly want, in time, to take on a younger wife – or two! If a wife did not bear children (and infertility due to pelvic infection was common) then a man would certainly expect to take another wife. These were difficult issues for Christians. And what if a man who already had more than one wife became a Christian? Was he supposed to abandon all but the first wife? Surely not! What would the discarded wives do? Who would support them? What chance would they ever have of marrying again? These were real issues that had to be faced.

Alcohol was a major stumbling block for Christians. Home brews, made from maize or honey, could be very potent indeed. And the whole purpose of drinking was to get drunk. Drunken rows and fights and injuries were very common indeed. Over the years I had to repair many people who had suffered alcohol-related violence. I stitched back ears and fingers that had been almost cut off, and sutured gaping knife wounds. One wife who was brought to hospital had been slashed repeatedly over the head with a *panga* (a machete) by her drunken husband. Apart from several deep wounds exposing the skull bone, she also sustained fractures of the skull. The idea of having just a social tipple of alcohol was not a prevalent concept. It was all or nothing. When we first arrived in Amudat we thought we would vary our fluid intake by making ginger beer. In no time at all the news got around that the doctor was himself brewing beer in his house – the implication being that therefore beer-brewing must be all right. We realised that, in that situation, we ourselves needed to be teetotal – and that included ginger 'beer'. Alcohol was at the root of so many social problems. It was alcohol that destroyed the life and marriage of little Samson Adio, our Health Worker. At times we despaired and wept over the set-backs of promising Christians. It was a case of 'here a little, there a little', but slowly Christ's Church in Amudat grew.

An issue that Christian girls had to face was that of female circumcision. According to Pokot tribal custom all girls are circumcised at puberty. The procedure is carried out, without any anaesthetic or hygiene, by a senior woman of the village. The extent of the surgery varies from tribe to tribe, but in the case of the Pokot it consists of clitoridectomy. An arrowhead or knife, or even a razor blade, would be used. The girl would be held with legs apart by other women and would be expected to be stoical. There could be considerable blood loss (on occasion the victim was brought to hospital, and required a blood transfusion). There was often infection. Even fatal tetanus could occur. Certainly the resultant scarring caused marked narrowing of the introitus, making subsequent childbirth more difficult. The rationale of female circumcision was difficult to establish. Some would say it diminished the wife's sexual pleasure, and therefore meant that she would be more inclined to be faithful to her husband. Others maintained that it actually increased the wife's pleasure, as well as that of the husband. To our western understanding it was a form of mutilation and subjection of the woman, and carried significant risks. As Christians we, and our Christian African colleagues, discouraged the practice. But Christian girls were put under enormous pressure by non-Christian parents to conform to tribal practice. It was, for them, a prerequisite of marriage. As soon as a girl had been circumcised – and age-sets were done together – she would be dressed in a plain goatskin, and she and her peers would live in a special *manyatta* until their wounds were healed. Groups of circumcised girls, in their dark goatskin attire, could sometimes be seen moving through the bush together. During this time of isolation they would be taught by older women about marriage, sex, the duties of a wife, traditional treatments and tribal lore. They would then (at the age of twelve or thirteen) be ready for marriage. This might be to a young man of their choice, or it could be to an older man as a second or third wife. It all depended on negotiations by her parents over the bride price. This would usually be paid in cattle. A young man might first need to rustle some cattle from a neighbouring tribe in order to afford a wife. An older, richer man might be in the enviable position of being able to make a down payment. Once married a girl's simple adornment, with a few strings of beads, gave way to multiple bead and copper necklaces and bangles, which made our western wedding rings seem pathetic in comparison.

Less contentious was male circumcision, which was universally practised, but at a later age – usually late teens. Again this would be done with an arrowhead or knife, and without anaesthetic. The young men were expected to be silent and stoical throughout. Circumcision was their passport to manhood, and to joining the young warrior clan. Increasingly, especially in the case of youths who had been to school, they asked to be circumcised at the hospital, with the benefit of anaesthetic and sterile instruments. We were happy to oblige.

During 1970 Kenya took back control and administration of the Karapokot area to our east. Amudat was now firmly in Uganda proper, and it seemed logical for the church to leave the Kenya diocese of Nakuru, and to come under the wing of the Uganda diocese of Soroti. We would have a new bishop. We were sad to leave Nakuru Diocese, because of historic links, and because of its new bishop, Manasses Kuria (who later became Archbishop of Kenya, and who was an old friend of my father). Our new Ugandan bishop, the Right Reverend Athanasio Maraka, made his first visit to Amudat in November 1970. We were impressed. He preached a helpful, simple sermon on Jesus the Good Shepherd. As is always the African custom his retinue of his wife, and archdeacon, and archdeacon's wife, each had the opportunity to 'say a few words of greeting'. The phrase 'a few words' is relative, and we had in effect four sermons. The bishop's wife said (amongst many other things), 'When I became a Christian I prayed for a husband who would be a church member – and look what God has given me! A bishop! When I married I prayed for a child – and God gave me eleven!'

Among those baptised and confirmed that day were girls from Ruth's hostel. It was exciting to see God at work in those young lives. It would not be easy for them to live out their new Christian faith, especially as girls. There would be enormous pressures on them over such issues as circumcision and arranged marriage. There would be a tension between their Christian faith and their tribal loyalty, which they would have to work out for themselves. It was a great joy when they married young Christian men, and showed all the evidence of Christian marriages, with mutual love, and respect, and faithfulness. It was also a joy when, as Christians, they felt able to retain the positive and constructive values of tribal life. Christ was not calling them out of their community, but rather calling them to live as Christians within it. To be salt, to be light, right where they were. This mattered so much, not just for them personally, and not just for the Pokot people, but for their nation. After all, these young people were the future of Uganda.

Chapter 16
EXPANDING THE MEDICAL WORK

By 1970 the hospital staff were working really well as a team. Lilian Singleton, in her kind, quiet, low profile way, stuck faithfully to her work. Every now and then things would get too much for her, and she would suddenly announce that she was going out on the next passing lorry for a break. We knew that as soon as she had recovered her energy she would be back again at work. Life did get very stressful at times, especially in the heat. Ruth Stranex, outwardly tough, was inwardly sensitive and very caring. She related well to the hospital dressers, and did sterling work with her girls' hostel. Both Lilian and Ruth became part of our family, and would often come over from their houses at bath time to help with the children, and to read them a bedtime story.

The six to eight hospital dressers were, on the whole, loyal and very competent. Because they had had no training other than what we gave them there was no professional arrogance about them. They were just keen to learn, and to improve their skills. John Tait, whom I inherited from Peter Cox, went off to Mvumi Hospital in Tanzania to train as a laboratory technician. He came back very capable, and well able to do all necessary tests. Andrew Kases chose to focus on the operating theatre, and became an excellent theatre assistant, learning the names of surgical instruments, and how to sterilise them, and to lay up trolleys for surgery. He would assist me with operations if required, or take over the anaesthetic EMO (ether/air) machine once the patient was asleep.

Late one night a Landrover arrived with a patient from the Sudanese refugee camp. The lady had been in labour for three days, and was moribund, with bleeding and severe abdominal pain. She had almost certainly ruptured her uterus, and the baby was already dead. The team sprang into action. John Tait went to find potential blood donors, and to bleed them and group and cross-match several pints of blood. Andrew got the generator going, and prepared the operating theatre. I meanwhile put up an intravenous drip on the lady. In a remarkably short time we had blood pouring into her, and were operating. Andrew took over the anaesthetic, and Ruth assisted me. The uterus had indeed ruptured, from side to side, with dead baby and placenta lying in the abdomen. The bladder was also torn open. All this took some sorting out and repairing, and we were up for much of the night. Meanwhile moths, beetles, sausage flies and every nocturnal flying insect in the district seemed to be attracted by our light to come and see what was going on. I sometimes wondered how many insects ended up inside operation wounds. At least it gave some variety to the surgeon's usual instructions to his assistant: 'Swab, please! Retractor! Cut! Remove that sausage fly please! Swab!' Within two weeks our patient was well, with catheter out, and able to go home. We had been too late to save her baby, but at least we saved her. Such successes encouraged and bonded us as a hospital team.

By this time we were seeing over fifty-two thousand outpatients per year. On one fairly typical busy morning I saw thirty outpatients, and admitted thirteen. They included cases of goitre, hydatid cyst, salivary gland stone, tetanus, kala-azaar and chickenpox. Tetanus occurred all too often, although so easily preventable. In older children it was often due to cuts or thorns. In adults it was sometimes the result of dressing leg ulcers with cow manure. It was almost invariably fatal, and a very unpleasant way to die – with contorting spasms of the body, and inability to swallow. The worst form was neonatal tetanus – tetanus in babies just a few days old, invariably caused by the village 'midwives' cutting the umbilical cord with a dirty instrument, such as an arrow head. As already described, the Pokot had their customary way of delivery, in the squatting position, with a lot of downward pushing and thrusting from the onset of labour. This, together with the large episiotomies (perineal incisions) they made, resulted in a high incidence of prolapse of the uterus. All this pushing, together with the cutting of the cord with dirty instruments, were things we wanted to change. But we did not want to take deliveries out of the hands of the village 'midwives'. Rather, we wanted them to be involved in hospital deliveries, and to learn better ways. The simple act of distributing new razor blades and a piece of clean string meant a considerable reduction in neonatal tetanus. Apart from learning better ways, it was important for the 'midwives' to be present during labour because, according to Pokot custom, this was the time the expectant mother must confess all her past misdeeds, and come clean. Each labour pain brought with it new revelations to the 'midwives' – a sort of confession by contraction. Without it they believed the baby would be weak or would die.

Trying to run a hospital on a drug and equipment budget of £800 a year made one very aware of the exorbitant cost of modern medicines. Many are quite beyond the reach of third world countries, and western drug companies do little to help. I was approached by one drug company to do a trial on the treatment of tropical ulcers – large, wet, suppurating ulcers that occur on the legs, and seem to be caused by a combination of trauma and malnutrition. Normally we treated them with the simplest of old-fashioned antiseptics, such as acriflavine or gentian violet. This drug firm had come up with a very fancy and expensive enzyme ointment, which was supposed to clean away all the suppurating tissue and bring about rapid healing. They offered us free supplies of the ointment if I would do a trial, and write it up. I agreed. We allocated patients randomly to two groups – to be treated with the enzyme ointment, or with simple antiseptics. I photographed the ulcers at the start, and we kept regular measurements of their size. It became clear before very long that the ulcers treated with simple antiseptic did better. This was not what the drug company wanted to hear, and withdrew their support when I said that I would, as agreed, write up my findings. They wanted to sell their product rather than know the truth, and a drug trial in the depths of Africa was, for them, a cheap way of doing it. John le Carre's novel, 'The Constant Gardener', is uncomfortably close to the truth.

Whenever possible, for operations below the waistline, I used a spinal anaesthetic. It was safer than a general, and it meant that, once the anaesthetic was in, I could concentrate on the operation. It was ideal for a one-doctor situation. The anaesthetic used for spinals was heavy nupercaine. It was injected through the outer covering of the spinal cord at the level of the lower back, and because it was a heavy solution it stayed at the correct level of the spinal cord. On one occasion, when reordering our supply of heavy nupercaine, we were told that it was no longer available. There was, apparently, insufficient demand worldwide to make it worth manufacturing. Suddenly, without warning, third world hospitals, especially one-doctor ones like Amudat, were deprived of one of their most essential, life-saving drugs. To the drug company it was not profitable enough. To us, and our patients it was vital. I, and no doubt many other doctors in similar situations, wrote in the strongest possible terms to the manufacturer, and, to their credit, it did become available again. But one was reminded that a bush hospital such as ours, struggling to provide a medical service to very needy people, came very low indeed on the priority list of the drug industry.

Treatment of disease was often costly, time-consuming, and sometimes too late. Prevention of disease was so much more satisfactory. Charles Ndege, and then Samson Adio, were dressers who 'specialised' in Health Education. They taught basic hygiene. No child with conjunctivitis was given eye drops until the mother had first washed the child's face, to underline the importance of cleanliness. But we had to be realistic – this was not a society with access to running water. The message was – when you are at the borehole or the pool in the riverbed, in other words whenever you can, wash. It was no good using visual aids such as posters for health education. We had access to any number of pictures of flies, or mosquitoes, or running taps. They meant nothing to the Pokot. 'That is not a fly,' they would say. 'A fly is not as big as that!' Samson was deft at catching flies. To get the attention of his audience he would stalk among them, studying the many flies feeding on the festering eyes of the children. Then suddenly he would snatch with his hand and catch one, and holding it up for all to see would explain that this was the cause of their children's illness – their conjunctivitis, their trachoma, their diarrhoea. Killing flies was a waste of time, but washing eyes so that they would not attract flies was very worthwhile. And so, little by little, the message went home.

Immunisation was their other theme. This again was a long-term process, convincing parents of the value of having their children protected. On any medical safari Charles or Samson would always come along, vital members of the team. While the rest of us treated the sick they talked to the waiting crowds, and immunised as many as possible. A typical medical safari was one we made to Katabok, at the eastern foot of

Kadam mountain, in October 1970. To get there involved twenty-seven miles of very rough track. We camped for three days and nights under a clump of acacia trees. The thorn-clad slopes of the mountain rose up just behind our tents. News soon spread of our arrival, and people began to appear along winding animal tracks through the bush. On the first day we treated one hundred and eighty patients and immunised eighty children. That was a worthwhile day's work. Sometimes it was the little things that caused greatest gratitude. On that occasion there were two children who had had seeds in their ears for two years – presumably put there in the way children do. I syringed them out, they could hear again, and the parents were so pleased that they offered to bring me blood and milk to drink at any time I chose. In total on that safari we saw five hundred and forty-seven patients, and immunised one hundred and fifty – and were given gifts of a hen, eggs, milk, and a lamb by grateful people. We decided that Katabok really warranted a small dispensary, which we would service from Amudat. We resolved that, when time allowed, we would come back and build one. The decision was met with great acclaim and applause from the crowd.

The dressers and I took advantage of that trip to climb Kadam from its eastern base. Samson, Joshua and I set off at 4.30 a.m. from our campsite. We climbed and climbed, up and up through increasingly thick and lush vegetation, which then gave way to dense forest, festooned with lichens and ferns. At 9.30 a.m. we reached the highest eastern summit, at nine thousand feet – we had climbed six thousand feet. The view across the plain to distant Amudat, and the blue range of the Karapokot hills beyond, was stunning. So too was the view the other way towards the forested slopes of the two main ten-thousand-feet peaks of Kadam. I determined that one day we would climb those too. On the way back we passed the villages of cave-dwelling Tapeth people. They are the small remnants of a tribe who once occupied the surrounding plains, but who were driven out by the stronger Pokot and Karamojong people. They now live in isolated pockets on three mountains in the area, Kadam being one. We stopped to talk to them, and I treated a couple of sick people. At one cave dwelling the man roasted maize cobs for us, and we sat in the entrance to his cave, gnawing at the cobs perhaps much as primitive man had once done. We were intrigued later to learn more about these mountain, cave-dwelling people. Larry Robbins, an anthropologist who was making a study of their way of life, based himself in Amudat for some months and we got to know him well. He worked in cooperation with Hamo Sassoon (nephew of Siegfried) from the Department of Antiquities in Kampala. Hamo Sassoon was studying ancient artefacts that had been found in old cave-dwellings. Another authority on Kadam and its cave-dwellings was the traveller John Weatherby. He had explored Kadam extensively, and studied the Tapeth people. He was indignant at the work Larry was doing, and clearly regarded Kadam as his mountain, and his preserve, and the Tapeth people as his people. We were caught between them, but rather than get involved in their dispute we chose to listen to and learn from each expert.

To study and try to understand the beliefs and mind of the local people was essential. It was essential from the point of view of evangelism – explaining the Christian message in a relevant and meaningful way. It was also essential medically – to understand why people often delayed so long before coming to the hospital; why patients disappeared from the ward to make sacrifices just when they were beginning to respond to treatment; and why some patients turned their faces to the wall and died for absolutely no diagnosable reason. I am sometimes asked, 'Did you see evidence of evil spirits, or of people being possessed?' Certainly we saw people who had been cursed, and who therefore expected to die, and did die. We saw people who previously had been mentally absolutely stable become raving lunatics because they had been cursed. It was precisely because of their fear that they might have been cursed, either by *Tororut* or by an evil spirit, that sick people were so anxious to make sacrifices. They dare not neglect the spiritual aspect of their illness. It is understandable that if one has no concept whatever of microbes and infection, or of physiology and pathology, then all illness is explained in spiritual terms. After all until the likes of Dr John Snow in England, cholera was thought to be due to harmful miasmas that hovered over the land. We did regularly pray for patients, for their healing and for release from the fears that bound them. Did we see dramatic miracles as a result of prayer? No, not dramatic in the sense of dying people getting up and walking. But we saw answers to prayer time and again, when patients made remarkable recoveries against all the odds.

Sometimes our prayer was answered in unexpected ways. We had admitted a very sick lady to the ward. She had general malaise and weight loss and was clearly deteriorating. But she had little in the way of specific symptoms. We did routine tests on her, and nothing showed up. Yet day by day she was getting worse. One day, on the ward round, I said to the dressers, 'I am defeated. I have no idea what is wrong with her, or how to treat her. Let us just pray now for her.' As we prayed round her bed the word 'Brucellosis' came into my head. We had not tested her for that because she had had none of the usual symptoms – no fever or joint pain or swelling. (We never did tests that were unlikely to be helpful because of their expense.) When we had finished praying I said that we ought to test her for brucellosis. The test was very strongly positive. We commenced treatment for brucellosis, and she immediately began to improve. That was an answer to prayer, a kind of miracle.

Chapter 17
FIBRE MAN

One of the first doctors to set up practice in Nairobi in the early part of the century was the renowned Dr Burkitt – known affectionately as Dr 'Kill or Cure' Burkitt. Famous for his eccentric ways Dr Burkitt would strip patients who were running a fever to their underwear, and then drive them at speed around Nairobi in his open car to cool them down. Legend has it that on one occasion the female patient became so cold that by the time they arrived back from the therapeutic drive the patient was wearing Dr Burkitt's clothes and he was in his underwear.

It was Dr Burkitt's nephew, Denis Burkitt, who came to be our most remarkable and stimulating visitor in Amudat. Denis qualified as a surgeon in Dublin, and served in the RAMC in Kenya during the Second World War. Having been turned down by the Colonial Medical Service before the war, because he had only one eye following an accident, he was accepted after the war, and posted to Lira District Hospital in northern Uganda. Here he showed that remarkable perception and incisive reasoning that were to mark his life. As surgeon Peter Bewes once commented, Denis saw with his one eye what most of us would miss with two. He was in due course posted from Lira to Mulago Hospital in the capital, Kampala. Here one day he was asked by consultant paediatrician Dr Hugh Trowell to take a look at a young lad called Africa, who had swellings in all four quadrants of his jaws. Both doctors were puzzled. Biopsies were taken, but the results were inconclusive. Some weeks later Denis was visiting Jinja Hospital, to the east of Kampala, when he chanced to look out of the window and saw another boy with identical swellings of the jaws. Denis's enquiring mind began to churn. What happened next is described in Bernard Glemser's book *The Long Safari*. Together with a missionary doctor, Ted Williams, Denis travelled the length and breadth of central and southern Africa, ten thousand miles in total, visiting over sixty hospitals, Government and Mission. Everywhere they asked about, and sought out, cases of jaw tumours. They plotted them on a map, and discovered that they only occurred below a certain altitude, only in areas of certain rainfall, and that the distribution coincided exactly with that of malaria. Pathologically the tumours were a form of lymphoma, but their cellular appearance differed in some respects from other lymphomas. The picture began to emerge of a tumour that might be caused by a virus, and one that could be mosquito-borne. This was revolutionary stuff. The idea came as a bombshell to the scientific and pathological world. An insect-borne virus causing cancer? Could it be? Further research linked the jaw tumours with the Epstein-Barr virus of glandular fever. The tumours were also found to be very amenable to chemotherapy. A new form of cancer had been identified as a result of careful study of its distribution. It was called Burkitt's Lymphoma.

Denis Burkitt's astute and enquiring mind led him to question why many other diseases are distributed in the world as they are. Why, for instance, within East Africa, is cancer of the oesophagus so prevalent in one geographical area, while just over a range of hills it is never seen? Why are diseases such as hypertension, coronary artery disease, diabetes, appendicitis, varicose veins, diverticulitis and colon cancer so prevalent in the developed world, whereas in rural Africa they are rarely if ever seen? And why do they begin to appear in those parts of Africa that have been developed – in the cities and towns? One of Denis's maxims was 'If you are consulted by an African with pain in the appendix area, speak to him in English and examine his pockets. If he speaks English and has cash, then it is appendicitis. If he speaks no English and has no cash then it is not!' Of course this was tongue-in-cheek advice, but there was truth in it. In nine years in rural East Africa I saw and operated on just one case of appendicitis, and that was in a nurse from downcountry (who earned a salary and spoke English!)

Denis used to compare what he called 'microscope medicine' with 'hot air balloon medicine.' 'There are too many doctors peering down microscopes looking for the cause of diseases,' he would say. 'More need to get up in the air in balloons, and look down on the world, and ask, 'Why is that disease there and not there?'' If it could be explained why rural Africa is spared so many of the West's illnesses then we would better understand what causes them. His observations marked the birth of what has come to be called 'Geographical Pathology'.

Another turning point in Denis Burkitt's life came when he met, and read the writings of, a naval doctor, Surgeon Captain Peter Cleave. Cleave's proposition was that many of the Western World's diseases – such as appendicitis, colon cancer and diabetes – are due to the high intake of sugars. Cleave called it the 'saccharine disease'. This rang bells with Denis. By now he was working for the Medical Research Council, based in London, and he was in an ideal position to recruit doctors, particularly mission doctors, throughout the Third World to actually look out for western diseases – not just to assume their absence, but to look for them and record their absence. The more Denis thought about it, and studied patterns of disease, and questioned why 'civilisation' or education brought in its wake new disease patterns, the more he felt that it was not too much sugar but too little fibre in the diet which was responsible for many of the west's ills. He became very interested in 'bowel transit times' – the time it takes for food to pass from one end of the body to the other. By feeding radio-opaque pellets to volunteers, and asking them to collect their next three productions of faeces, and then x-raying the samples, and counting the pellets, it was possible to work out how long it took for those pellets to pass through. He demonstrated that in an average English public school boy (presumably living on a refined diet of doughnuts, burgers and other stodge) the time was seventy-two hours. In a rural African (living on a very high fibre diet, of maize meal, cassava and bananas) the time was about eight hours. Denis postulated that chemicals generated by the slow-moving, hard, concentrated stools of a westerner, and the effort involved in passing them, were responsible for much western disease. In contrast the rural African's stool was soft, and bulky, and travelled quickly through the bowel, and was passed with little effort. Denis published his findings and theories, the idea captured the imagination of the press, and Denis became widely known as 'The Fibre Man'.

One conundrum remained, however. People such as the Pokot, and the other nomadic and semi-nomadic tribes who live in the deserts of northeast Uganda and northern Kenya, are cattle people. Their diet consists largely of meat, milk and blood. They eat very little fibre. And yet they do not suffer from any of the western diseases. What are their bowel transit times? So it was that Denis Burkitt asked to come and stay with us for a few days, to do some bowel transit time studies on the Pokot, and to see for himself the sort of disease patterns that we were experiencing. By now Denis was of world renown. For his Burkitt's lymphoma and his work on fibre and geographical pathology he had become well-known and widely respected in the medical world. He had been showered with more honours and degrees than probably any other doctor – CMG MD DSc FRCS FRS, and many more. We awaited the arrival of the great man with anticipation and some awe.

I shall never forget his arrival. The Volkswagon Beetle pulled up outside our house, he leapt out, said 'Hello', and before we had even reached the front door he had launched into his theme. 'You see it's not the diseases that you do get that I'm really interested in. It's the diseases that you don't get!' In his Irish accent the words tumbled over one another. He was one bundle of enthusiasm, energy, excitement. He couldn't wait to get started. And yet he was also one of the humblest, most self-effacing people I have known. He gave me, from the start, the feeling that I was the one doing great work in the world. That my views, my experience, were invaluable. That it was the bush doctors of the world who were doing the real medicine. He was a great encourager. And he was also a great Christian. Not because he flaunted his faith, but because he was so natural, so real, so matter-of-fact about it. He had that servant heart that is the mark of all truly great Christians. And he would have been the last person to think that he was anybody special. The following few days with Denis were some of the most privileged of my life.

Next morning, without delay, the Bowel Transit Time study began. We recruited about thirty Pokot patients, and, with translation from one of the dressers, Denis explained to them what it was all about. As the details of the study were unveiled, and it was explained about the pellets, and the collection in plastic bags of the next three specimens of stools, I could see the eyes of the Pokot getting wider with amazement. They kept glancing from interpreter to Denis to make sure that they were not imagining what they were hearing. Could the Mzungu really be saying these things? They were well aware that white people had very strange habits and ideas, but this one took the Pokot equivalent of the biscuit!

Nevertheless they obediently swallowed their pellets, took their three plastic bags in readiness, and wandered off into the shade of the trees, no doubt to discuss in depth what they had been asked to do, and to speculate as to what the Mzungu might do with their samples. During the following days bulky and rather smelly plastic bags were surreptitiously handed in. We had no x-ray at that time, so, having weighed each sample and measured its bulk (by water displacement), they accumulated in a box, ready for transport by Denis to Kampala.

One thing troubled Denis. He noted that our patients, while in hospital, were eating a rather atypical diet of the maize meal which we provided. This might affect their bowel transit times a bit. Could we perhaps visit a Pokot village well away from Amudat, where the diet would be more typical? There would not be time to do a bowel transit time study, but there might be an opportunity to examine the stools of people living on a meat, milk and blood diet. So Denis, a dresser and I set off by Landrover into the bush. We drove as far as we could, and then walked for several miles through the dry thornscrub, following a cattle track to a remote *manyatta*. The acrid smell of wood smoke and cattle dung told us we were getting close. The clouds of flies increased, persistently trying to settle on our red, sweating faces. Finally we came to a clearing in the bush, and a huddle of dome-shaped mud and stick huts, surrounded by a thorn barricade.

We appeared unannounced. The men of the village were having a *baraza* under a spreading thorn tree, squatting in a circle on their wooden stools, their plumed heads nodding at one another, their spears staked in the red earth beside them. The skin-clad, beaded women were decorating gourds under another tree, while their naked children played with an empty gourd in the dust beside them. They all raised their eyes at us with some astonishment. Where had the *Wazungu* suddenly appeared from, and why had they come? One could see the question written on their faces. Never before had *Wazungu* visited this *manyatta*. Denis was in seventh heaven. He was on a quest for motions, and his preoccupation caused him to overlook the niceties of politeness. 'You go that way round the village, and I'll go this way,' he said to me. 'Look behind rocks and bushes and if you see a nice stool give me a shout. I'll come and photograph it.' Before I could get in a word he was off on his quest, nose to the ground, as it were. I briefly spoke to the Pokot men, greeted them, explained what our visitor had come for, and said we would come and greet them properly in a bit. There was a shout from beyond a thick bush. 'I've got one! There's a good one here! Come and have a look!' The sheer excitement in Denis's voice was palpable. Meanwhile the expression on the faces of our hosts was one of total bemusement. Even more so when they saw Denis get out his camera, and with close-up lens start taking pictures at various angles of the small, offensive pile. They had experienced the desire *Wazungu* have for taking pictures of them and their women folk, in their tribal finery. But never before this. When Denis was done, and every possible venue had been searched, and several specimens eagerly photographed, I introduced him to the elders. As they gazed into his face, with its false eye, I could almost read the question going through their minds. 'Is this Mzungu completely mad, or is he so wise that his ways are beyond knowing?'

The next day Denis left. He gave Rosemary an enormous hug – he had treated her like a much loved daughter. He urged me to specifically look for those diseases which we said we never saw. I began from that day to examine every patient for, for example, varicose veins, and could say categorically that in several hundred examined I found varicose veins in only one. This sort of information I fed back to Denis in the months ahead, and he incorporated it in his papers. We had been greatly stimulated and inspired by his visit – both medically and spiritually. In my farewell speech to him at the hospital I said how we had noted his intense interest in stools. We were too small a hospital to have a Chair of Pathology, but in his honour we were appointing him to our first Stool of Pathology. We presented him with a Pokot stool (the wooden variety) in honour of his visit. I know he treasured it, and had it in his Cotswold home until he died.

All the bags of stool samples – about ninety of them – had been loaded onto the back seat of Denis' car for the journey to Kampala, where they would be x-rayed, and the bowel transit times calculated. It was some time later that we heard about their arrival at Mulago hospital. A doctor there, a friend of Denis, saw him driving in to the hospital, just back from Amudat. The friend flagged Denis down, and went over to the car to speak to him. The car windows, in spite of the heat and humidity of Kampala, were closed. As Denis' friend leaned forward to speak to him, and Denis wound down his car window, the friend was hit by a wave of stench that he said was indescribable. Denis, with his precious cargo, was blissfully unaware of the fetid atmosphere in which he had just driven two hundred and sixty miles.

The study showed that Pokot have equally rapid bowel transit times, and equally soft and bulky stools, to their fibre-eating countrymen. How does one explain that? Denis' theory was that people like the Pokot have eaten a low roughage diet for centuries. Their traditional way of life has not changed. Their bowels have adjusted to cope with that sort of diet. We in the west, by contrast, have had a significant dietary change during the last century. Our grandparents ate far more roughage than we do. Food was far less refined one hundred years ago. Fast foods were unheard of. We have cut out the fibre, and have suffered the consequences. Denis attributed the increase in cardiovascular disease, hypertension and diabetes, amongst other things, to our dietary change. Exercise could also play a part. Pokot walk often many miles in a day. They are wiry, and fit, and I never saw an obese Pokot man or woman, other than those who had received an education and were living a more sedentary life. Denis left me with much encouragement, and the challenge to make simple observations in a scientific way. It was as though a whirlwind had swept through Amudat, leaving us breathless but invigorated. Denis and I were destined to meet again in London the following year.

Chapter 18
MARSABIT REVISITED

We were due for our first proper home leave at the end of 1970. We would have completed three years in Amudat. The question was, 'Where after that?' Would we return to Amudat, or was this the opportunity to move to Marsabit, as originally planned? In order for this to happen another doctor would be needed for Amudat. And this is exactly what appeared to be working out. Dr John Malcolm and I had lived at the same hostel, the Medical Missionary Association, when we were medical students in London. John had then followed me to Swindon for his house jobs. We were old friends. And John, and his wife Gill (an ophthalmic nurse), with their two small daughters, Philippa and Rosemary, were interested in coming to Amudat. Peter and Liza Cox would then move from Marsabit back to Pokot country, to Kapenguria Hospital (where the Frasers had been until Graham's death). We would replace the Coxes at Marsabit . It all seemed very neat and to everyone's benefit. A period of six months' overlap was planned for John and myself in Amudat. Where would the Malcolms live during that time? We could not ask them to squash into our small guesthouse. Lilian nobly agreed to move into our guesthouse, and we extended her house, a double rondavel, for John and Gill. We did our best to make it welcoming and homely. They arrived in May. For John there was, as for me, the interest and challenge of the hospital. But Gill, as had been the case for Rosemary, felt very lonely and isolated. After their first few days John confided in me that, in spite of all our attempts to prepare them for Amudat, they had been 'absolutely shattered' by everything – the isolation, the basic living conditions, the heat. We knew how they felt, and just hoped and prayed that, with time, they would find it easier, especially when they moved into our house.

John threw himself with great energy and enthusiasm into the hospital work, and for me it was wonderful to have a colleague to share the workload, and the decision-making. Once he had settled it was the opportunity for us to take some overdue holiday. And that was where this book began. We went back to Marsabit, to renew acquaintance with my childhood haunts, and for Rosemary and the children to see the place to which we would return after our leave. We broke our journey at Nanyuki, on the slopes of Mount Kenya. We stayed at the Sportsman's Arms Hotel, the very hotel where my parents, brother and I had stayed on our first trip down from Marsabit to boarding school, when I was six. Nothing had changed. The accommodation was in little self-contained cottages, with roaring cedar log fires, to ward off the icy winds blowing down from the glaciers of Mount Kenya. What a change from Amudat! The next day we headed north, towards the hot, dry scrubland of Kenya's Northern Frontier District. The entrance to the NFD was fifty miles north of Nanyuki, at the dusty wild-west town of Isiolo. A permit was needed to pass the barrier. We were entering untamed bandit country.

Memories of childhood journeys to and from school flooded back on the one-hundred-and-seventy-mile-stretch of the journey from Isiolo to Marsabit. The vast horizon was broken by jagged mountains rising sheer from the plains – mountains that we had each 'claimed' as our own on childhood journeys. Warages, Lodomot, 'the Dog and the Bone', Ol Lolokwe (which was mine). The flat topped acacia trees, bedecked with weaver bird nests, the towering termite hills, the corrugated murram road stretching to the horizon, the relentless juddering of the car, and the clouds of dust which found their way into the car through every nook and cranny – it was all so familiar. We saw herds of elephants; we saw narrow-striped Grevy zebra, and the beautifully marked reticulated giraffe – both unique to northern Kenya; we saw graceful Grant's gazelles, long-necked gerenuk, jackals, ostriches, and much more. As children we had vied with one another to be the first to spot animals, and we kept a tally of varieties and numbers. So now we did the same with Andrew and Paul. As we reached the edge of the Kaisut desert we saw, racing across its surface, dust devils – snaking vortexes of dust, rising high into the sky, sucking up bushes and debris from the desert floor like giant vacuum cleaners. Beyond the desert we could discern the hazy forested slopes of Marsabit mountain. I had a lump in my throat. We were coming home.

We stayed the next few days with the Reverend Stephen and Eve Houghton, the BCMS missionaries who were originally destined to teach us Kiswahili on the boat trip out to Mombasa – the boat trip that we never had. We met so many old friends, saw so many familiar faces. Tears were shed at the recollection of days gone by. And, as I said at the beginning of this tale, always the question, 'David, when are you coming back to be our doctor?' The answer was, 'Soon. Next year. After our leave in England.' We made our nostalgic visit to the old mission site, where I had grown up. I preached at the Swahili and Boran services on the Sunday, and, of course, we looked round the hospital. This was the Government District Hospital for Marsabit District, an area of twenty-five thousand square miles. It was larger than Amudat Hospital, and had a trained staff of about eighty, but was still a one-doctor set up. The hospital was set on the forest edge, and the house that would be ours was right up against the forest. At an altitude of five thousand feet it was all so cool and green. Much as we had come to love Amudat and its people, we looked forward to our move.

On our return journey from Marsabit, when we reached the great rock face of flat-topped Ol Lolokwe mountain, some way before Isiolo, we took a track off to the right. This led us through fifty miles of elephant-decimated bush to the foot of Wamba mountain. And here we found the home of my aunt, Edith Webster, who had moved to the area from Marsabit in 1937 when my mother joined my father in Marsabit. She had gone first to Maralal to work as a teacher among the Samburu people, but by 1970 her home was in remote Wamba, still among her beloved Samburu. We stayed with her in her little cedar wood home for a few days, and here I celebrated my twenty-ninth birthday. What struck us at Wamba was that whole Samburu *manyattas* had accepted the Christian faith, without jettisoning their culture. Their *manyattas* were the same. Their way of life, with their cattle, was unchanged. Their dress was traditional, with all their finery of beads, and, for the men, ochre-dyed mud headdresses. But they were cleaner, and healthier, and – the impression was – happier. Their newfound faith had set them free from fear of God and spirits and curses. The lesson we learned, which was so relevant to the Pokot also, was that it is very difficult, if not impossible, for an individual to become a Christian, and then remain in tribal society. It needed villages in their entirety, from the chief down, to turn to Christ.

Africans are not individualists. They have strong family, and social and tribal bonds. Just as, in the book of Acts (chapter ten), Cornelius 'and his whole household' were converted and baptized, so Africans (or at least rural, tribal people) need to respond collectively to the Gospel.

Continuing in the missionary tradition of the Websters my brother Dennis, and his wife Priscilla, with young Timothy and Peter, had meanwhile come out to Kenya with CMS (the Church Missionary Society). Dennis had been appointed Chaplain to Thika High School, twenty miles north of Nairobi. They visited us in Amudat shortly before we left for England. It marked the beginning of a close relationship between the cousins, who were of similar age. At my last Staff Prayers at hospital I spoke on the verse of St Paul to the Ephesians (1:16), 'I thank my God always for you . . .' We had made many good friends in Amudat, both amongst our colleagues in the hospital and church, and also among our many visitors. We were leaving a good part of our hearts there.

So we flew back to England. It was going to be a significant leave in at least two respects – Rosemary was expecting again, due in the May; and I was booked to do the Diploma in Tropical Medicine and Hygiene course, at the London School of Tropical Medicine. Our home church in Ashtead had wonderfully provided us with a bungalow, so we could live independently over the coming months, and yet be just round the corner from Rosemary's mother. It was an ideal arrangement. That Christmas it snowed heavily. As we trudged to church through the thick, crunching snow, to the sound of the pealing bells of St Giles; as we opened an extravagance of presents by the roaring fire, and ate until we could eat no more; so then our thoughts went to Amudat, where it would be blisteringly hot, and a dry wind would be blowing up eddies of dust, and the patients would be receiving their extra ration of maize meal and an empty tin. What a world of contrasts!

Chapter 19
A COMMUTER

For the first time in my life I became a commuter – taking the train each day from Ashtead, in Surrey, to Waterloo, and then the Underground to the School of Tropical Medicine and Hygiene. It involved skills that I had yet to master, and I was up against lifetime experts. Where, for instance, should one stand on Ashtead Station platform to have the best chance of a seat on the train? I thought, after a few days, that I had discovered the secret – wait for the front end of the train, and there was a half-empty carriage. It was the disapproving looks, and side-ways glances, of my compartment companions that drew my attention to the sign on the carriage window – 'Ladies only'! I changed carriages at the next station – and stood for the rest of the journey. And then there was the skill of reading a newspaper on the train, especially when standing. Mine either spilled over onto the laps of adjacent commuters, or spread between their faces and their own papers, or it ended up in a crumpled heap. Why did nobody else seem to have a problem? I observed the sharp, neat flicks, elbows tucked in, with which they turned their pages, keeping their papers neatly folded into small squares. I tried a sharp, neat flick, with my elbows tucked in – and nearly hit my neighbour in the face. I was conscious – or perhaps imagined – pitying looks from the rest of the carriage. Another skill I found it hard to master was (having abandoned the crumpled heap of newspaper) that of staring into the middle distance without appearing to be looking at anyone (which would have drawn hostile stares in reply), and yet without falling asleep and missing my station. All in all I was so glad that I was not condemned to spend the rest of my life commuting to London on the 8.03.

The Tropical Medicine course was excellent. I was so glad that I had had three years of experience in Amudat before doing it. Clearly for exam purposes I had to learn about Chagas' Disease of South America and the use of human manure in the paddy fields of south China, but I could concentrate on, and pick the brains of world experts about, diseases relevant to East Africa. I could apply the course to my needs. It was a five month course, and during that time I got to know some of my fellow students well. In particular it was the beginning of a lasting friendship with a German doctor, Reinhard von Kietzell. Reiner, as he was known, was not very impressed by the canteen food at the School, so his wife, Liese-Lotte, made him sandwiches each day. They contained a non-descript white meat. I asked Reiner what kind of meat it was, but he was not sure. I studied it closely, and told him authoritatively that it was badger, commonly used in England for sandwiches. It was a little while before Reiner came to recognise deadpan English humour. (Years later, when they had been staying with us, we made them chicken sandwiches for their journey, and I painted the meat with black and white stripes. The badger joke lived on.) Another friendship forged was with a lovely Salvation Army doctor, Murray Stanton, working in India. Tragically Murray died from Weil's Disease (Leptospirosis) soon after his return to India. Being the only doctor on site he had self-diagnosed his illness, and given instructions to his staff as to how to treat him before he lapsed into a coma. There were, on the course, doctors from across the globe, and they were as interesting to talk to as the lecturers.

One of our lecturers was none other than Denis Burkitt. Having given us a riveting lecture on geographical pathology and bowel transit times, he said how very interested he was to know what effect a sudden change of diet had on the bowels. 'For instance,' he continued, 'some of you doctors have come from countries with healthy, high-roughage diets, and suddenly you are having to eat refined, low-fibre, sugar-rich English food. What has it done to your bowel transit times?' I sensed trouble approaching. I tried to look inconspicuous in the middle of the lecture theatre. But there was no escape. 'Now my friend there, David Webster,' he said, fixing his one eye on me, 'knows exactly what is needed, and I am going to ask him to recruit you all for a bowel transit time study.' Recruiting Pokot was a walk-over compared with recruiting doctors. Our Indian and African colleagues were particularly reluctant, although I knew that they were the ones Denis most wanted to study. I had to use all my charm and persuasion. The study time happened to coincide with a very hot Bank Holiday weekend, so by the Tuesday, when the

School re-opened, some of the samples coming in by train, underground and bus, were getting quite ripe. Embarrassed colleagues sidled up to me with brief cases at the ready, and, with knowing nods and winks and little said, slipped packages into my waiting case. I then had to take my fragrant collection up Gower Street to University College Hospital, where Denis Burkitt had arranged for them to be x-rayed. Did I imagine that people I passed in the street turned to look at me, and that others were giving me a wide berth? My reception at UCH's x-ray Department was understandably unenthusiastic. In due course I felt that my passing of the DTM&H exam had been well earned.

Meanwhile other dramatic events had occurred. On 26 May 1971 Rosemary, who was at term with her pregnancy, suddenly had a sharp bleed. I took her in to Epsom Hospital, where initially her treatment was casual. But, following further bleeding, an excellent Indian Registrar took matters in hand. She had a third degree placenta praevia, the placenta completely overlying the outlet to the uterus. There was no possibility of a normal delivery, and there was a high risk of losing the baby. In those pre-ultrasound scan days such discoveries were often not made until the last minute. She had an emergency caesarian section, and Stephen Jeremy was safely delivered. How glad I was that we were not in Amudat. Folks there had said, 'Doctor, you deliver our babies. When Rosemary has a baby she should have it here, with us.' As it happened the delivery coincided with our home leave. But what if we had decided to have the baby in Amudat? It did not bear thinking about.

Andrew and Paul were enjoying life in England, but perhaps not adapting to it. They had been loaned a tricycle each, and would pedal at high speed along the pavement, and then suddenly divert up people's drives, hurtle round their flowerbeds, and then shoot out again. They left not a few astonished Ashtead gardeners in their wake. They did not understand the difference between the freedom of the bush, and people's private gardens. A delightful elderly couple, Tubby and Mary, lived next door to our bungalow. Mary loved to take the boys out for walks, but she was prone to vertigo. On one occasion Paul, pedalling furiously around her legs, put her off balance, and she fell on the pavement. Ever concerned, Paul leapt off his tricycle, rushed over to her, and asked 'Are you going to heaven right now, Auntie Mary?' Andrew had an ever-enquiring mind. He helped me post a letter to Amudat in a postbox – a new experience. In Amudat letters went into a postbag which we padlocked and put onto a lorry. I explained how in England the postman would collect it, and take it to the post office, and then how by van, sorting office, plane, train and lorry it would reach Amudat. He looked puzzled. I went through the process again. He was still puzzled. 'But how will the postman get his hand through that hole in the letter box to get the letter out?' he asked. Taking their first trip on a double-decker bus Paul asked, in a loud voice, if the space under the stairs was the toilet. 'No!' said Andrew authoritatively. 'The toilet is upstairs!' 'No it isn't,' argued Paul. 'It's up at the front like on the plane.' They both had a fascination for toilets, and the variety of levers, chains and buttons used for flushing. It was all so much more interesting than a long-drop – although the wild life in English toilets did not bear comparison with that in our Amudat long-drop.

Rosemary's mother revelled in having the grandchildren to hand, and loved to show them off to her friends. She was Chairperson of the Ashtead Townswomen's Guild, and sometimes held elegant tea parties in her drawing room. On one such occasion the children were summoned to be shown off. The assembled company of august ladies were sipping their afternoon tea. Grandma told Paul to sit quietly at her feet. As he did so his gaze turned upwards, and his loud question broke the silence: 'Grandma, why do you wear nappies?' He had espied her woolly underwear. He was not shown off at a tea party again.

Before, during and after the Tropical Medicine course, and the birth of Stephen, deputation work had to be fitted in – visiting churches and groups that supported our work, to talk about it, show slides, preach on Sundays, speak to school groups and meet key people. Apart from Ashtead itself, where we had tremendous support from the church, we, or I, visited Bury, Rawtenstall, Kingswood, Malvern Girls' College, Amersham, Charlbury, Edgware and Romford. I spoke to Rotary Clubs and Inner Wheels – and to anybody who cared to listen. We needed all the support we could get. A particularly enjoyable weekend was back at Ashburnham Place, near Battle, with the St Thomas's Christian Union

Houseparty – the very place where, on a similar occasion, Rosemary and I had been challenged by Peter Cox, and where we later met. On this occasion it was I who was the 'missionary speaker'. Some lasting friendships began that weekend, and a number of those students came out to us for their elective periods. Several ended up working in the Third World, so in a sense it was history repeating itself.

Dramatic events had been unfolding in Uganda. On 25 January 1971, while President Milton Obote was on his way back from the Commonwealth Conference in Singapore, his military leader, Brigadier General Idi Amin, staged a coup. There were troops and tanks on the streets of Kampala, with pro and anti-Obote factions of the army fighting one another. Soon Amin got the upper hand. Obote sought refuge in Tanzania. The Baganda people, of the Kampala area, came out in celebration. After all, Obote had deposed and exiled their King, the Kabaka. In fact, with the exception of the people of Obote's own tribe, the Lango, there was widespread support for the coup. Obote had not been popular. The British Government, though cautious in its language, also welcomed Amin's accession to power. Obote's left-wing, pro-China stance had not gone down well with Britain. Amin, it was said, was a simple soldier, British-trained, favourable to Britain. He was a hearty, straightforward, honest sort of chap, we were told – in the best tradition of NCOs in the British army. He would no doubt take the advice of wiser, more literate people when it came to political decisions. The British community in Uganda were, by and large, delighted by the coup.

In Amudat Amin was remembered as the Sergeant who had once been in charge of an army detachment there. Amudat people had rather different recollections – of a soldier who had been only too happy to shoot up the locals. At first the coup itself had little direct impact on Amudat. John Malcolm and the nurses and hospital dressers continued their work as normal. But within three months of the coup Amin issued an edict that all Ugandans must wear clothes, or be shot. Numbers at Amudat Hospital began to drop off, and it was suspected that people were afraid to be seen by the army. On a personal level the message that had been coming through from John and Gill Malcolm for some time was that they would not be staying at Amudat. We had to reconsider our next move. A young couple, Dr Ralph and Ceri Settatree, were available for Marsabit. It looked more and more as though our place should be back at Amudat. Again, it seemed, our going to Marsabit had been thwarted. But we had peace about it, and felt that in due course, in God's time, the opportunity would come. By August 1971 the decision was made. John and Gill would leave Amudat soon after our return. John subsequently found an opportunity for private practice in the town of Nakuru in Kenya, and they were very generous in hospitality to those of us who lived further afield. John also became school doctor to St Andrew's, Turi, a Christian primary boarding school. There he cared medically for many missionary children, including, in due course, our own. John had done an excellent job in Amudat over the year. We flew out to Nairobi, en route once again for Amudat, and at one minute past midnight on 19 September, at thirty thousand feet, Rosemary and I exchanged seventh wedding anniversary cards and gifts.

Chapter 20
DEATH AND DISCOURAGEMENT

As we approached the flooded Alakas, ten miles short of Amudat, we saw a note in a cleft stick at the side of the road. It was addressed to us, and was from John Malcolm. He had been out to meet us, and tow us through. Finding us not yet there he had gone home but would return in an hour, the message said. We arrived in Amudat to heart-warming greetings. Having felt apprehensive about returning it somehow seemed right to be back. We would live in Lilian's former house until the Malcolms left in a month's time. Three things struck us. First, Amudat was so green – there had been a lot of rain. Second, there was also a lot of cattle raiding going on, with Karamojong frequently seen skulking in the vicinity of our houses. Third, the army, with its new-found power since Amin's coup, was active in the area, and very trigger happy.

The greenness was refreshing. Aloes were ablaze with their orange-red flowers. Wild lilies had appeared among the newly sprung grass. The Kanyangereng was flowing gently, and ideal for the children to splash in. The bird life was at its best. Until now our only binoculars had been an old, cracked ex-army pair that had belonged to my father in the war. Now we had new ones, a gift from Rosemary's mother, and we could begin to identify and to appreciate to the full the stunning variety of colourful birds – superb starlings, paradise fly-catchers, lilac breasted rollers and black and crimson gonoleks, all with their iridescent plumage, regularly visited the trees around us. Perhaps due to the wet, scorpions had sought refuge in the house, and we had a few close encounters – Rosemary had one that was too close and very painful. The wet weather also led to a plague of ants. I picked over three hundred out of the marmalade one morning. (Yes! I counted them.) Mosquitoes were rife.

The wet weather brought with it great advantages for the Pokot – grazing and water, of course. But also flying ants. In rainy weather flying forms of termites emerge from their anthills to mate and start new colonies. The flying forms have swollen sausage-like abdomens, full of a protein-rich goo, much loved as a delicacy by the Pokot. They are eaten either raw, after first removing the legs and wings, or roasted, having a pleasant nut-like taste. During rainy weather, when the flying ants were emerging in their thousands, the Pokot would cover the exit holes of the anthills with skins, and direct the flying ants into pits from which they could scoop them and feast.

It was a puzzle as to why cattle raiding had increased. Not infrequently we would see groups of young Pokot men, armed with two or three spears each, their blades unsheathed – a sure sign of serious business – running through the bush past our house. This would follow a sighting or a rumour of Karamojong raiders in the area. On one occasion this happened when the school Christian Union was meeting in our house. With one accord they leapt up and joined the chase. Not many Christian Union meetings end so abruptly for such a reason! On a number of occasions Karamojong footprints were seen in the sandy gully that ran past the house. A raiding gang of over one hundred were seen at the Kanyangereng. One night Rosemary set off for the long drop and returned very rapidly – by torchlight she saw a man sitting on the bonnet of the Landrover. It was all a bit unsettling. Probably our lives were not at risk, but the lives of the Pokot most certainly were. Lokitare was a young lad who caused us a number of problems, not least his predilection for stealing Landrover keys. But our feelings for him changed when his father, out collecting firewood near to our house, was speared to death by Karamojong. Two young herd boys were killed at the Kanyangereng at the very spot where we regularly went with the children. The uncle of our dresser, John Makal, was speared. His body was not found for several days. I had to do a post mortem for the police. In the heat the body had decomposed, and was infested with maggots – very distressing for John Makal. Almost daily we heard of Pokot who had been speared.

Some people were lucky. A Tapeth boy from Kadam was speared through the groin, the spear emerging from his buttock. He was also badly wounded in the arm and twice in the chest. He had been left for dead. He was brought to hospital, having lost a lot of blood. At one point, while we were setting up a blood transfusion, his heart stopped and we had to resuscitate him. We bled every possible donor, and poured blood into him. It took four hours to repair his wounds. He fortunately made a good recovery. Another entire night was spent in the operating theatre. Initially it was to patch up a man who had been mauled by a lion – he had a badly chewed arm, with compound fracture of radius and ulna, deep bites in his groin, and penetrating his abdomen, and gashes from claws that had ripped open his thighs. We had just finished three hours of work repairing him when a policeman who had been speared, on this occasion by Pokot, was brought in. He had been trying to recover cattle that the Pokot had rustled from the Karamojong. His arm was badly injured, with severed muscles and tendons. That took some more hours of work.

One Pokot victim of spearing had a penetrating injury of his left lung with a tension pneumothorax – air leaking from his lung had built up pressure within the chest cavity, causing increasing collapse of the lung. He was desperately ill, and fighting for breath. I put a drain in his chest to relieve the pressure. It then became evident that he was also leaking air from his right lung, and needed a drain on that side too. By the third day he was doing well. Rosemary was giving him regular physiotherapy, to help re-expand his lungs. We felt really encouraged. His wife was responsible for his care. On the fourth morning we found his wife fast asleep and the patient dead, the chest drains having become disconnected in the night. It was this tragedy which decided us that, however short of staff we might be, we must always have a dresser on night duty, and not rely on patients' relatives. I carried out a post mortem on the man, and found that the spear had gone through his left lung and penetrated deeply into the right. Yet he would have lived if those tubes had not disconnected. It was a sad and salutary lesson.

As well as the busyness resulting from tribal raiding it was also busy thanks to the Uganda army. They despised the Pokot. Amin had already made his edict about clothing, and any Pokot seen naked or in traditional goat skins was shot on sight. Most of the victims that we saw at hospital were women and children. One small baby had had her leg shattered by the bullet which killed her mother. It made us very angry, and we protested, but could do little else. The army was now in control, and were answerable to nobody.

Trauma of various kinds featured a lot in our day-to-day work.

On the day after the Malcolms left we planned to move back into our original house. I intended to have the day off for the move. But it was not to be. During the night a Ministry of Works lorry overturned some miles from Amudat. One man was killed outright. Twenty two were injured. We roused all the hospital staff (two nurses and five dressers), and set into motion our equivalent of a Major Incident plan. Injuries included a fractured base of skull, three fractured arms, two fractured knee caps, a dislocated shoulder, severed tendons, an ear torn off, and multiple lacerations and bruises. Seven patients had to go to theatre during the night, five of whom required general anaesthetics. It was at times like that that I felt incredibly proud of our staff – their skills and their commitment. After all, just a few years before they had been herd boys, with no schooling. Now they were carrying out complicated medical procedures with skill and confidence.

It was not always a story of success however. One of our dressers, Wilson Akiru, had a delightful wife, Cheposera. She had had no education, but was very keen to learn. She was always cheerful, and so delighted when she delivered their first child, a little boy. Before long she was pregnant again. When nearly at term she began to bleed. I took her to theatre and examined her under anaesthetic. She had placenta praevia, and needed urgent caesarian section. I delivered a little girl, but not without difficulty. The placenta lay right under the incision into the uterus, and I had to go through it. The baby was fine, and cried lustily. Cheposera came round from the anaesthetic. She and Wilson were thrilled. Then suddenly she collapsed, and became pulseless. We did everything we could to resuscitate her, but to no avail. In retrospect I think she had a rare amniotic fluid embolus. Wilson was distraught. I was devastated. It would have been distressing for this to happen to any patient, but to the wife of one of our own staff, and someone we all knew and loved, was almost unbearable. There was no question of a post mortem – it was not required by law, and doubtful if I would have been able to identify the cause of death with any certainty. Instead we did what one does in a hot climate – we went to dig the grave. We dug into the hard rocky ground. We dug into the night, by lamplight. We needed a grave deep enough to be proof from hyenas. The Pokot usually left their dead out in the bush for the hyenas. Wilson wanted his dear wife's body to be protected and respected. We all took it in turns to chip away at the hard rock with pick axes. For me the hard digging was a way of expressing my grief. As the pickaxe rang out on the rocky ground so the tears flowed. I felt responsible for Cheposera's death. I felt guilty, a failure. At one point Wilson came over to me, and put his arm around me, and said, 'Doctor, it was not your fault. You did everything you could. Cheposera is with God.' They were generous words. The next day we had the funeral. Cheposera's body was gently wrapped in a new piece of cloth. We made a coffin out of crates. Many gathered round that dusty, rocky graveside. The Catholic Fathers joined us. Daudi Chebtwey spoke of the hope that the Christian has even in death. Wilson stood there, under the hot son, cradling his precious new baby. The immediate problem was that of feeding her. Mary, the wife of our health worker Samson Adio, had recently stopped breast feeding their baby, and she still had enough milk for Wilson's baby. Wilson set off to find his younger sister, to come to help him. He knew that her village was somewhere in the Karapokot hills, but did not know exactly where they had moved to. In the end he walked one hundred and twenty miles to find her and bring her back with him. Never at any time did Wilson show or express bitterness or anger. But for me that was perhaps the blackest day we had in Amudat.

And yet, on the positive side, we saw the arrival and installation of our x-ray – the building donated by Oxfam, the machine and generator by Bread for the World. For the first time we could diagnose and assess properly fractures and chest infections, including tuberculosis.

The US army kala-azaar project had folded up soon after George Barnley's accident, and the death of his wife. The two years of research had come to no very helpful conclusions, and the loss of most of the sandfly collection in the accident had not helped. But now the possibility of a new project arose. Paediatricians working with the Medical Research Council (MRC) in Kampala, and in liaison with Newcastle University, wanted to study the nutritional state of Pokot children. Malnutrition is one of Africa's major health problems – in those days before AIDS it was, along with malaria and gastroenteritis, a leading cause of death in children. In many parts of Africa malnutrition presents as kwashiorkor, caused by protein deficiency. Children get bloated tummies, and swollen limbs and faces, and reddish hair. But in the Amudat area malnutrition was caused by both protein and calorie deficiency, and this leads to marasmus – failure to gain weight, or weight loss, with stick-thin limbs and shrivelled bodies. It was to study marasmus, as opposed to the kwashiorkor prevalent in other parts of Uganda, that the MRC team wanted to come. They were also interested in the high prevalence of gastroenteritis – the biggest killer of children. In the Amudat area at that time two out of five children died before the age of five, and this was mostly from gastroenteritis. The general lack of hygiene and abundance of flies made the spread of diarrhoeal diseases very common. If for any reason a mother could not breast feed her baby that baby would inevitably die. Even if formula milk was available (which it wasn't) they had no way of sterilising bottles and teats. Untreated cow's milk would be given to the baby from a filthy gourd, and it was only a matter of time until that baby got gastroenteritis and died.

In November 1971 the MRC team came on a preliminary visit, and we drove together into the bush, to a remote village called Achorichor. There we set up clinic. Never before (or since) have the people of Achorichor had three paediatricians, a bush doctor (me), a senior medical student, a nutritionist, a biochemist, a nurse and two dressers to attend to their needs. We saw and assessed seventy-two children that morning. We then returned to Amudat to do a ward round. They saw cases, not only of marasmus and gastroenteritis, but also of cholera, amoebic dysentery, amoebic liver abscess and kala-azaar, amongst other things. By the end of that day they had decided to go ahead with the project, and were quite excited. They would build a complex of rondavels for their accommodation, and would set up a mobile laboratory next to the hospital. I sensed that this was going to be a much more productive project than the US Army one, and that they would be very much easier to get on with than Max had been. It was an exciting prospect.

Lilian Singleton had gone on well-earned home leave at about the same time as the Malcolms left. In her place came a young nurse, Di Wildish, who fitted in well to the tough new life. Another boost to our morale came from the visit, on his elective period, of medical student Keith

Knox. Keith was President of the St Thomas's Hospital Christian Union, and we had met the previous year when I spoke at their Houseparty. Keith was the son of a well-known Christian speaker and Town Clerk of Harrogate, Neville Knox. He had clearly inherited a lot of the dynamism of his father. Keith came like a breath of fresh air, throwing himself into the activities of the hospital with great enthusiasm. He was very popular with the schoolboys, with whom he played endless games of football. Also with the girls in Ruth's hostel, who spent happy hours with him splashing in the Kanyangereng. He spoke in church, and on safari, and had a great knack of communicating his faith in a real and attractive way. He taught new songs to Rosemary's Sunday School, now over seventy strong. And he taught all sorts of tricks and songs to our own boys. Keith was, without doubt, a hit. There was great sadness when he left at the end of his elective, but what pleased us all was that he indicated that one day, when qualified, he would be back.

Chapter 21
KATABOK

On our previous medical safari to Katabok, at the eastern foot of Kadam, we had promised the people we would build a dispensary there. For a number of reasons it was a good site. There was always a substantial Pokot population in the area, and it was also within reach of the Tapeth people on the mountain. There was a water supply – a borehole, but also a spring in a nearby valley if the borehole pump should break. It was within reasonable reach of Amudat – twenty-seven miles of rough track, but negotiable with four-wheel drive. Our plan was to build two mud houses, one for the dispensary, one to house the dresser. Dressers would rotate from Amudat, a month at a time. We made a reconnaissance visit in February 1972, and initially we were disappointed. The borehole was broken, and there was nobody in sight. After a while a man emerged cautiously from the bush. 'It's all right!' he shouted. 'It's the doctor! We are safe!' And then people began to emerge from all directions. We discovered that the army had been around, and a number of people had been shot. Not surprisingly at the sound of our Landrover they had gone into hiding. When we told them of our plan for a dispensary they were very happy. We looked at possible sites, and decided to build under a clump of shady thorn trees where we had previously camped. We discovered some sheets of corrugated iron, the remains of a *duka* that had once been there. The owner, a Somali man in Amudat, would no doubt be glad to sell them to us. That evening we walked to the spring in a green valley tucked into the mountainside. Wild fig trees provided cool and shade. Ferns clung to the rocks around the spring. Clear water trickled musically over the pebbles. A pack of baboons on the rock face above us protested loudly at our visit – or perhaps they were barks of welcome. Katabok felt to be the right place for a dispensary.

The next day we pegged out the site for our proposed buildings. We found a source of sand in a riverbed two miles away. There were very few suitable trees for poles, so we noted that we would need to bring them from Amudat. (The only poles able to resist termites were those of the iron-hard terminalia tree.) We saw about eighty-five patients, and returned to Amudat excited at the prospect of the dispensary. On the way back we did some work on the track, filling in gullies, and smoothing the way through riverbeds. The dressers set to in their spare time to cut poles in readiness. We needed to hire a lorry to take all the building supplies – cement, roof timbers, poles, drums of water. Not surprisingly lorry owners were not too keen, because of the state of the track, but in the end I persuaded one. He obviously did not know what he was committing his lorry to because a mile short of Katabok he refused to go any further, and threw everything off. We had to ferry it all for the last bit by Landrover.

Building began in April. My brother, Dennis, and family were visiting us from Thika. He and the four older cousins came along too, together with five of the hospital staff. We worked solidly for the next five days, camping on site. Terminalia poles, roof trusses and corrugated iron went up first. Then we cut hundreds of 'fito' – thin poles nailed horizontally to the uprights, and between which mud would be packed for the walls. The four cousins, aged between four and six, joined in, carrying 'fito' and making themselves useful. The only people who refused to make themselves useful were the local Pokot for whom we were building the dispensary. They were quite content to watch. On the next building trip, a month later, when we had to pump water and mix mud for the walls, we insisted on some help from the Pokot men, and they condescended. They considered what we were doing to be women's work, and beneath their dignity.

The first of July 1972 was the Grand Opening of Katabok dispensary. Twenty three of us, including the Akapolon (the Chief), packed in to two Landrovers for the laborious journey. What a sight awaited us at Katabok! Over five hundred people had gathered, in all their best tribal finery. As we arrived the men began to dance, rhythmically jumping into the air to the clapping and high-pitched singing of the women. The pace increased. Drums throbbed. Dust rose from their stamping feet. The ostrich feather plumes in their mud headdresses waved in synchrony. The air vibrated with the resonant rhythmic base chants of the men, and the shrill voices and ululating of the women. Their song was telling the story of the day. The rhythm, the chanting, the clapping, the dust, the heat were mesmerising. It went on without a break for over two hours. A bull, a sheep and a goat, which had been tethered under a nearby tree, were then slaughtered – not a pretty sight. The bull's abdomen was slit open and the entrails slid out onto the ground. The tribal elders gathered round them to 'read the signs'. The position of each bit of the innards was important, and used for divining the future. Apparently the portents were good. The meat was roasted on an open fire. The prize bits, such as the liver, were reserved for guests (us) and the elders. Pieces of charred liver were passed round, and as we each took a piece a detachment of bluebottle flies peeled off and followed it to our mouths. The trick was to open the mouth for just long enough to allow entry of the liver, but not the pursuing flies. Then came the speeches. The Mukungu, the local chief, spoke, thanking us for the dispensary. Then it was my turn. Using the illustration of the key to the new building, I spoke of Jesus who is the Key to God. Then came the Akapolon, the Government appointed Head Chief. As I rather feared, he used the occasion for a harangue about paying poll tax and wearing clothes. The crowd got angrier and angrier, and began to shout him down. One old man angrily asked how a man could possibly be expected to pass urine when wearing trousers.

Meanwhile there was a welcome diversion. Shrieks of laughter from behind the dispensary drew some of the crowd away. While the men waffled on the women had got Rosemary and Di to dance with them, a cause of great amusement. Daudi Chebtwey wanted to end the proceedings with a prayer. He prayed a beautiful prayer, asking God's blessing on this new venture. But an old Pokot man was determined to have the last word. He rose to his feet, gathered a bunch of grass, and then began to bless us. He waved the grass as he chanted his prayer. After each petition there was a deep, reverberating rumble from all the men – 'Sera' ('Thank you!') 'Karam' ('Good!' – the equivalent of 'Amen'). He prayed repeatedly for me. He prayed for the effectiveness of our medicine, for good supplies, for safe travelling. He and the other elders chased away diarrhoea and other illnesses with a waving of their arms. Finally another wizened old man reviewed all that had been said. The grunting and 'Amens' rose to a crescendo. Then all the elders spat on the bunch of grass and, as a sign of blessing, it was rubbed on our heads. The bunch was then broken up, and bits of grass placed on each item of furniture in the dispensary. There were more staccato sentences, a rising cadence of grunts, a crescendo, and the old man fell on one knee in a bow of reverence. It was a most moving experience. Dancing began again, and we departed for Amudat (leaving two dressers at the dispensary) with the sound of singing and merriment ringing in our ears.

I returned to Katabok with supplies a week later. The dressers, Michael and Moses, had treated over five hundred people during the week. Numbers settled down to about eighteen hundred patients treated each month. The dressers were happy to rotate, a month at a time. Katabok dispensary had been well worth all the effort, and our medical care helped to counterbalance the aggression of the army.

On each visit to Katabok I would look up to Kadam and long to climb to its highest peaks – the sheer-sided plateau of Obda, at ten thousand feet, and craggy Tebtho, just a little lower. I had already climbed the third highest peak, Ayas, from Katabok. So it was that one weekend I set off, with some of the hospital staff and a Tapeth guide, approaching from the northern side of the mountain. As we reached the foot of the mountain we moved from thorn bush plain to high canopy forest, and saw troops of beautiful, long-haired, black and white colobus monkeys swinging and chattering in the high branches. Up and up we climbed, on a steep forest path. Before dusk we reached a cave, where we were to spend the night. There was a pool of greenish water alive with creatures. I filtered them out with my handkerchief before we made tea. As we unpacked to prepare a meal I realised that I had left behind probably the most vital commodity – sugar. I had promised to bring enough for everyone, and there was none. Undaunted the guide went off into the forest with a smoking log from the fire. He returned not long afterwards with a hat full of dripping honey, fresh from a wild hive. Our carbohydrate requirements were abundantly met. We had a fitful night in the entrance to the cave. A thought in my mind was what animals normally lived in that cave, and would they return during the night? Certainly there were leopards living on Kadam.

The next day we followed a very ill-marked track, cutting our way in places through thick undergrowth, and always climbing. We passed beautiful waterfalls, and crystal clear water. What a contrast from the hot plains below! Next came a belt of cedar trees, festooned with lichen. Finally we came onto moorland, not unlike the highlands of Scotland. And then the flat summit, from which there was a vista for a hundred miles in every direction – mounts Elgon, Moroto, and Napak loomed on the horizon, and even the blur of distant Lake Kyoga to the south. The tin roofs of Amudat glinted in the sun twenty miles to the east. A sheer rock face, three thousand feet high, dropped away at our feet to the broccoli-like forest canopy below. My legs felt weak even at a safe distance from the edge. That was nothing to what I felt when two of the dressers, John Makal and Justus Okiru, had a mock fight on the very edge of the cliff. We read Psalm 92 together – 'I sing for joy at the work of Your hands; how great are Your works O Lord! The Lord is my Rock!' We could not but sense the majesty of God on that mountain top. And then we began the long climb down.

On another occasion I climbed Tebtho, the craggy peak of Kadam, with the MRC team. Again we camped in the same cave, and had more time to explore the one hundred feet high waterfalls crashing down the mountain into deep fern-ringed pools of icy water. Again we saw troops of colobus monkeys. The meadow-land on Tebtho was lush, with carpets of wild flowers, including gladioli. Always, in East Africa, the difference that altitude makes is striking. One can pass, as we had done, from arid thornscrub to lush forest and meadows of wild flowers within a very short distance – or, as on Mount Kenya, from desert to glacier.

No times were more enjoyable than expeditions with the hospital staff. Most Bank Holidays we did something together. One of our most memorable expeditions was along the dry course of the river Kanyangereng, which rises on Kadam and flows when Kadam has rain. We decided to walk the riverbed from a point near to the mountain, and follow it to Amudat. Because of the winding course of the river it would mean a walk of about thirty miles. We set off early, before the heat of the day. The sand was soft, and the going tiring. All along the way were the footprints of animals, and the dressers had little problem identifying them – giraffe, eland, dik-dik, lion. The riverbed was lined with cool trees, some bearing wild fruits. The dressers knew exactly which were good to eat and which poisonous. We refreshed ourselves along the way with tart apricot-like fruits. From time to time we came to deep pools in the riverbed, and plunged in to cool off. We were splashing around in one particularly large pool when a herd boy appeared, and after watching us for a bit with unusual interest, asked if we knew that there was a crocodile living in the pool. I think I was the first to the bank. He may well have been right – when the Kanyangereng is in flood crocodiles from the River Suam, into which it flows, come upstream, and can be stranded in isolated pools. At one point on that long walk we came across a broad, smooth, undulating track in the sand – the trail of a large snake. We followed it along the riverbed and came on a five-foot puff adder, as thick as a man's thigh, basking on a sand bank. Puff adders are lethargic snakes, which is why people often tread on them and get bitten. I would rather have let this one sleep on in peace, but to the Pokot every snake is an enemy, and a potential cause of death. The dressers cut a forked stick, pinned the sleeping snake down, and beheaded it with a *panga*. Its head joined my collection; its skin made an attractive belt for Justus.

One of our expeditions was to the Turkwell Gorge. Situated forty miles from Amudat the gorge has been formed by the River Suam, which arises in Mount Elgon to the west, carves its way through the Karapokot hills to join the River Turkwell on the eastern side, and finally meanders across the desert to Lake Turkana in the north. The Turkwell gorge is remarkable for its narrowness, and the sheerness of its two thousand feet deep sides. The water plunges down through a series of labyrinths and waterfalls, until finally emerging onto the Karapokot plain. It was a dramatic place – alas no longer so, since the gorge has been dammed. The track we followed is now submerged under the Turkwell dam. It used to wind it way for thirty miles through the bush, from the main Kitale to Amudat road, crossing thirty riverbeds, some with steep-sided banks, and loose sandy beds. Four-wheel drive was a must. In the rainy season the gorge was totally inaccessible.

Imagine, therefore, my surprise when one day a British teacher from downcountry Uganda turned up at the hospital in Amudat in a Ford Cortina. 'I am on my way to the Turkwell Gorge,' he said. 'Can you tell me how to get there?'

'I can certainly tell you,' I replied, 'But there is no way you will get there in your car!'

'Oh, don't you believe it,' he said. 'This car gets me anywhere!'

'Not to the Turkwell Gorge,' I said.

'We'll see!' was his only answer.

Seeing that he would not be dissuaded I offered to ask one of the dressers to go with him, as guide and mentor. He agreed, and Wilson Akiru offered to go. The story of that trip we heard many times from Wilson, in vivid detail, in the months ahead. They drove the first ten miles, along the 'main' Kitale road, without a problem. The Cortina even negotiated the dry Alakas riverbed. It was when they turned off the road onto the Turkwell Gorge track that things began to get interesting. After just one mile they came to the first of the thirty riverbeds – steep eroded banks, and thick soft sand. Wilson advised leaving the car, but that idea was unthinkable to the teacher. They dug a slope, drove down onto the sand, and the car sank up to its axles. Fortunately before too much revving and further sinking had occurred a group of Pokot men came along from the direction of the gorge. With persuasion from Wilson, and no doubt a little financial lubrication from the teacher, they bodily lifted the Cortina out of the sand, and placed it back on the bank from whence it had come. 'We will walk!' agreed the teacher. The Pokot men asked what their plans were, and said they were leaving because Turkana raiders were near the gorge, and it was very dangerous to go on. The teacher was not impressed, and said he was going anyway. Wilson felt a responsibility for him, and so went too. On the thirty mile walk to the entrance of the gorge they met other Pokot hurrying away. All advised them to turn back, but the teacher was not for turning.

At dusk they finally arrived at the entrance to the gorge. It was time to make camp for the night. The teacher had a sleeping bag. Wilson just had his transparent plastic mackintosh. The teacher began to light a fire to heat his supper, but Wilson urged him not to. With Turkana raiders in the area the light of a fire would attract them as sure as a candle attracts moths. The teacher had his baked beans cold. Wilson chose a spot high on the riverbank to bed down. The teacher chose a smooth soft spot in the sand on the edge of the water. Wilson advised him against that place for two reasons – the danger of crocodiles, and the risk of the river rising in the night, if rain fell on distant Mount Elgon. But, as in all things, the teacher knew better. He wanted comfort. He stripped naked, and climbed in to his sleeping bag, carefully placing all his belongings at his side – the river side. During the night he was woken by a gentle lapping against his sleeping bag. He was almost afloat. The river had risen. He reached out for his things, and, with the exception of one walking boot, they were all well on their way to Lake Rudolf. Clothes, money, car keys and one boot – all gone! The naked teacher emerged from his sleeping bag, and waited for dawn. He was still determined to see the gorge. 'Anyway,' as Wilson told us later, to our great merriment, 'By good luck I could lend him my mackintosh and one shoe!' Now Wilson's shoes were quite fashionable winkle-pickers, and his mackintosh was plastic and transparent. We had this vision of the hirsute pink teacher, in transparent mack, and wearing one walking boot and one winkle picker, exploring the gorge. Perhaps the sight scared off any Turkana!

The long walk back to his car then followed. When they eventually reached it he could not unlock it to get clothes, or start it, because the keys were somewhere the other side of the gorge. They walked the mile to the road, and waited for a passing vehicle. It could have been a very long wait, but fortunately for him two Asians came along, who ran a garage in Kitale. Having adjusted to the unusual sight of this naked Englishman in a transparent mackintosh they drove to his car, forced the door, and hot-wired the engine. Unfortunately he had spare clothes in the car, and we were denied the sight of him in Wilson's mackintosh and shoe when he arrived back at the hospital slightly chastened. He was only slightly chastened, because one of his first questions was how to get to Lorsuk, one of the remotest of the Karapokot hills. 'My car can get anywhere – almost anywhere!' he assured me.

Chapter 22
GENERAL AMIN

The third of August 1972 was a watershed day in the history of Uganda, and also in our lives. The President of Uganda, General Idi Amin, was due to attend an Agricultural show at Iriri, a small town about one hundred miles west of Amudat. We were invited to attend. We found ourselves sitting in the row just behind the President. Amin, a hulk of a man, was in a jovial mood. There were the inevitable long speeches. Amin himself made quite a sensible speech. He said that the bride price in Karamoja District should be reduced, so that there was no longer the temptation or necessity to make cattle raids – a very practical suggestion. Entertainments followed, including a tug-of-war in which Amin participated. Choirs from various schools in the district sang, and our school from Amudat sang so well that the President gave one thousand shillings to the school. We all travelled home in high spirits. It had been a good day. It was the last good day for a very long time.

Amin spent that night at the Karamoja District headquarters in Moroto. Whether it was the effect of his lunch at the show, or the bed he slept in, we shall never know. But that night he had the dream in which, he said, God told him to expel all Asians from Uganda. He announced on the radio that they were all to go within three months. From Uganda's point of view the decree was disastrous – the country's economy was heavily dependent on the Asian community. From wealthy businessmen like Madhvani, who owned vast sugar estates, to small shop owners like Kanti Patel in Amudat, the prosperity of Uganda was largely due to the hard work and business acumen of Asians. From the point of view of the Asians themselves the decree was disastrous – most had been born in Uganda, and their lives and wealth were totally tied up in the country. They knew no other life and no other country. From the point of view of Britain the decree was disastrous – of the eighty thousand Asians in Uganda many had British citizenship, and suddenly Britain was expected to absorb this enormous number of immigrants within a very short space of time. The British Prime Minister, Sir Alec Douglas-Hume, protested, and talked of reviewing Britain's aid to Uganda. This resulted in a quick response from Amin - he cared nothing for British aid, and now not only British Asians but also those with Uganda citizenship would be expelled. 'All Asians are sabotaging the economy,' he declared. In a very short time a war of words was escalating. But it was more than just words. Within two days the Uganda army had set up a road block in Amudat to ensure that no Asians escaped with their money and belongings via the back door to Kenya. All passing vehicles, even those Kenya vehicles travelling to and from Lodwar in the north, were searched. We were relieved that our friend Kanti Patel must have had a premonition of what was to come, and had already sold his shop in Amudat, and left for the sunny climes of Morecombe in Lancashire, where he had bought a corner shop. (He now owns a chain of supermarkets in California.)

Britain pursued the diplomatic path in the hope of persuading Amin to see sense. A cabinet minister, Geoffrey Rippon, flew out to Uganda, but Amin refused to see him, nor would any other Ugandan minister. Radio Uganda's news programmes were vitriolic against Asians, and increasingly so against Britain. The situation began to change from day to day. Our source of news was the BBC World Service, which we listened to frequently, and the lilting notes of the signature tune, the Lully Bolero, became very familiar. By mid-August Amin had made it very clear that the expulsion order applied, as well as to businessmen, to professional Asians – teachers, doctors, dentists etc. It was going to knock an enormous hole in professional services. Asians who presented their Uganda passports to prove their citizenship had them torn up before their eyes. They were rendered stateless. I had to make a trip to Mbale to get cash and supplies, and everywhere was dealt with most courteously by Asian shopkeepers. They were very philosophical about their plight. They stood to lose everything, because Amin was allowing them to take nothing out – no goods, no money. One said to me 'Sometimes good can only come through suffering. We will suffer. Uganda will suffer. But in the end good will come!' I admired his lack of bitterness, and his optimism. (On a return trip to Mbale three months later it was a dead town. Ninety per cent of shops were boarded up. Most supplies were unavailable. The only shop where paraffin was available was run by an Arab.)

Movement even within Amudat became more complicated. An army road block lay between the hospital and the shops. If I drove the few hundred yards to the shops for any reason I was stopped and the Landrover searched, and then again on return. As the soldiers had seen me leave the hospital, and saw me enter the shop, I wondered what they thought their search might find. I asked them what exactly they were looking for, but they didn't know. I felt sorry for them. They were under orders, and must have found it as embarrassing as I found it irritating. There was great temptation – and from some directions pressure – for us to pack up and leave Uganda. Why put up with all this nonsense? Tension in the country was running high. Amin was totally unpredictable, and his often drunk and trigger-happy soldiers equally unpredictable. One did not know what Radio Uganda would announce next. We were due at a BCMS conference at Limuru, in the highlands west of Nairobi. It was an enormous relief to get away for a bit from the stress of Uganda, and to unwind in the cool green hills. I was asked to lead our worship one morning, and shared what I strongly felt God had been saying to me through Psalm 11: 'How foolish of you to say to me "Fly away" . . . there is nothing a good man can do when things fall apart." The Lord . . . has His throne in Heaven. He watches . . . He knows . . .' (TEV) Rosemary and I knew that our place was in Amudat, and we must go back come what may.

In early September Palestinian terrorists killed two athletes and held hostage other members of the Israeli team at the Munich Olympic Games. Subsequently all the hostages died in a bungled rescue attempt. Amin praised the action of the terrorists, and accused Israel and Britain of jointly plotting to assassinate him. Radio Uganda repeatedly warned Ugandans to keep a close watch on British people. The Asian sugar magnate, Madhvani, and one of his British managers were arrested and put in an army gaol. We feared nothing from the local people in Amudat, but the army was completely unpredictable, and hung on every word from Amin. The tension was constantly ratcheted up. We met with our fellow Christians in Amudat for prayer, and found encouragement in Psalm 46:

'God is our refuge and strength, an ever present help in trouble. Therefore we will not fear . . .' (NIV). By 7 September the threats from Amin were beginning to focus not just on British people, but more specifically on British missionaries. The radio announced that British missionaries were spies, with guns under our mattresses. What was the right and responsible thing to do, for my family, and for our nurse, Di Wildish? (Ruth was already out of Uganda at that time). That night we prayed together, and prayed for very clear and specific guidance as to what to do. The next morning I drove to the shop to get matches, going through the army roadblock. While in the shop I felt a tap on the shoulder. It was our resident Assistant District Commissioner, Mr Owor – a lovely Christian man. 'David, can you just come out into the road a moment?' he asked. He led me away from the crowded shop, and in the road, in full view of the soldiers but out of earshot, he said, 'I have some bad information. I cannot tell you what it is, but Rosemary and the children and your nurse must go to Kenya!' 'When?' I asked. 'Now!' he said. 'Immediately!' 'And what about me?' I asked. 'You carry on with your work, but be ready to go at any time on foot to Kenya. Not by road! Go through the bush. I will try to send you a message if you need to go, and then just go!' We could not have had a clearer answer to our prayer. (It was only later that I discovered that the 'bad information' had been orders from Amin to all his local army commanders that if any attempt whatever was made on his life then any British people should be dealt with 'accordingly'. There had already been several assassination attempts. Mr Owor and I both knew what that would mean to our local army commander, Major Juma, who had a record of murder.)

I returned to the house, and told Rosemary and the children, and Di. They would go up to our BCMS colleagues at Nasokol, in the hills over the Kenya border. They packed, there was a tearful parting, and they set off, making their departure look as if they were just going out for a drive and a picnic. The soldiers at the barrier did not stop them. I went back to the house, feeling overwhelmingly lonely. It was so quiet. A little later I turned on the BBC World news. 'Kenya has closed its borders to all Britons leaving Uganda. Anyone attempting to enter Kenya will be turned back', the announcer said. I was devastated, and was worried for the rest of the day that the family would return. But a further news bulletin later that evening said that the order had been rescinded – Kenya had mistaken a sudden influx of British families for a mass exodus from Uganda. In fact it was British people taking their children back to boarding schools in Kenya at the start of a new term. Meanwhile Rosemary had reported their arrival to the Police in Kenya. The policeman responsible for immigration had a local newspaper open on his desk with the headline 'KENYA CLOSES ITS BORDERS TO BRITONS'. He carefully folded his paper to cover the headline, but not before Rosemary had seen it. He took their passports, stamped them with a Visitors Permit with no time restriction (usually it was two weeks), and told her that they were welcome. She went on to report their presence to the District Commissioner responsible for Nasokol, Mr Ohare – like our Mr Owor he was a committed Christian, a Pentecostal, and a most kindly man. He said to Rosemary, 'You stay as long as you like. Rest and be at peace! My Special Branch officers will keep a watch that nobody troubles you.' They were able to collapse into the care and hospitality of our Nasokol friends. That night Rosemary found in Stephen's nappy a needle which he must have swallowed, and which had passed right through him, pulled blunt end first by its thread.

All this I did not know until a message from Rosemary came on a passing Landrover the next day, to tell me what had happened and that all was well. Meanwhile I had been agonizing over the question, 'What to do next?' I was consoled that evening when I happened to read the words of the angel to Joseph and Mary when they fled to Egypt with the baby Jesus. The angel said to them, 'Stay there until I bring you word!' (Matthew 2:13). That was good enough for me. Just as we had had very clear guidance about the family and Di going out, so too it would be made very clear when it was safe for them to return. I settled in to my lonely existence in Amudat.

Even before the family's departure I had been under surveillance by two members of Amin's 'Special Force'. It was the dressers who first recognised them. They were several shades lighter than Pokot, and wore sunglasses and fashionable shoes. The dressers called them 'The brown men'. Once it was realised by the army that the family and Di had 'escaped', the Brown Men stepped up their surveillance of me. It was actually quite amusing, because they stood out like sore thumbs as they hung around the hospital, watching my every move. The dressers would sidle up to me and whisper, 'Doctor, the Brown Men are just round that corner', and I would nod and wink knowingly. Mr Owor had told me to be ready to set off on foot for the Kenya border if he sent me a warning, so I carried with me my 'flee bag', containing passport, water and biscuits. I knew that the dressers would do everything they could to assist me. It was about ten miles direct through the bush to the border, and then it would be a rough sixty mile walk along the hills to Nasokol.

My worst moments were at night. I was totally alone in our cluster of houses, one mile from the hospital and shops. If needed at night at the hospital a vehicle would drive up to call me. It would come to a stop with its headlights beamed onto our bedroom door, and a voice would call out 'Daktari! Daktari!' I would emerge into the glare of the lights, like an actor under a spotlight, unable to see a thing. Then a voice would tell me what the problem was, and I would relax. Always there was the possibility that it was an army vehicle come to arrest me – or worse. To keep myself busy during that lonely time, I made a solar heater for the house. I had started work on it previously, but then put it aside. Now I put my mind to it. It was a simple affair – a shallow water tank, painted dull black, mounted at forty-five degrees, and facing the sun. As the water in the tank heated it rose by convection into a lagged drum in the roof, displacing cooler water down into the heater, and so constantly circulating during the day, getting hotter and hotter. By evening we had forty gallons of piping hot water.

I was working on the solar heater one Saturday afternoon. It was very quiet. I felt very isolated and alone. Suddenly one of the dressers burst through the bush. I nearly fell off my ladder. 'Doctor! Doctor! Come quickly! The army has arrested Justus!' It turned out that our hospital dresser Justus Okiru had been arrested at his home thirty miles away, accused of spying for the British. I had given him my father's old ex-army binoculars, so cracked and fogged that it was difficult to see much at all through them. Justus had been thrilled. He took them to his home where a passing army patrol caught him bird-watching. They said that with British army binoculars he was clearly a spy. They trussed him up, kept him in a hot rondavel without food or drink for twenty-four hours, then brought him back to Amudat to the police post. Fortunately by the time I arrived the army had left on another patrol, leaving him in the custody of the police – who were our friends. I explained to the Inspector the story behind the binoculars, and he released Justus immediately.

During the weeks that the family were out at Nasokol I was able to join them from time to time. There were ways and means of by-passing the barrier in Amudat. My intermittent absences must have caused the Brown Men great grief, but always I turned up again. The army sergeant in Amudat came to see me to have his eyes tested. He told me that he had difficulty focussing on distant objects, such as when shooting; and that his eyes could not bear to look at white things. On both counts I was secretly relieved! Tense as life could be in Amudat we were better off than many parts of Uganda. In mid-September there was a small invasion from Tanzania. The army arrested eighty Britons in Kampala in reprisal. Most were soon released. The British High Commissioner in Kampala was expelled, adding to the feeling of insecurity of Britons. But for us the day came when Mr Owor took me aside and said that it was safe for the family to return. Ruth also returned from leave at this time. Life became more normal again.

Chapter 23
UNSETTLED TIMES

On the domestic front life resumed its 'normal' pattern – if anything in Amudat could ever be considered normal. By now Andrew and Paul began each day with 'school'. I taught maths and science, and Rosemary taught the rest. Bearing in mind that Andrew was only five years old and Paul four, the titles 'maths' and 'science' may be rather too grand. We went on nature walks, and studied such things as thorns (which are, of course, modified leaves), and termite hills, and ant lions. The boys' nature table displayed mason wasp nests, larva rock, dead scorpions, shed snake skins and lizard tails. We even branched into applied biology, in the form of poultry keeping. We were given in Nasokol the gift of a cockerel. We brought him home, made a house for him, but discovered at nightfall on the first evening that he had gone missing – no doubt taken as supper by a serval cat or mongoose. It was a relief, therefore, to find him snuggled down and comfortably asleep on an armchair in the sittingroom – the house I had made for him evidently did not meet his expectations. A few nights later we were disturbed by a tremendous squawking from the direction of the cockerel's house. Torchlight showed him to be in the jaws of a mongoose. I chased them in my pyjamas, around the garden and into the bush, where finally the mongoose dropped the cockerel. Apart from the loss of a few feathers and his dignity he was fine, and lived to grace our table at Christmas.

On the wider front life was tense and unpredictable. Asians were leaving Uganda by the planeload. They were humiliated at every step, and robbed by the security forces of any possessions that they tried to take with them. In October three of Uganda's very best medical specialists, all British, were declared *persona non grata* by Amin, and were expelled. They were Prof Sir Ian McAdam (surgeon), Prof Lawrence (paediatrician), and Dr David Barkham (physician). Between them they had given thirty five years to Uganda, and all three had been very supportive to Amudat Hospital. (David Barkham had taught me as a medical student at St Thomas's.) At a stroke Mulago Hospital and the Medical School had been seriously depleted. The cardiothoracic surgeon, Prof Summers, left soon afterwards, before he had a chance to operate on a lad with severe mitral stenosis whom I had referred to him. The lad went into severe heart failure and died. Uganda was losing some of its most valuable people, and one could only despair. On the local front the MRC Team in Amudat sadly but understandably decided that they could not function under prevailing circumstances. It was too risky. Safari work, essential to their research, became difficult due to army activity. The team was pulled out of Uganda. It was a sad loss to the local people and to research. We gained in that they kindly left us their complex of rondavels, which Ruth soon turned into an excellent girls' hostel – far superior to the mud houses they had occupied until then.

At regular intervals Radio Uganda made announcements about missionaries, declaring us to be mercenaries, and on another occasion saying that we were all to be counted. In November the Roman Catholic Fathers in Amudat received a police message, summoning them to District Headquarters in Moroto to be counted and checked. There were at the time over one hundred Catholic missionaries in Karamoja District, and just ten of us Anglicans. We BCMS folk in Amudat did not receive any message, and assumed the count did not apply to us. Two days later a police message came. Because we had 'failed' to report to Moroto we must now proceed immediately to Kampala, and report there to Immigration, and explain ourselves. This meant leaving the hospital without any doctor or nurse. We told the dressers that we would be back as soon as possible. In the event we were treated with great courtesy by an official at Immigration, and we were away for only two nights. We returned to Amudat to find the hospital running smoothly. The dressers had, of their own accord, done a lumbar puncture on a patient suspected of having meningitis. They had stained the spinal fluid, diagnosed the correct type of meningitis, given the appropriate antibiotics, and put up an intravenous drip. They had also done a forceps delivery on a mother. We felt very proud of them. Three days later Amin announced that fifty-eight missionaries were to be expelled immediately from Uganda – they were 'mercenaries in disguise'. These turned out to be all Roman Catholics who had had some deficiency in their paperwork. Amin assured us that all missionaries would in due course of time be expelled.

Lest the level of tension should fall Amin announced in December that, in retaliation for the cancellation of British aid to Uganda, he would be taking 'drastic action' against British people, but would not announce it for another three weeks. That kept us on tenterhooks, although by now we were becoming somewhat immune to threats. One incident did shake me. I was examining a lady in my consulting room. A dresser was with me. Suddenly the door burst open and a man in military uniform swaggered in, demanding to be examined immediately. I saw red. I told him to leave my room immediately, and never again to barge in to a doctor's consulting room when a patient was being examined. I said I would see him when I was ready, and to wait outside. He left without a word. If it is possible for a Pokot man to look pale, then the dresser looked pale. 'Doctor, do you know who that was?' he asked in awed tones. 'No!' I retorted, 'And I don't care!' And then, after a moment's hesitation, 'Anyway, who was he?' 'That' he pronounced 'was Major Juma!' Now, I knew of Major Juma. Everyone knew of Major Juma. But I had not met him before. He was the commanding officer of the army in Karamoja District. And he had a notorious reputation. When in charge of Mbarara Barracks in southern Uganda two American journalists had disappeared – certainly murdered by Major Juma. Soon after coming to Moroto he had arranged for all soldiers of ex-president Obote's tribe, the Lango, and their associated tribes, the Teso and Acholi, to be put in a separate lunch queue. They had been machine gunned, and about one hundred killed. Their bodies were tipped into a nearby valley. Major Juma was ruthless. And I had just thrown him out of my room. It did not auger well if Amin was to order any kind of action against Britons.

From time to time we went out to Kenya, to Nasokol and Kitale, via our back road. We needed breaks to restore us. My absence on these occasions was obviously noted by my 'guardians', the Brown Men. I was astonished when, on two occasions, Radio Uganda announced that Amudat Hospital had been 'abandoned' by its doctor. It was quite upsetting to hear Amudat being specifically mentioned when I had in fact stayed on through thick and thin. The Minister of Health had admitted that the number of doctors in Uganda was down to one third of what it should be. Ten brand new Government Hospitals had been unable to open because of lack of staff. Yet here we were, giving a full service, and yet being described as 'abandoned'. I wrote to the Minister of Health to put him right.

For a long time we had planned and looked forward to a visit to Amudat by Rosemary's sister, June. She had taught for many years at Malvern Girls' College and was due for a sabbatical. Then Uganda's troubles began, and it looked as though a visit was out of the question. Britons were strongly advised by the Foreign Office not to visit Uganda, and Uganda was not issuing Visitors' Permits to Britons. We were very disappointed. I kept in touch with our friendly Assistant District Commissioner, Mr Owor, about it. Towards the end of 1972 he said that he thought a visit would be possible after all. June would have to enter Uganda unofficially, via the 'back door' through Kitale. She must then stay in the Amudat area, and not proceed further into Uganda. He would vouch for her at a local level, but she would not have an official Visitors' Permit. We were delighted and June flew in to Nairobi on 4 January 1973.

We made our journey to Amudat in easy stages, to give June time to adapt. We stayed at Lake Naivasha, in the Rift Valley, where the son of my godfather, Dr Bunny, took us on a wonderful birdwatching trip on the lake. Fish eagles, jacanas, purple gallinules and other abundant bird life thrived along the papyrus-thick shores. Lake Nakuru was our next port of call. Vast pink flocks of greater and lesser flamingo whirred over the water, and filtered for algae in the alkaline shallows. Groups of pelicans did their synchronised dipping and ducking. The sharp stench of the soda water mixed with that of the droppings of millions of birds. Waterbuck and reed buck browsed among the yellow barked fever thorns on the lake shore. On again to Kaptagat in the eight-thousand-foot highlands on the west side of the Rift Valley. Here we feasted on rich farm cream and fresh vegetables. Then it was time to introduce June to the real Africa. It was down on to the hot plains, to Amudat. She went to sleep that first night to the sound of Pokot singing in a nearby *manyatta*, and the grunting of a lion.

June appreciated the many varieties of exotic birds which frequented our garden – red and yellow barbets, black headed orioles, slate-coloured boubou shrikes, paradise fly-catchers, glossy starlings, and the raucous 'Go-away' bird – all so rich in colour. Our resident boomslang snake made an appearance for her in our wild fig tree. She was intrigued at the way hens wandered in and out of the hospital wards, looking for scraps of food. One enterprising patient used to catch a hen each day, and keep it under the blanket on her bed until it had laid its egg, which she then fed to her child. But if June thought that life in Amudat was different she had a shock coming to her when I took her on safari to our dispensary at Katabok. Here she really saw life in the raw. A Pokot man had just speared a warthog, and he cooked it outside the dispensary. She watched in fascination as the head, eyes, feet and all were devoured. June was mesmerised by the skin-clad or naked people, the smell of unwashed bodies, the total lack of any facilities, the dust and dirt, the flies, the heat. On our return journey to Amudat two days later we ran over a cobra, which reared up at the side of the Landrover, its hood outspread in anger. We got back to a crisis in the hospital – two girls who had undergone ritual tribal circumcision had bled heavily and needed urgent transfusion. It was all somewhat far removed from Malvern.

A few days later I had to go to Mbale to get petrol, diesel, tyres and salary money. Because June was in Uganda unofficially, she was not able to come. She looked after Andrew, Paul and Stephen, so that Rosemary could accompany me. We had an uneventful trip, except that Landrover tyres were unavailable in Uganda – the army had commandeered them all. We arrived back that evening to find June distraught. Soon after we had left for Mbale Mr Owor had come to our house to find me. He was horrified to hear that we had gone to Mbale. He told June that a guerrilla camp had been discovered there, and there was fighting in the streets. Seven 'guerrillas' had been caught and were to be publicly shot. Furthermore Amin had announced that Europeans were trying to slip in to Uganda as visitors. Mr Owor told June that in view of these developments she would have to leave Uganda immediately. She spent the day envisaging that she had been left in the middle of nowhere with sole responsibility for three small children. But we had encountered none of these disturbances in Mbale – although we later heard that a

British doctor in Mbale was beaten unconscious at a roadblock that day. Our immediate concern was to get June out of Uganda. Carefully laid plans for a holiday in Kenya the following month would all have to be cancelled, and we would need to make alternative arrangements at very short notice. I asked the ever-helpful Flying Doctor radio staff to do some ringing around for us. Meanwhile we needed to get June into Kenya while awaiting some replies.

Instead of heading south to Kitale we drove north into Kenya's remote Turkana District, to a small fishing resort, Eliye Springs, on the west shore of Lake Turkana. The deep blue-green of the lake, Teleki's 'Jade Sea', in the midst of a burning wilderness of sand and larva rock, was a refreshing site. We pitched our tents next to a clump of doum palms, just a few yards from the shoreline. A constant strong easterly wind blew off the lake, keeping us cool in the scorching heat. We wallowed in the waves at the water's edge of the crocodile infested lake, and tried to unwind. News from Uganda was that, overnight, all old currency had been cancelled. New notes were to be issued. Anyone who had smuggled cash into Kenya had wasted their time. So had I, when collecting salary cash from Mbale. It would all have to be changed. We tried to forget all that by enjoying the magnificent sunrise over the lake, the flocks of brightly coloured lovebirds in the palms around us, and the crashing waves on the black sand shore.

After two days we headed back to Amudat. By now there should be some replies from the Flying Doctors about alternative holiday plans. As we approached Amudat a man stepped in to the road and flagged us down. It was Justus Okiru (of the binoculars). He had been waiting all day for us, to warn us that, because of the currency change, there was now a new roadblock up in Amudat, and he was concerned for June. Fortunately the roadblock was manned by police, not army, and we had no problem. June went on into Kenya with Ruth, while we had a day or two to leave hospital and home in good order. A quick visit to Katabok dispensary revealed that the army had been there, and everyone had fled. At Amudat I patched up an Italian priest who had been badly beaten at a roadblock in Mbale on the day of our visit. We left to meet up with June in Kenya, and to start our hastily rearranged holiday.

Our first port of call was Marsabit, a six-hundred-mile drive from Amudat. Marsabit was cool and green and misty. We met up at the hospital with Ralph and Ceri Settatree, who had come to Marsabit in our place when we returned to Amudat. The really good news was that my brother Dennis and Priscilla and family were to move from Thika High School to Marsabit Secondary School. If the opportunity did come for us to move to Marsabit we would be there with them – both brothers back in the place of our childhood. After three nostalgic days it was time to head south again, to Nairobi and then the coast. We camped that night at a dry riverbed, the Merrille, half way to Isiolo, setting up our safari beds next to the car. During the night a herd of elephant passed silently around us, undeterred by our campfire, but leaving as their calling cards steaming piles of droppings. In the morning a pack of wild dogs and a leopard came to drink at waterholes in the riverbed. Two further days of travelling brought us to the coast, just south of Mombasa island. Here at last we really could unwind, as we and the children revelled in the warm waters of the Indian Ocean, the endless white sandy beaches, and the coral reef, with its wealth of colourful fish and shells.

It did seem though that nothing would be straightforward during June's stay with us. Driving in to town on Mombasa island involved a crossing on the Likoni ferry – a flat, open ferry which carried about forty vehicles and several hundred foot passengers. We were first in the queue of cars waiting to board one day. It was morning rush hour, and hundreds of pedestrians were crowding down the ramp. As we drove on to the ferry I discovered that petrol was pouring from underneath our car – a fractured fuel pipe. Already a large pool was spreading over the ferry floor. And passengers in all directions were smoking. By now the ferry had left the shore, and we were heading into the deep, shark-infested waters of Likoni creek. I tried to stem the flow of petrol with my thumb while Rosemary and June pushed their way through the crowds on the ferry, asking them not to smoke. There was little time to explain why. Some no doubt took them for two bossy, colonialist memsahibs. Others, who smelt the petrol, understood. It was the longest ferry crossing of our lives. I had visions of the ferry exploding into flame, and of those who escaped the inferno being eaten by sharks. We drove off the ferry with great relief, and headed for a garage – where the rapidly spreading pool of petrol on the garage forecourt ensured us very prompt attention.

During our stay at the coast Rosemary developed a high temperature. We had taken our anti-malarials without fail. I took her to see a doctor in Mombasa, and she was admitted to hospital. Blood slides were positive for malaria. The doctor insisted that she could not have taken her Daraprim regularly. We knew that she had, and it turned out that she was the first known case of Daraprim-resistant malaria to be reported in East Africa. It soon became a common phenomenon, and Daraprim was abandoned as a preventative. We were finally able to return to Nairobi, and June, reeling no doubt from her many experiences, returned to the quieter climes of Malvern. One final gesture on my part was secretly to pack in June's case an appropriate memento of her visit – an elephant dropping. Her beans grew particularly well that year.

It had not been possible to let our colleagues in Amudat know that our return had been delayed by Rosemary's illness. My Special Branch 'minder' had yet again reported that I had 'fled'. We drove in to Amudat, past the open-sided church, just as the Sunday morning service was ending. Our arrival was announced to the congregation, and we had a great reception. The following morning I saw my 'minder' peering up the hospital verandah with a look of disbelief on his face. The disappearing doctor had turned up yet again.

Overseas leave was soon due and once again the question arose as to whether we might move to Marsabit. Unless we could find a doctor to replace me in Amudat I could not and would not move. But to get another doctor for Amudat was not easy. The Uganda government was not issuing new work permits, and who would want to come to Uganda anyway? The policy of BCMS was, rightly, not to send a family until and unless the situation improved. Once again our prayers were answered. Dr John Wattis, and his wife Libby, a nurse, offered to come to Amudat for two years, knowing full well the situation in Uganda. They had no family, and were prepared to face the risks and tensions. Furthermore the Immigration Department agreed to issue work permits. After six years in Amudat the way was opening up for us to move.

On our last Sunday in Amudat I preached on Ephesians 6:10–14:

'Finally be strong in the Lord, and in His mighty power . . . Therefore stand . . . stand . . . stand . . .' We could choose to leave Amudat. Our many African friends could not. They had to stay on amidst all the tensions and frustrations. Christians were under real threat from the new Muslim-dominated regime, and who knew what the future might hold? They would need to be strong in their faith, and, in the midst of all the pressures and difficulties, to stand firm. A farewell party was held for us. The Reverend Timothy, in his speech, said how I used to go out with them to cut poles for the new church 'without a shirt on'. This was translated 'naked' – which, for anyone who did not know me, must have conjured up a strange image of the departing doctor. I was glad to see that my 'minder', one of the Brown Men, had invited himself to the party. He would now be able to report with confidence that I had indeed finally 'fled'.

We had come to Amudat six years previously with reluctance. We now left with reluctance. We had experienced loneliness, illness, exhaustion and stress, and yet they had been profoundly happy, fulfilling years. We had enjoyed family life, without the distractions of television, computers and ready-made amusements. Above all we had learned to trust God more. We had had the huge privilege of working among very needy people, and of making a real difference to their lives – often the difference between life itself and death. We had seen the hospital more than double in size, with new and better facilities. We had seen a new church building go up, and had added our sweat to the labour. More important we had seen the living Church, Christ's body in Amudat, grow. We had seen lives changed – people set free from fear and evil to live new lives in Christ. We had seen people grow in their faith, and progress in their walk with God. Yes, of course, there had been many set-backs, disappointments, discouragements. In many ways it was, then, a time of seed-sowing. The harvest is being seen now, over thirty years later.

Lake Turkana

Ileret

Alia
Bay

Dukana

ETHIOPIA

Sololo

North Horr

Moyale

Huri Hills

Dida Galgalu

Chalbi Desert

Loiyengalani

South
Island

Mount
Kulal

Kargi

MARSABIT

MARSABIT (NORTHERN FRONTIER) DISTRICT

Koroli Desert

KENYA

Nyiru Range

Kaisut Desert

Ndoto
Mountains

Laisamis

River Merille

Maralal

Wamba

0   50   100

Isiolo

Chapter 24
RETURN TO MARSABIT

Our home leave in England in the summer of 1973 was, in several ways, unsettling. We had left Amudat with the full intention of returning to Marsabit, in northern Kenya. But those intentions were challenged. I did a three month locum in General Practice in Nuneaton. It was my first real experience of General Practice, having done only a few locum surgeries in Ashtead before we first went to East Africa. Now I was doing General Practice proper, including on-call. I enjoyed looking after, and getting to know, whole families. I valued the privilege of the supportive role that a GP has at critical times in people's lives – in pregnancy, at birth, at times of illness or stress, at death. I saw the role of a GP as being more than just a medical adviser to patients, but also a friend. In all this I had an ideal mentor and role-model in Dr Tony Barney-Adshead, the senior partner in the practice, with whom I stayed for part of the locum. It was very tempting to settle down in General Practice in England, and to enjoy a more normal sort of existence.

Another tempting factor was the buying of a house in Ashtead – the very first house of our own. At the time house prices were beginning to soar, and we felt it wise, whatever the future held, to have a base. We enjoyed turning our 'semi' into our home. Andrew and Paul went to school – where Andrew's somewhat wild behaviour was noted. When he dived under a crate of milk, as it was being carried up the stairs by two sedate little girls, his exasperated teacher asked, 'Why can't he behave like other children?' Our boys missed the freedom of the bush, and we were concerned lest their unusual life-style in East Africa would make it increasingly difficult for them eventually to settle in England. Nor did we relish the prospect, if we returned to Kenya, of them having to go away to boarding school.

A further factor that caused us to question our return to Africa was that Britain's Overseas Development Administration seemed reluctant to sponsor me. If I returned to Marsabit it would be as the Medical Officer of Health for Marsabit District. This would be a Government post, and I would be seconded by our mission, BCMS, to the Kenya Government. I would be paid a local Government salary. We could live off that, but it would not cover such things as boarding school fees for the children, and flights to and from Britain. For this we needed sponsorship by the ODA, and sponsorship did not seem forthcoming. It was very tempting to stay in Britain. I had been surprised at how much I had earned as a GP locum, and we had enjoyed a financial security that we had never had before. We felt torn, and confused. We prayed, as we had done on previous occasions, for clear guidance as to what God wanted, rather than what we wanted. The answer came at the Keswick Convention in the Lake District. One of the speakers, the Reverend Keith Weston, said something which stuck in our minds: 'Affluence and ease (or the desire for them) are perhaps the greatest stumbling block to the excitement of serving God in the place of His choice for us!' It was clearly a word from God for us – it was not yet time to settle down to a secure life in England. God still had things for us to do in Kenya. At about the same time we heard that I had been accepted by ODA, and the Kenya Ministry of Health had granted me a work permit. The way ahead could not have been made much clearer.

On 18 August 1973 my sister Marilyn married a solicitor, John Denman. When Dennis and I were both abroad we had been concerned for Marilyn. She had had a rough time since her teens, with our parents' illnesses and deaths. Dennis and Priscilla came from Kenya for the wedding, which was at St Giles Church, Ashtead, where Rosemary and I had married. Dennis took the wedding service, and I had the privilege of giving Marilyn away.

News from Amudat was mixed. Keith Knox, who had done his elective with us, and was now newly qualified, was helping out at Amudat until such time as Dr John and Libby Wattis could replace us. But Ruth Stranex was having a hard time from the army. The NCO in charge, Sergeant Nyoka (meaning, appropriately, 'Snake') was harassing her, and also the rest of the hospital staff, at every opportunity. We had a few desperate letters from Ruth, urging that the Wattises go out as soon as possible, which they did. After I had finished my GP locum there was a very busy round of deputation, speaking at our link churches around the country, and at any and every other opportunity to which I was invited. Our return to East Africa in December 1973, and the temptation to stay in England, were made much easier to bear by the situation in Britain – miners' strike; ambulance, rail, gas and electricity strikes; three-day working week; blackouts. It was all doom and gloom. The Heath Government was teetering, and the weather was very cold and utterly dismal. Even Amin's Uganda had its attractions. But we were heading for Kenyatta's Kenya, and a whole new challenge.

Dr Ralph Settatree had been the MOH Marsabit for the previous two years. A hand-over from him would have been helpful, but his departure and my arrival dates did not allow for any overlap in Marsabit. Instead we met briefly in Nairobi over lunch. When arranging a rendezvous I suggested to Ralph the café on the roof of the supermarket (Rosemary's and my usual meeting place in Nairobi). There was a silence on the phone, then Ralph said, 'I think the Hilton Hotel would be preferable!' Perhaps this venue symbolised our move from missionary to government service. So the Hilton it was, and Ralph gave me a quick resume of my many duties as MOH, and of the various staff members – whom to trust, and whom not to trust. No longer would I be working with a handful of carefully selected Christian dressers, as in Amudat. I would now be in charge of eighty-five government-appointed staff, some local, some from downcountry; some Muslim, some Christian, most nothing; some friendly, some resentful at having a white boss; some excellent at their work, some not, or with drink problems. The remoter hospitals, such as Marsabit, were sometimes a dumping ground, a disciplinary posting, for staff who had misbehaved themselves elsewhere. It was going to be a challenge. I would be the Medical Officer in charge of a district twenty-five thousand square miles in area, stretching from Lake Turkana in the west to the deserts east of mount Marsabit; and from Ethiopia in the north to the Merrille riverbed seventy miles south of Marsabit. It is a vast area of rugged mountains, thornbush savannah, wastes of burning larva rock, and pure desert. It was then populated by about seventy-five thousand people, mostly nomadic, and representing a number of tribes – the Boran, Gabbra, Rendille, Samburu, Turkana, El Molo, Shangilla, Somali and Burji. The distances and wild terrain would be a challenge.

So would language. There would be one other government doctor in my district – Robby Gurney, also seconded by BCMS, who was the doctor at Moyale Hospital, on the border with Ethiopia. A Roman Catholic mission hospital at Sololo, near Moyale, had an Italian doctor. There were scattered dispensaries, mostly mission-run. Overall responsibility for all medical services in Marsabit District would, as MOH, be mine. Transport around this vast and inhospitable area would be provided for two to three days each month by the Flying Doctor Service. Ralph wished me well. I could not help feeling that he was quite glad to be leaving.

We set off for Marsabit in our Peugeot 404 estate on 15 December. The first one hundred and twenty miles was on a relatively good, though pot-holed, tarmac road. It was, for me, familiar country from my childhood. Green hillsides were dotted with thatched mud houses, the homes of Kikuyu people. Foaming, red-brown rivers, their water stained with eroded topsoil, wound through the cultivated valleys. Maize, cassava, beans, bananas, sugar cane and coffee grew in profusion in the fertile soil. We passed women, their backs laden with enormous bundles of firewood, or carrying heavy water containers balanced on their heads. We passed roadside markets, selling everything from chickens to goats to baskets to sticks of sugar cane. Runny nosed children waved cheerily at the car. Every now and then the windy road ran alongside the single-track railway to Nanyuki, the very track which first took Dennis and me to boarding school as children. As we neared the lower slopes of the seventeen-thousand-foot Mount Kenya the green hills gave way to extensive grassy plains with their black cotton soil, the beginnings of what had been European farmlands – growing wheat, and raising pedigree cattle. Even by 1973 the process had begun of Africanising many of these highly productive farms. Soon after Nanyuki, at the small centre of Timau (near the farm where our family had holidayed in 1952), we called in at our friends, Richard and Joan Carles. Richard's parents had farmed there for many years, raising cattle and sheep, and growing wheat. Richard had inherited the farm. Their lovely sprawling house looked up onto the jagged, glaciated peaks of Mount Kenya – a mountain much loved by Richard, but which, in three years time, was tragically to take his life.

Feeling suitably refreshed we continued our journey, heading down from the cool slopes of Mount Kenya to the hot plains of the Northern Frontier. Isiolo is the wild west town which marks the entry to Kenya's remote north. A permit has always been required to pass this point. At many times in history it has been obligatory to travel in convoy beyond Isiolo, because of the risk of *shifta*. By 1973 travel in convoy was not required, and we passed the barrier just as the cool of the evening was dispersing the shimmering heat haze of the day. I hoped thereby to avoid any blow-outs of overheated tyres. We headed north on what was now a corrugated, teeth-rattling, nerve-jangling earth road. One thing soon became clear – the Peugeot 404 was not designed for such roads. If I drove too slowly the corrugations shook every nut and bolt in the car. If I drove fast enough to ride the corrugations the car would begin to slew alarmingly, and at times it was difficult to hold the road. Even for the children the excitement of the Great Adventure began to wear off. Hopes of avoiding punctures were not realised, and we had three. We carried two spare tyres, so the last puncture had to be repaired at the roadside. On we pressed, past familiar craggy mountains, and over one rattling wooden bridge after another. These were an improvement on years gone by, when, as often as not, we had to drive through soft sandy riverbeds. As always on that road to Marsabit, wild life was abundant – giraffe, zebra, gazelles of various kinds, jackal, warthogs, elephant. An animal that we used to see on childhood journeys, but alas no longer, was the rhinoceros. By dark we had reached the village of Laisamis, on the edge of the Kaisut Desert. This was just a waterhole in our childhood, but was now the site of a small Catholic Mission hospital – one that I would become familiar with in the years ahead.

We crossed the barren Kaisut in the cool of night, and reached the foot of Marsabit mountain. As we began to climb we had yet another puncture, and again one that I had to repair at the roadside in the headlights of the car. As I was in the process of doing that a man in a loin cloth with a spear suddenly emerged out of the darkness. He wanted a lift to Marsabit, but not just for himself. It was for his goat as well. We might just have squeezed him in, but not the goat. He couldn't see the problem, and was quite persistent. The headlights of another vehicle appeared on the horizon – the first other vehicle we had seen since leaving Isiolo one hundred and seventy miles back. It was a Kenya Police Landrover. They insisted on stopping to help with the tyre, and would not leave until they were sure we were all right. As I shook the hand of the policeman in charge he said, in that open, unembarrassed way so typical of African Christians, 'I want to tell you that the Lord Jesus Christ has saved me. I was a sinner, but He has forgiven me.' We were able to share that greeting so widely used in East Africa: 'Bwana asifiwe!' (Praise the Lord!).

So we arrived in the dusty little town of Marsabit, nestling at the edge of the forest on Marsabit mountain – the place of my brother Dennis's and my childhood, and also that of Dennis's wife, Priscilla. (Priscilla's father had been the Police Inspector in Marsabit during part of our childhood). Now Dennis and Priscilla, and their children, Tim, Peter and John, were back living in Marsabit. They welcomed us to their home at the Secondary School, where Dennis was teaching, and then accompanied us to our new home at the hospital. We were, once again and after two attempts, back in Marsabit.

The road to Marsabit with Ol Lolokwe

Zebra crossing

A Marsabit elephant

Marsabit town centre

Camels at waterhole, Marsabit

The track in Marsabit forest

Lake Paradise

Marsabit district hospital

In theatre with Mohammed

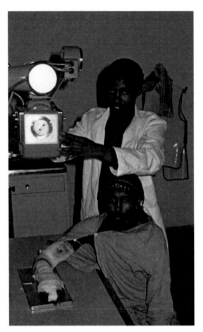

X-raying a man with a lion bite

Visiting Naomi and Jarso

Our house at Marsabit

Anne Spoerry, doctor and pilot

The Chalbe Desert from the air

Flying Doctors' plane at Ileret

Loiyengalani oasis

Preparing to leave Loiyengalani

Top: plane at North Horr airstrip.
Middle: polluted water hole, Maikona.
Bottom: health inspector at the hole in
Maikona which is now protected.

Drought: the ground is scattered with skeletons

A child with marasmus

Starving child begging for food

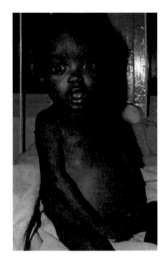

A recovering child

The congregation of St Peter's Church

Landcruiser on the lower slopes of Marsabit

The Reverend Stephen Houghton and his team collecting salt at the Chalbe desert.

Camping at Kalacha on trip to Lake Turkana

The Landcruiser with Lake Turkana behind and South Island in the distance

Mount Kulal

Mount Kenya from the Carles' farm

Miracle Rocks at Merille

Rosemary and Naomi on a return visit to Marsabit in 1991

Me with Elisha, then a cabinet minister, 1991.

Chapter 25
MEDICAL OFFICER OF HEALTH

Our very first night in our new home was somewhat disturbed by the sound of elephants in the garden, eating the new euphorbia hedge that had been planted along the forest edge. The house and its situation could not have been more different from our home in Amudat. We had a fairly new three-bedroom bungalow, situated on the edge of the hospital compound. Adjacent to it were similar bungalows, the homes of the Hospital Administrator, the Health Visitor and the Nurse in Charge. Our home looked out over the hospital compound, and beyond it the prison and lines of whitewashed police houses, and then the *shambas* of Sagante, a cultivated area on the slopes of the mountain, and finally, in the far distance, the blue haze of the Dida Galgalu – that vast plain of burning hot lava wastes, stretching away toward Ethiopia in the north. To one side our garden bordered the forest which clothes the peaks of Marsabit mountain. Wild olive trees, festooned with green-grey lichen, made a refreshingly green and cool outlook. The melodious calls of birds echoed through the forest canopy, perhaps the most beautiful sound of all being the clear, bell-like notes of the shy tropical boubou shrike – three notes ringing out in a descending cadence. Packs of marauding baboons patrolled the forest edge, looking for opportunities to raid the vegetable and maize *shambas* of hospital staff – including ours. The shrieks and squeals and barks of squabbling baboons could frequently be heard from the depths of the adjacent forest. An elephant ditch had been dug along this border, supposedly to prevent elephants crossing into the gardens of the townspeople. It had not taken long for elephants to find or make ways across. So, pleasant as the forest was, it was also the source of constant forays into our garden – of baboons by day and elephants by night.

Gracing the centre of our garden was a huge wild fig or *dhambi* tree, similar to the one that had shaded our house in Amudat. A mauve bougainvillea sprawled rampantly at the side of the house. We were soon reminded that the rich red volcanic soil of Marsabit goes from one extreme to the other – it either billows as a fine dust, covering everything in and out of the house; or it is a glutinous mud, that collects in thick clods on the feet, and stops all but four-wheel drive traffic. It did not take us long to plant grass in the vicinity of the house, and to keep cars at a distance.

It was a change from Amudat to be living right next to the hospital. This, in theory, was bigger, and more sophisticated than Amudat Hospital – after all, it was the Government District Hospital, the centre of medical care for an area of twenty-five thousand square miles and seventy-five thousand people. But closer inspection showed that it left much to be desired. There was a very old, stone-built Outpatient Department – which, in my childhood, had been the full extent of the hospital. This was cramped, and the walls and floors stained with the red soil of Marsabit. There were two relatively modern wards, male and female, each with twenty beds, and an old maternity ward. There was a quite separate stone building which served as the operating theatre. Patients had to be carried by stretcher, come rain or sunshine, along an outdoor pathway to get to or from the theatre. It was a not uncommon sight to see a huddle of staff around a stretcher, two carrying, one holding the drip set, one the drainage tubes and bag – and possibly yet another an umbrella to keep the patient dry. There was an x-ray block, and an x-ray machine about to be installed; and a generator house. Behind the wards was a horrendous small and smelly mortuary, with torn fly mesh over the windows – clearly a favourite port of call and trysting ground for every bluebottle fly in northern Kenya. There was a small office block, and then the houses of the hospital staff. All this comprised phase one of the new Marsabit District Hospital. Phase two did not materialise in my time.

My first priority was to meet, and get to know, and hopefully win the friendship and support of, the hospital staff. It was not going to be easy. For a start there were eighty-five of them, as opposed to six in Amudat. And, as mentioned before, they came from all sorts of backgrounds. Of the three qualified Medical Assistants (trained to diagnose and treat illness) one was a childhood friend of mine, Mattayo Yonah. Mattayo had been working as a medical assistant at Marsabit for many years, and, being local, spoke the local language, Boran. This gave him a head start over the downcountry medical assistants. The hospital secretary, Mr Ndururi, a Kikuyu man, was pleasant and trustworthy – essential for the person holding the purse strings of the hospital. In my early months there was a rapid turnover of nurses-in-charge. One or two excellent ones were soon posted elsewhere – anyone who proved to be very good was snatched up by bigger and more important hospitals, or transferred to Ministry of Health Headquarters. The person I could see that I would have most problems from was one of the health visitors, Mr N. He was arrogant, defiant, and clearly resented very much having a white doctor in charge of him. He was using the hospital Landrover as his private vehicle, and at times driving it when drunk. He and I entered a period of prolonged battle, which involved verbal and written warnings and finally the involvement of my boss, the provincial medical officer. I had to become accustomed to official procedures and red tape, which at times were extremely frustrating. A similar situation arose with the hospital pharmacist, who, it turned out, was regularly stealing ethyl alcohol from the pharmacy and drinking it. (He was finally posted elsewhere, where he tragically drank himself to death). Sometimes I longed for our in-house trained, enthusiastic, faith-motivated Amudat dressers. My new staff, being all officially trained and qualified in their various disciplines, in some instances had a professional arrogance which was not justified by their performance.

Those early days were not easy. I had no consulting room and therefore converted a small storeroom to provide somewhere to roost – a desk and examination couch and a few bookshelves. Ralph Settatree had done an excellent job at Marsabit, but the rapid turnover of staff meant that no sooner were staff trained up than they were replaced. There seemed no protocol for dealing with emergencies. In the middle of the night a lady needed a caesarian section for an obstructed twin labour, but the night staff had no idea where the instruments were, or how to prepare the theatre. On another occasion I was called to hospital at 1 a.m. by a patient's relative. He said that there were no staff on the ward, and he was having to look after all the patients. I went to investigate and could find no nurses. A patient got out of bed to let me in to the locked Maternity Ward – and there were the three night nurses, all fast asleep on spare beds. From time to time there were stories of patients having to pay staff to get a bedpan. These were the horror stories that one heard about Government hospitals, and I was determined that Marsabit Hospital was going to be different. But to change the attitudes of staff without changing their hearts was difficult. They needed the compassion and servant-heart of Christ. And I had little say in staff selection – the first I would know about a new member of staff was a 'posting order'. A new Medical Assistant turned up one day, having been posted to Marsabit. I really did not like the look of him – he seemed very shifty and evasive. The next day he had disappeared – he caught the first lorry back downcountry – and we never saw him again. Presumably he liked me (and Marsabit) no more than I liked him. Such were the vagaries of staff appointments.

One of my first administrative tasks was to do the hospital returns for that year, 1973, for the Ministry of Health. I discovered that no outpatient records at all had been kept since Ralph Settatree left, and the records for the half-year before that had been torn out and used to wrap patients tablets. I looked back to the previous year's returns, 1972, and found that the Medical Assistants had reported themselves as having seen three hundred and sixty thousand outpatients. According to their statistics three hundred and sixty patients had been treated every day, including Sundays, for malaria alone, and eighty-five per day for tapeworm. The figures were clearly the figment of someone's fevered imagination, and presumably were not the returns that had been officially submitted. We began to keep accurate figures of attendances and diagnoses, and to do some auditing.

There were two jobs that I hated most. One was that of post-mortems. At least in Amudat I had had the option of refusal – I could say that I was not a Government doctor, and was not obliged (although I usually did agree). Now it was my duty, as MOH, to establish a cause of death in all cases of violent death, or unknown or suspicious cause of death. With frequent raiding by armed *shifta,* especially in the wild border regions with Ethiopia, there was never a dearth of bodies to examine. They were often several days old, and had lain in the heat until brought to Marsabit by police patrols. They had often been mutilated by their attackers – raiders from Ethiopia cut off genitals to take back as trophies. Some of the bodies had been speared to death, some shot. They would often be in an advanced state of decomposition. I would do the least cutting and probing necessary to establish a cause of death, and all the while, in the awful little mortuary, clouds of buzzing, bloated bluebottles would circle my head, and land on my face, and try to crawl into my mouth and ears. Often maggots in profusion fell out of the corpse. On one particular occasion the police informed me that they had brought in four bodies, and would I do post-mortems and reports. The stench on that occasion was particularly nauseating, as the bodies had come from a very remote part of the district, and were already several days old. I gritted my teeth and sealed my lips to keep the flies out of my mouth, and did what had to be done – though I found only three, not four, bodies. A week later the police asked for the report on the fourth body. 'There was no fourth body', I said. 'Did you look in the sack under the bench?' they asked. Back I went, and there, in a sack, was a human head. It was that of one of the raiders, whom the police had shot. They had brought back the head as evidence that they had killed him. But how do you establish a cause of death on just a head? My report on that one was brief – what one might call a 'truncated' report.

The other job I hated, but which I was obliged to do, was to witness corporal punishment in the nearby prison. Lashings with the cane were a frequent punishment, meted out particularly to young offenders. My job was to examine the prisoners before the beating, and to pronounce if they were fit enough for it. If they were they would be strapped to a frame in a spread-eagled position, a wet cloth placed over their buttocks (to prevent cutting of the skin), and the due number of strokes (usually twenty or thirty) applied with a cane by a burly prison officer. My role was to witness and count the strokes, and finally to examine the prisoner again. If I said that they were not fit for the beating it would either be deferred, or they would be given a prison sentence instead. This they usually did not want, and so, on the whole, wished to be pronounced fit. At least the punishment was soon over, and was probably in many cases quite an effective deterrent. And at least it was done under medical supervision, and not secretively. It made me realise, however, how very much more awful it must have been for my father, when he was Kenya's senior prison chaplain, to be with condemned prisoners before their execution, and then to have to witness their hanging. My prison role extended to a monthly inspection of the prison, to ensure that conditions and treatment were humane. Many prisoners were quite content with their free board and lodging, especially during times of famine. The old colonial name for prison, 'Hoteli ya King George', still applied.

The District Commissioner at Marsabit during most of our time there was a delightful man, Mr Samuel Oburru. He had an equally charming wife, Mary. Like our Assistant D.C. in Amudat (Mr Owor) Mr Oburru and his wife were committed Christians. He was a man of real integrity. Mr Oburru came to see me at the hospital one day with severe toothache. Already Mattayo had made three attempts to extract a rotten molar under local anaesthetic. Mr Oburru could stand the pain no longer, nor any more injections. He begged for a general anaesthetic. I was not happy. A general anaesthetic, with no anaesthetist, carried a real risk. I urged him to go down to Nairobi and see a dentist, but he insisted that he had no time for that, and wanted me to do it. At that time a new anaesthetic on the market was Ketamine. It was much safer for short operations than other general anaesthetics because the swallowing reflex was not lost. I decided to do Mr Oburru's extraction under Ketamine anaesthesia. The extraction was difficult enough, but what I did not know about was the odd, twilight-world effect that Ketamine can have. Mr Oburru took about forty-five minutes to wake up, and during that time he kept up a running conversation, revealing the thoughts on his mind. He began the monologue by saying, 'Let us pray! It will help!' He then proceeded to pray a long prayer for me, followed by the revelation of what was written about me in my confidential personnel file. He said how I had dedicated myself to help the Borana of Marsabit, and how my 'Daddy' had helped the Borana very much for many years. He then preached a long and lucid sermon about coming to God through Christ – to the bemusement of Mohammed, the Muslim theatre assistant. He finally woke up.

It was not the only time that Mohammed had a Ketamine-induced rendition of the Christian faith. I removed some nasal polyps from a policeman. As he came round he repeatedly pronounced, slowly and deliberately, 'Dokita! Eeet ees painfool!' He then suddenly, to

Mohammed's surprise, burst into a rendering of the hymn, 'My faith looks up to Thee, O Lamb of Calvary'. We had the whole hymn, in English, at full volume, and as he was borne away on his stretcher to the ward the strains of the hymn drifted back.

Chapter 26
SCHOOL AND HOME

Andrew, now just seven years old, had only a few weeks to settle in to his new home before going off to boarding school at St Andrew's, Turi, four hundred miles away in the Kenya Highlands. We promised to do some special things with him during his last week of holiday. He was keen to have some modelling clay, and I recalled a place in the forest, behind the old mission site, where clay could be dug. We drove up the rough, and now little used, track to Karantina, where my childhood home had been. Leaving the car at the site of the former mission we walked into the forest to search for the clay. We followed an animal trail through the undergrowth – the footpath of childhood days had long since become overgrown. Suddenly, just ahead of us, there was a crashing of branches, and an enormous black buffalo emerged from the undergrowth. He lowered his head, with its spread of massive horns, and gave us a mean stare. Buffalo are probably the most unpredictable and aggressive of the large wild animals, and we made an instant decision to retreat. As we did so Rosemary (never one to miss an opportunity) rapidly filled the bag that had been intended for clay with elephant droppings from the forest floor. They made excellent fertiliser for our budding vegetable patch. On arriving back at the old mission site we wandered over to the remains of my old home when we heard, just a few yards away, branches cracking. Two elephants were feeding off a tree. Once again we retreated, this time taking some roots of my mother's old yucca plants. The Karantina site had been thoroughly reclaimed by the wild.

On a later occasion I was walking there with a visiting medical student when we rounded a clump of bushes and came face to face with an enormous elephant. 'Don't run!' I commanded. 'Keep still!' In theory, running away could provoke a charge. At that moment the elephant appeared to make a lunge towards us – and I fled. The student, Steve, obediently stood his ground. Later I commended him. ' Always do as I say, never as I do!'

The day of departure for school inevitably arrived. How my heart ached for little Andrew. It brought back strong and painful memories of the many times Dennis and I had had to set off tearfully from Marsabit for our boarding school in Nairobi. At least Andrew was going with his cousin Tim. And he was going to a very happy school, with a caring, Christian ethos (unlike Nairobi Primary School, which Dennis and I went to at that age). Dr Robby and Priscilla Gurney's eldest was also going to St Andrew's, and they had driven down from Moyale to take the school trip. The party set off at 4 a.m., leaving Dennis and me behind to get on with our work. Being their first time to boarding school, the departing children left in a state of high excitement. It was all a great adventure. I was reminded of the lines from Gray's 'Ode on a Distant Prospect of Eton College':

> Alas, regardless of their doom,
> The little victims play!
> No sense have they of ills to come,
> Nor care beyond today.

The saddest person was Paul, who was going to miss his big brother a lot. Three days later the party arrived back, less the three boarders. It had been, predictably, a traumatic time. For Rosemary the separation was very hard – it was one of the costliest things that a missionary mother may be called to do. It did not help when Andrew's first letter arrived from school. He said that he had 'cried all yesterday, and a little in the night, and again today.'

Before he left for school I had promised Andrew that I would make a tree house in the wild fig tree in the garden. I rather forgot the promise after his departure, but he did not. A letter from school said that he hoped I was getting on well with the house (not even on the drawing board at that stage). He said he would like it to have 'a ladder which winds up, doors, windows and window sills, chairs and a table. Mummy can help with the curtains if she has time'! In fact it turned out to be quite a splendid tree house, and it did have a window, made from a cracked car windscreen. In the holidays Andrew and Paul sometimes slept in it.

There was one drawback – the tree was a favourite spot with elephants, who rubbed against it at night, so we could not let the children sleep there alone. I had to join them. This had a further disadvantage. On one occasion I was sleeping in the tree with the boys when, in the middle of the night, a nurse came from the hospital to call me to see a patient. He knocked on the door, Rosemary answered, and she told him that the doctor was sleeping in the tree, but she would call me. The nurse was puzzled by my odd habits, and it gave rise to strange rumours.

Something we missed in Marsabit were the evening walks to the Kanyangerang. Of course we could go for walks, but if we ventured into the township we would pick up a retinue of excited and persistent children and other hangers-on, which did not make for a peaceful walk. To walk into the forest was not advisable because of wild animals. Our favourite pastime, when the opportunity presented itself, was to drive into the forest to one or other of Marsabit's two crater lakes. The smaller one, Suqurti Diqo ('Little Sugar' – which, strictly speaking, was for most of the time a bog rather than a lake) was about two miles into the forest behind our house, along a rough earth track. At any moment one might meet elephant or buffalo on the road, or possible a graceful greater kudu, or a shy bushbuck.

As already mentioned, Marsabit is famed for its elephants, which are particularly large, with record-breaking tusks. During my childhood Marsabit's most famous elephant was Mohammed, who, having had one tusk broken off in early life, remained with just one enormous tusk. It was so large that, in rough terrain, he had to walk in reverse, otherwise the tusk dug in to the ground. By 1973 Mohammed had long since died, and the reigning elephant king was the massive Ahmed, who had two huge tusks. A special Presidential decree had been declared to protect him from poachers, and armed game rangers kept a watch over him. My godfather's daughter, Diana Bunny, an artist, was commissioned to paint Ahmed's portrait. Perhaps because of the frequent attention he had from human beings, and the absence of attacks by poachers, he was a gentle, non-aggressive beast. It was our privilege to see him in the forest on a number of occasions. It was towards the end of our time in Marsabit that I returned from a medical safari to find the hospital deserted by all staff and mobile patients. There was an eerie silence reminiscent of the Marie Celeste. Ahmed had died in the forest. He was found leaning against a tree, as though asleep. The whole of Marsabit township had gone into the forest to witness the spectacle. He was taken to Nairobi, where his preserved body can now be seen, in all its immensity, at Nairobi Museum.

Herds of elephant or buffalo were often to be seen grazing in the grassy crater of Sukurti Diqo. It was a beautiful picnic spot. But this was spoiled for us during our time in Marsabit by the building of a tourist Safari Lodge on the edge of the crater. So we preferred to drive on further into the forest to the even remoter and more beautiful crater lake, Lake Paradise, known locally as Suqurti Guddo ('Big Sugar'). To reach it required a four-wheel drive vehicle. The forest track passed a spring, deep in a forest valley, at Barquli ('The Basin'). This was the source of Marsabit's precious water supply. Festooned with ferns and mosses, and swarming with colourful butterflies, the spring was a beautifully cool and refreshing spot. In the season the forest floor would be ablaze with the red pompoms of 'Fireball' lilies. The track wound on through the forest, sometimes deviating to by-pass trees that had been felled by elephants. Suddenly it emerged onto the edge of a steep crater, and a most breath-taking view. Far below, in the hollow of the crater, was a circular azure lake, about half a mile in diameter, its shores rimmed with lichen-draped forest. There would commonly be herds of elephant or buffalo, or greater kudu with their graceful spiralling horns, or maybe a giraffe or two, drinking at the water's muddy edge. Flocks of coots broke the sparkling surface of the water, and the haunting cry of a fish eagle would echo round the crater. No wonder the explorers and journalists, Martin and Osa Johnson, named the crater lake 'Paradise' when they lived there for those three years in the 1920s.

Lift ones eyes from this sapphire lake and the distant view was spectacular. The broccoli-like forest canopy gave way to the thorn-clad lower slopes of the mountain, dotted with volcanic hillocks. Below that, at the southern foot of the mountain, lay the barren brown Kaisut Desert, which we had crossed on our journey to Marsabit. Beyond that, in the blue haze, the rugged mountain ranges of the Northern Frontier – Ol Lolokwe, Warages, Lodomot, and the cedar-forested Ndoto Mountains and the Matthews Range. On a very clear day the snow-clad peaks of Mount Kenya, two hundred miles to the south, could just be discerned.

A rough track wound round the edge of the crater and down to the lake shore. We passed the remains of the 1920s home of Martin and Osa Johnson. During the time that they lived here the lake was full, as it was during our time in Marsabit in the 1970s. But in my childhood, in the 1950s, the lake had dried up – the crater floor was covered in grass. In those days, on school and Sunday School outings from the mission, we used to play football on what was the lake bed. I remember my father having to fire his shotgun over the heads of browsing elephants in order to clear the pitch so that play could begin. On one occasion the game was interrupted by a rhino and her calf, who suddenly trotted out of the forest into the crater. The footballers scattered with record speed, and the rhinos charged back into the forest. Now, once again, and for reasons that seemed unrelated to annual rainfall, the lake had filled again. We had many a happy picnic under the trees on the lake shore, relaxing and unwinding away from the pressures of hospital and home.

We needed an occasional 'bolt-hole' like that. Life in Marsabit was no less busy than it had been in Amudat, especially with the coming and going of many visitors. Sometimes we felt overwhelmed. Not all had to be accommodated, but many had to be fed and entertained at some point. On one particularly busy day in early 1974 the Provincial Medical Officer (my boss) and entourage arrived on a visit of inspection. They had just left when the Flying Doctors brought in our old friend Malcolm Harper, Field Director of Oxfam, together with an expert on bee-keeping and the radio engineer. We were soon joined by a doctor studying Buruli ulcers, and another investigating the incidence of xerophthalmia (from vitamin A deficiency). Dr Robbie Gurney then arrived with a deputation from Moyale Hospital to meet the PMO. They had no sooner been fed and watered than the Missionary Aviation Fellowship (MAF) plane flew in with an orthopaedic surgeon, two nurses, and four patients for surgery the next day. The day ended with the arrival of the Bishop and a team of twenty four for the start of a week-long mission in Marsabit. This involved our missionary colleagues, Stephen and Eve Houghton, rather than us, but we were nevertheless expected (and wanted) to take an interest.

As in Amudat one never knew who might turn up next. I recall the day when there was a knock on our front door, and there stood a tall, gaunt white man, his face gnarled like a tree trunk, his nose craggy from old breakages, the skin of his arms deeply bronzed and leathery from years of exposure to the sun.

'I am Wilfred Thesiger!' he announced.

To my shame at that time I had never heard of Wilfred Thesiger. I replied, 'Oh hello! I'm David Webster.'

I suspect he had never heard of David Webster. I invited him in, and he had a meal with us, the first of many. He was a fascinating raconteur, and in due course we heard all about his classic books *The Arabian Sands* and *The Marsh Arabs*. Whenever he came to Marsabit after that he always called on us, and we had some interesting discussions. After one such evening I noted in my diary, 'Wilfred Thesiger came to supper, and we had a long discussion covering, amongst other things, ticks, bilharzia, DDT, army worm, bedbugs, drought, game conservation, anthropology, circumcision, uvulectomy – all seasoned with accounts of his time with the Marsh Arabs, his treks across the Empty Quarter of Arabia, fighting with the Yemeni Royalists, and his camel treks round Kenya.' I became an avid fan and reader of this great traveller, and the next trip to Nairobi ensured that his two enthralling books on Arabia were added to our bookcase.

The journey to and from St Andrew's School, Turi, was long, tiring and often eventful. On one return journey to Marsabit we had an unnerving experience. The car was packed to the limit, and by dark the children were all asleep in their various nooks amongst the luggage. We were crossing the Kaisut desert towards the foot of Marsabit mountain. My eyes were glued to the road ahead, looking out in the headlights for wash-aways and potholes, and yet trying to maintain enough speed to ride the relentless corrugations. Then I saw in the darkness ahead the dim light of a torch being waved up and down. We had passed the occasional person wanting to hitch a lift to Marsabit, and we had no room at all for anyone. I assumed that this was another hitchhiker, so did not slow down. Suddenly, as we were almost level with the torchlight, the headlights of a vehicle were switched on, blinding me. I jammed on brakes. We heard shouting, and as we juddered to a stop someone ran up to the open window at my side and thrust a rifle barrel at my head. For a moment I thought it was an armed robbery or a kidnapping, then, as my eyes adjusted, I recognised a police uniform. It was a police roadblock, set up to catch ivory smugglers. I did point out to the policeman that it was not a very safe way to run a roadblock, especially on a road where armed hold-ups by bandits were not unknown.

The journeys to and from Marsabit were not only exhausting, but also took a heavy toll on vehicles. Three kind and very generous Christian friends who owned small planes – Kit Bowen (an accountant in Nairobi), Mike Harries (a coffee farmer near Nairobi), and Hugh Pilkington (of Pilkington Glass, who lived outside Nairobi) – all at various times flew the Webster and Gurney children to and from Turi. It was a tremendous help to us, and meant that we often saw the children at Half Term when otherwise we would not. One end of term the children were flown home by Mike Harries. The great day dawned misty and wet, but then cleared. We reckoned on a late evening arrival, and went down to the airstrip. A bank of dense black cloud was approaching Marsabit from the north. We were anxious, and our eyes scanned the southern horizon for the sight of a small red plane. The huge bank of cloud drew closer, and began to blot out foothills of the mountain. I turned to the others and said 'There's no hope of him landing now!' when suddenly the plane appeared. Mike began to make the usual anticlockwise circuit to come in to land when he realised that the cloud was approaching very fast indeed, and was about to envelop the runway. He did a sharp turn and made a rapid clockwise approach. As the wheels of the plane touched the earth the cloud swirled around, and by the time the plane was at a standstill everything was blotted out, and rain was bucketing down.

It was on another school flight that Kit Bowen had problems with the battery on his plane. He dropped off the Marsabit children but then, to fly on to Moyale, he had to start the engine by swinging the propeller – quite a nerve-wracking business. On the return flight, at the end of Half Term, he kept the engine of the plane running while picking up our children. He did the same again when dropping them off at Turi. This meant that he used more fuel than anticipated. As he approached Nairobi on his return home his fuel gauge registered empty. The engine cut out as he touched down at Wilson Airport, and he freewheeled to a stop on the tarmac. Another very close-run thing.

Chapter 27
THE FLYING DOCTOR

It was not long after our arrival in Marsabit that Dr Anne Spoerry literally flew into our lives. Anne was of Swiss origin but born in France. As a medical student in Paris during the Second World War she worked for the Resistance. Being a member of the medical faculty she was issued by the Gestapo with an Ausweis – a pass which allowed her freer passage than most. Her role for the Resistance in Paris was to run a safe house, and to look after SOE agents coming in from Britain. In due course she, and her older brother Francois, were caught by the Gestapo. Anne was imprisoned in the notorious Ravensbruk concentration camp. Francois was moved from one camp to another, ending up in Dachau. Both survived the war. Anne completed her medical studies, and then, after a spell as a Government Medical Officer in the British colony of Aden she settled in Kenya, and began a new life. She was appointed medical officer to settler farmers and their farm workers at Ol Kalou, in the Kenya Highlands west of the Aberdare mountains. In due course she bought a farm of her own at nearby Subukia, learned to fly, and then offered her services and that of her plane to the surgeon, Michael Wood, founder of the then nascent East African Flying Doctor Service (now called the African Medical and Research Foundation). Michael Wood, incidentally, was married to Susan, the daughter of Alfred Buxton – 'AB' who first inspired my father to go to East Africa.

By the time we arrived in Marsabit in 1973 Anne had the regular routine of a monthly air safari round the vast and remote Marsabit District. She did some doctoring herself, but preferred to concentrate on the flying, and to take the MOH from Marsabit to do most of the medical work. It was an ideal way for me to get around my district, to treat patients in scattered dispensaries, both Government and Mission, to encourage and support nurses and dispensers in lonely places, and to keep an eye on the medical needs of the district. Anne arrived for one of these air safaris once we had settled in at Marsabit. From our first encounter we recognised a down-to-earth, no-nonsense person, with a heart of gold. Short, stocky, with close-cropped white hair (she was then aged fifty-five), she always wore a blue bush shirt, trousers and a cap. Such was her appearance that our two-year-old Stephen took to calling her 'Uncle Spoerry'! Anne spoke a form of Kiswahili that is sometimes called 'Ki-settler'. She spoke it loudly, and she had an explosive temper – expressed sometimes in a colourful mixture of English and Swahili, occasionally laced with French. On our many air safaris together I spent quite a bit of time soothing ruffled feathers after one of Anne's outbursts. But even the victims of her wrath – perhaps an over-demanding patient, or an indolent local official – usually accepted that her bark was much worse than her bite. She had great compassion for anyone in genuine need.

Anne's plane, for most of my time in Marsabit, was a blue and white Cherokee Six, Alpha Juliet Echo, marked with the red cross and insignia of the East African Flying Doctor Service. It was a plane I came to know well. Marsabit was (and is) a notorious place to fly in and out of, because of the thick mists which often envelop the mountain, and which can come down quite suddenly. Pilots who do not understand the vagaries of Marsabit's weather have come to grief (including the plane in 2006 carrying the Assistant Bishop and a number of Government and Opposition leaders to a tribal peace meeting). The airstrip is a dusty (or muddy) stretch of ground between volcanic hillocks just below the town. Safe landing depends not only on clear visibility, but also on an absence of stray goats or cows from the airstrip. Anne would usually delay her arrival in Marsabit until midday, to give any morning mists time to clear. We would be informed of her ETA by the Flying Doctor radio. Her arrival would be heralded by a low swoop over our house – the signal to drive down to the airstrip to meet her in. A police Landrover with a drum of aviation fuel would also head for the airstrip, to top up the plane before our air safari round the district.

Our itinerary varied from month to month. There were eight possible ports of call to cover in the three day safari. Having loaded on board medical supplies, gifts of food for remote outposts, perhaps a medical worker returning to his place of work, and on occasion a patient returning home after treatment in Marsabit, we would be off. Sitting next to

Anne in the co-pilot's seat I would wave goodbye to an anxious-looking Rosemary (she hated me going on these trips, because of her innate fear of flying). We would roar down the airstrip in a cloud of dust, then up and away, perhaps heading north. The lower slopes of Marsabit mountain, pock-marked with craters, gave way to the vast, scorching lava plain, the Dida Galgalu. This is the home of the nomadic Gabbra tribe and their camels. As we skimmed over it at ten thousand feet, the shadow of the small plane racing across the barely penetrable lava waste far below, my thoughts would turn to my father and his travels over these same wastes on foot, with camels for baggage, befriending the people, preaching the gospel, and bringing such rudimentary medical care as he could. The lava rocks were so hot in the midday sun that he found it possible to cook an egg on them. Prophetically he once wrote in his diary, in the 1930s, that the future for getting about this wilderness lay with air travel. And here was I fulfilling that prophecy.

Below we could see the road from Marsabit to Moyale, on the Ethiopian border, winding its way through the Dida Galgalu. From that altitude the road looked deceptively smooth. In fact it was a car-breaker, with corrugations, potholes, wash-aways and high, stony central ridges. What took four gruelling hours or more by road could be covered in forty minutes by plane. Ahead of the plane, in the distant haze, were the mountains of southern Ethiopia. On only my second flight with Anne Spoerry, on this stretch north from Marsabit to Moyale, she suddenly said to me, 'I'm going to have a nap. You take over. Just head for that mountain. Keep the nose of the plane up by pulling back a bit on the joy stick. Watch the altimeter.' And with that she was asleep. I sensed a palpable lack of confidence emanating from the passenger behind me, a medical student. I tried to disguise my own equal lack of confidence. After a while a nervous voice behind me suddenly said, 'Oo look! We're flying over an airstrip!' I realised that she thought we had over-flown our destination. As it happened I knew that the airstrip she could see was one at Turbi, half way to Moyale. But I did not tell her that. I just said, casually, 'Oh yes!' and flew on. She seemed profoundly relieved when Anne eventually woke up in time to take over for our landing at Moyale. I only ever flew Anne's plane when we were safely aloft, though she did let me do some turns. I have to admit that I watched like a hawk the process of landing the plane. After all Anne was no chicken, and her build was compatible with coronary heart disease. If ever she had collapsed at the controls I wonder if I would have managed to bring the plane down safely. Thankfully that speculation was never put to the test.

Moyale airstrip straddles the border of Kenya and Ethiopia. You touch down in Ethiopia and come to a stop in Kenya. Throughout our time at Marsabit the doctor at Moyale Government Hospital was Robbie Gurney, our fellow BCMS missionary. There was never any need to visit Moyale when Robbie was there – only if he was away down country for any reason. Such visits were occasioned by medical emergencies at Moyale, and usually I had to make them by road from Marsabit.

Our next stop would be Sololo, a Roman Catholic mission at the foot of a rugged mountain to the west of Moyale, and also very close to the Ethiopian border. Sololo mission was run by Italian Verona Fathers, and boasted a small hospital with an Italian lady doctor, Dr Dessi. We would quite often call there on our air safaris, and I would do a ward round with Dr Dessi, and discuss cases with her. She saw a lot of tuberculosis, and I was able to encourage her to do sputum staining, and to make more definite diagnoses. There was a language problem as I speak no Italian, and Dr Dessi spoke little English. So we tended to converse in Kiswahili. Although the various Catholic missionaries in Marsabit District knew me to be an Anglican (and an Anglican missionary at that) our relationships were excellent. I profoundly admired many of them for their dedication, and the lonely and simple life-style that they had committed themselves to. One of the few times that made me really sad about our denominational division occurred at Sololo. We were travelling with Enda Byrne, an Irishman who worked for Catholic Relief. We stayed overnight at Sololo, and Dr Dessi and Enda warmly invited me to join the priest and sisters at their evening mass in the church. We all, including Anne Spoerry, sat in a row. When the time in the service came for the giving of the sacrament the priest came down the row and distributed the bread to everyone – except me. He stepped past me, and carried on down the row. Although I knew that he was simply obeying the rules of the Catholic Church I felt a deep sense of rejection. It has made me realise in our own churches how exclusive Holy Communion can be, and how excluded people can feel, unless care is taken to make them feel welcome. I would have felt happy with just a word of blessing from the priest, just a token recognition that I was there, sharing with them.

From Sololo we would head west again to Dukana. Dukana was a name on the map but hardly a place. There was just a small, lonely police post in the bush, about two hundred miles northwest of Marsabit. The police were there to try to stop the frequent cross-border cattle raiding by bandits from Ethiopia. Most of the post-mortems I had to do in Marsabit derived from the Dukana area. In my early months there was no usable airstrip, but we persuaded the police to clear more bush, and flatten more termite hills, and so make a strip long enough for Anne's plane. The first challenge when flying in to Dukana was to find the strip – there were no clear markers to distinguish it from the surrounding bush. We then had to take particular care to check the runway for animals, both domestic and wild. Even one small dikdik in the way could cause a nasty accident. There were no buildings anywhere near the airstrip at Dukana, no trees worthy of the name, and no shade. We would hold our clinic in such scanty shelter as the wings of the plane afforded. The enervating heat parched us, the dry scrub shimmered in the heat haze, swarms of determined flies tried to drink from the corners of our eyes and mouths. Sometimes the heat was so intense that even the flies seemed torpid. The acrid wood-smoke, cow-fat smell of our patients mingled in the hot air with that of aviation fuel.

Local *manyattas* would have been notified by the police of our coming, and there was usually a good crowd assembled. Nobody wanted to miss the opportunity for medicine, the police included. They would push their way to the head of the queue, and often, in doing so, got the full blast of Anne's wrath. Given the opportunity people would try to get two or more innings, joining both Anne's queue and mine, so I would see and treat the men, and Anne would see the women and children. In this way we had a bit more control over the jostling crowds. Those Dukana clinics were very hot and very exhausting.

The people here, as at Moyale and Sololo, are Gabbra or Boran. The men wore white *woyas* (cloths knotted over the shoulder) and turbans.

The women wore goatskins, decorated with cowrie shells, their hair platted into many ringlets and greased with cow fat. They are people with strikingly fine features. The language of both tribes is the same, namely Borana. I remembered a little from childhood, but resorted to Kiswahili most of the time. The Gabbra are mainly camel herders, and the Borana cattle people. They can only survive in these desert areas because of their nomadic way of life – following the rain and the grazing. The number of patients we might see at a clinic at Dukana (and, remember, every single person was a patient – nobody ever admitted to being actually well) would depend on how many *manyattas* happened to be in the vicinity at the time. When the last patient had stridden off into the bush we would pack up and once again check the airstrip for animals before taking off in a cloud of red dust to Ileret.

Ileret is one of the remotest outposts in Kenya. Situated on the very northeastern shore of Lake Turkana it comprises a small, well stockaded police post, and a two-roomed Government dispensary, which we maintained from Marsabit. The people inhabiting that area are the Shangilla, a small tribe who live mainly by fishing in Lake Turkana's prolific waters, and survive on a diet of dried fish, supplemented by goat meat. A characteristic of the Shangilla, and their neighbouring lake tribe to the south, the El Molo, is the excellent state of their brown-stained teeth. I never had to extract a single Shangilla or El Molo tooth. The reason for this, and for the brown staining, is the high fluoride content of the lake water.

The country bordering the shores of the lake is desolate in the extreme. The strongly alkaline water of the lake does not support much vegetation, and in most places the desert extends right to the shore. Here and there coarse grass grows, and hardy shrubs, but there is little green along the shoreline except after occasional rain. Lake Turkana teems with fish – the tilapia and Nile perch are the biggest and best of any East African lake. And because of this so are the crocodiles. The lake teems with them too. Compared with river crocodiles, which depend for their gastronomic needs on animals (or people) coming to the water's edge to drink, the Lake Turkana crocodiles have such an abundance of fish to eat that they tend to be less aggressive to humans. Having said this two people, one of them a policeman, were taken by crocodiles at Ileret during our time in Marsabit. The crocs were never averse to a change in diet.

Ileret had the distinction of having two airstrips – a short one near the police post and dispensary, and a longer one about two miles away. Which one we used depended entirely on our load. The shorter strip had sandy banks along one side, and these were peppered with holes – the nests of beautiful carmine bee-eaters. On one occasion as we landed we were greeted by vast flocks of these brilliantly coloured birds, with their carmine breasts, greenish-blue heads, cobalt-blue rumps and streaming tail feathers. They were in their breeding plumage. It is interesting that von Hohnel and Count Teleki, who 'discovered' Lake Rudolf (now Turkana) and gave it its name in 1888, also (in von Hohnel's account) describe birds which must have been carmine bee-eaters, in a place which could well have been in the vicinity of Ileret. Perhaps we were witnessing the descendants of their birds.

Our visits were always a highlight for the dispenser doing his turn of duty at Ileret dispensary – especially if his rotational stint had ended, and we had brought with us someone to replace him. We would be met at the airstrip by an excited welcoming committee of dispenser, police, and locals. Children would offer to carry the medicine boxes and other supplies on their heads, and we would make a happy procession along the hot sandy track from the airstrip. Away to the left the blue-green lake glinted enticingly in the sun. How I often longed for a plunge. We saw patients in the little tin-roofed, cement-block dispensary, and encouraged the dispenser in his lonely work.

On occasion there were other medical matters to investigate. Once an outbreak of severe gastro-enteritis was ravaging the population. The possibility of cholera arose. We asked to see the source of water being used by the police and local populace. We were shown a shallow hole, dug in the sand, and filled with filthy brown water. A woman was filling her water vessels, her feet in the pool of water. Goat droppings abounded all around, and goats were using the same hole to drink. The water was not of course boiled, and it did not take much intelligence to guess where the infection was coming from. We took water and stool samples to test for cholera. Fortunately it proved to be simple gastroenteritis, and some advice on protecting the water supply brought dramatic improvement. There was always a high incidence of brucellosis at Ileret, and on another visit we took blood samples from a cross-section of the population, and milk samples from goats. They tested strongly positive for brucellosis, and the milk was clearly the source of that problem. What to do about it was much more problematical. The Shangilla were not favourably disposed to boiling the milk.

Flying south down the shore of Lake Turkana to our next stop, Alia Bay, was always a great thrill. Anne would fly low, skimming the shore of the jade-green lake and its many sandbanks. The coarse-grassed shore line would often be populated by herds of oryx, with their lance-like horns; or by the slender-necked gerenuk, a graceful buck which can live without water, deriving all it needs from foliage; or by ostriches, striding along at great speed at the sound of the plane, the proud black and white males with their rather dowdy brown wives. On the sandbanks along the shallows of the lake hundreds of crocodiles could be seen, sunning themselves. Some were huge, reaching up to sixteen feet in length, the largest crocodiles in East Africa. At the sudden approach of the plane they would slither into the water, sinister scaly leviathans, a threat to every living creature around them, and at risk from nothing except humans.

Lake Turkana is about two hundred miles long, and forty miles wide. Alia Bay is situated about halfway down its eastern shore. It is the site of one of Kenya's newest National Parks (the Sibiloi National Park), too remote to be visited by many. At that time there was a tented game rangers' camp, under the charge of a white Honorary Game Warden, Rodney Eliot. Our visits were to treat any sick rangers. 'Who is sick?' I would ask, and everyone's hand would go up. 'Are you really ill?' I would ask remarkably healthy looking game rangers. 'Ndio daktari! Mgonjwa sana sana!' ('Yes doctor! Very sick indeed!') came the reply. Rodney, who would be standing nearby with a bemused expression on his face, would tease them. 'If you are that sick, then you are too ill to be employed!' and there would be general merriment. It was usually more a morale-boosting visit than a medical one, but always enjoyable. Anne Spoerry, aware of Rosemary's fear of my flying each month, suggested that she and little Stephen should come along with us on one safari. It was a helpful experience for Rosemary, in that she saw how meticulous Anne was as a pilot. On that trip we spent a night at the Alia Bay camp. Rodney Eliot most generously vacated his tent for Rosemary and me. A lasting memory is of sitting that evening on the lake shore, the waves lapping at our feet, the tangy smell of the alkaline water, flamingos and herons wading in the shallows, and the great orange ball of the setting sun casting its reflection across the lake. The following morning, when Rodney drove us to the plane, we encountered two lions which had made a kill next to the airstrip. Fortunately neither they, nor hyenas which we had heard in the night, had chewed the plane's tyres. So off again, and southward to Loiyengalani at the southeast end of Lake Turkana, once again skimming the shore.

Chapter 28
WINGS OVER THE DESERT

Koobi Fora is a spit of land projecting into Lake Turkana just north of Alia Bay. Inland from the lake the terrain is like a moonscape – an inferno of barren, blistering, rock-strewn nothingness. It was at Koobi Fora in the late 1960s that Richard Leakey, anthropologist son of the famous Louis and Mary Leakey, discovered remains of early man. It was Leakey's contention that human life has its origins in these now desert wastes, and that once it was a fertile, forested region, populated by the ancestors of present day man and animals. The presence of abundant fossilised tree trunks certainly confirms its forested past. Leakey began excavations in the area, and established a base camp at Koobi Fora. On our flights south from Ileret we would pass over it – as remote a campsite as one could imagine. To assist with excavations, and as part of their work experience, Richard Leakey would have young, budding anthropologists to stay at his camp. It was one such American who was staying there in June 1974. As was the routine he was dropped off one morning at a dig site inland from the lake. The arrangement was that he would be picked up again in the evening.

It would seem that this young American finished his digging early, and decided to walk back to the camp. When the vehicle came to collect him that evening he was not there, but nor did he arrive back at camp. A search party went out that night, without success. The next morning he was still missing. Richard Leakey started an air search in his plane, and he called for any other planes in the vicinity to help. I became aware of the problem because I was, at the time, on a medical air safari to Africa Inland Mission dispensaries in the south of my district. The Missionary Aviation Fellowship plane that was supposed to be flying me around was diverted to take part in the search for the missing student. No sign of him was seen. He was apparently carrying no water, and hopes of finding him alive began to fade. On the third day of searching trackers came across his footprints well inland – he had been heading away from, instead of towards, the lake. In one place it seemed that he had been running in circles. By the fifth day all hope had gone. Then a vehicle driving from Alia Bay up to Ileret came across a piece of paper blowing in the track. Pieces of paper don't just 'happen' in that sort of area. They stopped, found more paper, and recognised it as the American's notebook. Then they saw him – lying under a bush a little away from the track, and still just alive. He was taken to Koobi Fora and flown straight to Nairobi. He was able to talk, and to tell what happened. But, tragically, severe dehydration had damaged his kidneys and other organs beyond repair, and he died of organ failure two or three days later.

Many questions arose in my mind over that tragedy. Why, in that sort of climate and landscape, was he not carrying a good supply of water? Why did he not have matches or a lighter, to make smoke in the event of him getting lost? Or even a mirror to attract attention? Why did he not lay out his notepapers in a pattern on the ground, to enable him to be spotted from the air? Apparently, he said, planes flew right over him on at least two occasions, but failed to see him. Why did he not just head west, towards the setting sun? He would have been bound to reach the lakeshore sooner or later, and would have had water in plenty, and could then have followed the shore line back to Koobi Fora? Why did he head east, away from the lake? If he was unsure about east and west, why did he not just observe, from grass caught around bushes in the dry river gullies, which direction the water had flowed when they were last in flood? All water in that area flows into the lake, and any one of these riverbeds would have led him to the lake. There seemed to have been an ignorance of basic bush craft. It reminded me of how our New York visitor in Amudat, Annie, had got completely lost in the bush. It can never be taken for granted that city-dwellers will understand the bush, and be able to find their way – any more than that a bush-dweller, like me, can find their way round a city. When Wilfred Thesiger and I were discussing this tragedy some time later he said that in his opinion the deadliest, most dangerous country that he had ever travelled in is that east of Lake Turkana. In his opinion the searing heat and waterless lava wastes are compounded by the hot, dry winds, which batter the body and dehydrate. It is indeed an inferno.

We never landed at Koobi Fora on our safaris – there was no reason to do so. From Alia Bay we would continue our flight southwards. The gentle flat shore of the bay gave way to rugged volcanic cliffs, dropping sheer into the lake, from the steep slopes of Porr mountain. To the west, across the jade-green waters of the lake, we could see the black, barren outline of Central Island. Ahead of us lay South Island, another heap of barren larva rock as it were dumped in the lake. This is sometimes called 'The Island of No Return'. In the 1930s an expedition to South Island was led by Vivian Fuchs. His party camped on the eastern shore of the lake, and two members set off for the island in a collapsible boat. It is known that they reached the island, because the shore party saw the light of their fire that night. But they never returned. It is likely that on their return trip one of the sudden, violent squalls for which Lake Turkana is notorious, or possibly a crocodile or hippo, capsized their flimsy boat. Certainly once in the water they would have had little chance of survival because of crocodiles. If they had been taken by a crocodile on the island their boat would still have been there. No trace of them was ever found, apart from empty food cans on the island shore.

Just short of South Island we would turn east to land at the little oasis of Loiyengalani – a refreshing patch of green on the southeastern shore. Across a narrow stretch of water from Loiyengalani lies the small, barren El Molo Island, home to some of the El Molo tribe. The El Molo are the smallest surviving tribe in Kenya, numbering now no more than a few hundred. Interbreeding within the clan has led to ill health and congenital abnormalities. They live in small, dome-shaped, palm-leaf huts, on the shore at Loiyengalani and on El Molo island. They live on a subsistence diet of fish, which they catch with spears from rafts of doum palms. The high fluoride content of the lake water has ensured that they, like the Shangilla, have healthy teeth, but the excessive levels have also led to brown staining of the teeth and to bone abnormalities. Loiyengalani consisted then, apart from the El Molo settlement, of a police post, a Catholic mission, and a small tourist lodge, Oasis Lodge. After the heat and barrenness of Ileret it was always refreshing to fly in to Loiyengalani. The buildings nestle amongst a grove of rustling doum palms. Warm, brackish water bubbles out of the ground, coarse green grass abounds, and flocks of brightly coloured lovebirds chatter and screech in the palms. After the glare of the desert it is Paradise.

The Catholic mission dispensary at Loiyengalani was run by a diminutive Italian nun, Sister Julietta. She would bustle about in her blue and white nun's habit, a Mother Theresa-like figure lining up patients for me to see, and keeping strict order with a quiet authority. We always stayed overnight at the Catholic mission, and the welcome and hospitality of the priest and sisters was inevitably warm. So was the weather. The luxury they provided was that of a small swimming pool, filled directly from one of the oasis's hot springs. It was a prospect I used to relish all day, as we held our various clinics in the scanty shade of the plane, or in hot, tin-roofed dispensaries. After a simple supper of perhaps goat meat and rice, washed down with powerful black Italian coffee, Anne and I, and any other passengers travelling with us, would wallow in the warm but refreshing water of the pool, washing off the dust and sweat of the day, unwinding, and discussing every subject under the sun – from faith, to anthropology, to art and literature. The sound of the trickling spring water, the rustling of the palm trees, the clear, clear black sky like a jewel-studded dome above us, always made me feel glad and privileged to be doing what I was doing. There were not many perks to the job, but this was one of them. After an hour or two of soaking we would retire to our simple rooms in the priests' quarters. The windows had mosquito-proof mesh, which made the rooms rather hot and stuffy. But always in the night a very strong east wind would begin to blow down from nearby Mount Kulal. It would arrive quite suddenly, rattling the windows, and bringing a welcome coolness. Outside the palm trees would rustle furiously, with a sound like pouring rain, and the Fathers' wind generator would spin noisily. Dogs at the El Molo *manyatta* kept up their barking and howling, and sometimes a hyena added its whooping call. Morning would be heralded by the excited chatter of birds in the palm trees, and the singing of children at Mass in the nearby church.

A short walk from the Catholic mission, through the palms and over the trickling stream, lay Oasis Lodge. It was not a well frequented tourist lodge because of it remoteness. Sometimes after work in the dispensary we would wander over there for an ice-cold drink – another prospect that would have been exercising my imagination throughout the hot day. The lodge too had a swimming pool fed from the spring, and, with its simple, palm-thatched buildings, it was an attractive place, a cool haven from the heat. It had had, though, a bloody history. During the 1960s *shifta* – armed Somali bandits, who laid claim to northeastern Kenya – were very active, especially to the east, nearer to the Somalia border. It was a time when Loiyengalani was being developed – the lodge upgraded, and the Catholic mission established. The local people had not been involved by the Government in these changes, and some understandably felt that their land was being invaded. *Shifta* bandits were encouraged by members of the local Rendille tribe to do their worst. Just before Christmas in 1965 the manager of the lodge (Guy Poole), the Catholic priest who was building the nearby mission (Father Stallone), and an Italian truck driver, were met together in the lodge for a drink. Sudden gunfire announced a *shifta* raid, which was on them before they had time to react. The three Europeans were tied up with flex in one of the bandas. The *shifta* ransacked the lodge, and helped themselves to alcohol from the bar. They then shot Guy Poole and Father Stallone. They made the Italian driver load his truck with their loot. Some miles from Loiyengalani the truck ran out of petrol and was abandoned. The *shifta* continued on foot, taking the Italian with them. No trace of him was ever found again. There were rumours that he had been skinned alive, but no real evidence of his fate. It was hard to believe, whenever we sat under the cool palm thatch of the lodge sipping our drinks, that it had been the scene of such brutality just a few years previously.

Take-off from Loiyengalani always required a careful check for stray Rendille camels or El Molo dogs. Sometimes we would have on board a patient, coming with us to Marsabit for surgery or treatment. Usually such patients had never flown before. They would cover their eyes for take-off, uttering whimpers, and cries of 'Ay ay ay ay ay!' When finally they ventured to peep out, and saw the land far below, the cries would resume. No doubt the tales of those flights were recounted in song around the fires in their villages time and time again in the coming years – how the big 'ndege' (bird, or plane) came and bore grandma away in its stomach.

From Loiyengalani we would head northeast, by-passing the rugged mass of Mount Kulal. Rising to an altitude of eight thousand feet, Kulal sticks out of the Koroli desert, its twin peaks separated by a deep precipitous gorge. Thick cedar forest crowns its heights. It is home to members of the Samburu tribe. An AIM mission nestles on its upper slopes. There is an airstrip, regularly used by MAF planes, but Anne Spoerry would not land there. I did not blame her. I once visited Kulal by air, on an MAF plane, and landing and take-off rather resembled a heart-stopping ride at the fair. The short airstrip ends abruptly at the rim of the two-thousand-foot gorge. On take-off we seemed to shoot off the end of the runway like a plane off the deck of an aircraft carrier. Not only did we not rise – we actually dropped into the gorge as we became airborne, pitching and tossing in the air turbulence. Anne had done it once, but never again, she said. Apart from that one occasion on the MAF plane, my visits to Kulal were by road – an almost equally breath-taking experience.

We flew north of Mount Kulal to our next destination, North Horr. North Horr is an oasis on the edge of the vast, sandy, salt-encrusted Chalbi Desert. Again there is a small administrative centre consisting of a handful of buildings, a police post, and a Catholic mission. The sandy airstrip runs alongside the pools of the oasis, where at times thousands of camels gather to drink. The Gabbra people water their camels every eight days. The camels can smell the water from miles away, and the herds begin to stampede towards it, kicking up vast clouds of dust. They appear to be running on water, owing to mirages on the desert surface. We always had to check North Horr airstrip particularly carefully for camels. By the time we had landed and come to a stop in a billowing cloud of sand the Landrover from the mission would be there, waiting next to the little palm-thatch shelter which we called 'Immigration and Customs'. The sister in charge of North Horr dispensary was not a 'nun' type of sister, but a 'nurse' type – a lay German worker, called Anna. She was first class. She knew her medicine, was efficient, and my visits to North Horr were always used to the best advantage.

Sister Anna asked me to see a Gabbra woman with a bulging blind eye (proptosis). The last patient I had seen with a similar problem, a young lad, had turned out to have a highly malignant retinoblastoma of the eye. I feared the worst for this lady. But removal of the eye showed her to have a hydatid cyst, not a tumour, behind the eye. Hydatid cysts are a stage in the life cycle of the dog tapeworm, Echinococcus. Normally the cystic part of its life cycle is spent in sheep or camels, and dogs become reinfected when they eat the offal. Humans are not a natural host, and only become infected by close association with dogs, and contamination of the fingers by dog faeces. Hydatid disease was common among the desert dwelling people, who live in close association with their dogs – the Gabbra and Turkana especially. Another patient at North Horr presented with a small cystic swelling on his chest wall. When I explored this it turned out to be the tip of an iceberg – an enormous hydatid cyst, full of hundreds of daughter cysts, and occupying half his chest cavity.

Visits to North Horr reminded me of a holiday there in my childhood. In those days there was no Catholic mission, dispensary or school. We stayed then in a small stone-walled, palm-thatched Government rest house, nestled among the doum palms. In an evening huge flocks of small sand grouse used to sweep in like clouds, to drink at the pools of the oasis. In order to provide our supper my father fired at a flock with his shotgun – and killed eighty-three with one shot. Some supper! We feasted on the tasty, plump little birds until we could eat no more – and took many back to Marsabit. Visits to North Horr not only reminded me of childhood days, and how privileged I had been to grow up in such a fascinating part of the world. But I also thought again of how my father had travelled the Chalbi Desert with his camels, visiting Gabbra *manyattas*, living among the people, and winning that respect and love which is a prerequisite for sharing the Gospel. I was always very conscious that I was following in his footsteps, and fulfilling his wish to have done Medicine .

On occasion Anne and I were accompanied on our safari by the media. No doubt there is something adventurous about air travel around Marsabit District. The concept of a Flying Doctor Service has a romantic appeal – 'Doctor flies in to remote outpost and saves life!' It made good material for documentaries to entertain and interest folks in the west. On one occasion a French Television film crew accompanied us. Everything was 'Formidable!' They had hired their own plane, which buzzed around us, getting good angles on our plane. At each stop they filmed us at work, and at North Horr they interviewed me as I sat on a sand dune in front of a doum palm. I spoke about the problems of delivering health care effectively to scattered nomadic people. 'Formidable!'

Someone who accompanied our trip on two occasions was Mohammed Amin (no relation to Idi Amin in Uganda). Mohammed worked as a freelance cameraman, but did a lot for the BBC, and it was for the BBC that he made his trips with us. He was a most likeable man, very professional. On one air safari with us it was literally a case of 'Doctor flies in and saves life!' We arrived at Loiyengalani to find Sister Julietta with a very sick little girl, unconscious and fitting. She had cerebral malaria, and needed urgent treatment. Every minute counted. I gave intravenous chloroquine and hydrocortisone, and by the next morning she was sitting up and drinking. Sadly soon after that, when filming riots in Addis Ababa with Michael Buerk, Mohammed was severely injured by an explosion. He lost an arm, but not one to be deterred he learned to handle his camera with an artificial arm. He had lived through many dangerous situations, but finally met his death when travelling in a hijacked plane which crashed into the sea off the Comoro Islands. Mohammed Amin's life and death gave me great respect for those news reporters and cameramen who frequently take risks to keep us informed of world events.

Chapter 29
MAIKONA

There would be one more port of call on a typical monthly Flying Doctor safari. Taking off from North Horr we would fly southeast again, heading towards Marsabit mountain. To our left were the bare, volcanic Huri Hills. To our right, and stretching to the distant horizon, the flat, glistening white Chalbi desert, coated with its crust of salt, leached up when the desert floods in times of rain. We flew over the oasis of Kalacha, with its pools and palm groves. There was no airstrip then, and just the beginnings of an AIM dispensary. It was at Kalacha that my father's camels were attacked by lions in 1932. On we flew until the glistening tin roofs of the small settlement of Maikona appeared, near the foot of Marsabit mountain. If anyone ever wants a foretaste of life on the moon I suggest Maikona as the place to go. It is utterly barren. Black lava rock is unrelieved by any green. Such vegetation as there might once have been has long since been eaten by goats. It is a place of black nothingness and scorching heat, reflected relentlessly off the black rock. There are a few huts, and a small Catholic mission. We would land on the strip which had been cleared of rocks and marked out with boulders, and then taxi right in to the mission compound.

There were always hazards to look out for. On one occasion the teacher in Maikona school had had a sports day for the children. The airstrip seemed a smoother place than most for the children to run, so he had marked out a track with large rocks – lines of which went right across the airstrip in two places. Fortunately we spotted them before touching down, and zoomed the mission until someone realised our problem and moved the stones. Anne's language to the penitent teacher is better left out of this account.

The Catholic mission here was different. There was something special about it. And that was because of the two priests who were in charge. Father Tablino and Father Venturino were Italians, but not members of any Catholic missionary order – such as the Verona Fathers or the White

Fathers. They were parish priests from Italy who had been seconded by their diocese to work in 'the missions'. So they were not beholden to any missionary order, and did not have that sometimes aggressive and competitive approach which some of the missionary orders displayed. The two priests lived, turn and turn about, for a month at Maikona (their 'luxurious' base) and then for a month out in the *manyattas* with the Gabbra people, travelling with them and their camels, and sharing their life. This was the approach my father had had, but because he also had the work at Marsabit to see to he could only do it sporadically. Fathers Tablino and Venturino had given themselves totally to this way of life. I came to admire them profoundly, especially Father Tablino. If it was his month to be at Maikona he would be there to wave us in, his inevitable cap protecting his bald head from the fierce sun. I sometimes wondered if he slept in his cap. (A Gabbra man once came to him asking for medicine for baldness. Father Tablino said nothing, but simply removed his cap, smiled, and replaced it. The man went away convinced but disappointed.)

The sisters at Maikona ran a small dispensary – it was expected of all missionaries to provide medicine. But none of them had any medical qualifications or experience. To make matters worse well-meaning folks back in their home churches in Italy kept sending boxes of medicines out to them – mainly free samples that doctors had given them. Some were time-expired, and some were entirely inappropriate. The sisters hadn't the faintest idea what most of them were for. So they had a system. If the medicine carton mentioned 'heart', it went onto the 'heart' shelf. If it mentioned 'kidneys' or 'lungs' it went onto the 'kidney' or 'lung' shelf. And so on. If then a patient came in and complained of a symptom, such as pain, that seemed to be roughly in the area where the sisters believed, say, the heart to be, the patient would be given the first box that came to hand off the heart shelf. The consequences of this haphazard approach to medicine can be imagined. A patient with a muscular pain in his chest wall, perhaps from wrestling with a stubborn camel, might go away with a box of Digoxin or a beta-blocker. Someone with a urinary infection might well be given a diuretic – not something they would benefit from or appreciate. It was a pragmatic approach to medicine, but rather a dangerous one. I remonstrated with the sisters, and urged them to stick to simple medicines. I cleared their shelves of many of their samples – pointing out that western illnesses such as coronary heart disease and hypertension are almost non-existent amongst the people of rural East Africa. Sister Serafino, who was in charge of the dispensary thought I was a bit fussy. After all, the patients just wanted medicine. They were not too bothered what it was.

Mother Angeleto, the senior nun, once approached Father Tablino about their simple little church at Maikona. It was in fact simplicity itself, and could well have passed for an evangelical chapel. 'Father!' she said 'Could we not have a statue of the blessed Virgin in the church?' 'Sister! Sister!' he replied 'Isn't Jesus enough?' And this summed up his and Father Venturino's theology. We had many a discussion, long into the night, sitting out on the verandah of their simple house, sipping strong black Italian coffee, gazing at the stars, and catching the night breeze. They longed for the Gabbra people to come to a real faith in Christ, not to a meaningless membership of the Church. They were not into the all too common Catholic approach of baptizing every person possible by every means possible – even if it meant handouts of food or clothes. They abhorred this approach as much as we did. And yet, as we agreed, there was a problem. When people are starving, when they are sick, when they are so poor that they possess nothing but the rags or skins they stand in, how can one, as a Christian, not help them? Of course we must. Christ told us to. But how do you not confuse compassion with bribery? How do you ensure that someone who professes a desire to become a Christian is doing so out of faith in and love for Christ, and not because they hope to get more food, access to schooling, or some other material benefit? Fathers Tablino and Venturino were very careful not to gather around them 'rice Christians'. They looked for evidence of true faith before baptising a new believer. I told them that they would have made excellent Protestants.

Staying at the mission with Father Tablino was a young Gabbra man who, having come to faith in Christ and been baptised, now felt a calling to the priesthood, to serve his own people. The Roman Catholic Bishop, Cavallero, had accepted him for training for the priesthood, and wanted him to go to Seminary in Nairobi for six years. Father Tablino baulked. 'If you take him to Nairobi for six years,' he told the Bishop 'he will lose contact with his own people and culture, he will change, he will have raised expectations of life-style, and he will never come back to live and work amongst his own nomadic people. Besides,' he went on ' of what use to him is a knowledge of western church history or of liturgy? Please let me train him here!' he begged. And, amazingly, the Bishop agreed – probably out of personal respect for Father Tablino. I asked Father Tablino how he planned to train him. 'What I really want is for him to have an understanding of Scripture,' he said. 'We will study St John's Gospel first, and then the Epistle to the Romans. When he really understands those, and takes them to heart, we shall have made a good beginning!' I could imagine my father – an evangelical Anglican, and from such a different background – agreeing with every word. The Reverend Stephen Houghton in Marsabit had a very similar approach to clergy training. His successor, the Reverend Andrew Adano, a Gabbra man, who became Anglican Bishop of Marsabit, was largely trained on the spot by Stephen.

On all my safaris around the district, whether by air or road, public health matters were an important concern, as well as the treating of sick people. After all, prevention is better than cure. Maikona, rather like Ileret, caused us concern because of the prevalence of diarrhoeal illnesses. The reason was obvious – the water supply for the local community consisted of a filthy pool from which camels, goats, dogs and people all drank. Animals waded in it, and contaminated it with their urine and droppings. The water was a murky green colour. Joseph Wakienda, our Health Inspector in Marsabit, supervised the building of a protective wall around the pool and a separate trough for animals. For the first time the people had clean water to drink, and the incidence of gastroenteritis (often resulting, in the case of children, in death) fell dramatically. Our Public Health programme was one of the most important aspects of the medical work.

Maikona lay not far from the western base of Marsabit mountain. The last hop home was only about twenty minutes flying time. We would never leave before midday in case the airstrip at Marsabit was still shrouded in mist. There was an occasion, seared in Rosemary's memory, when Anne and I were flying back directly from Loiyengalani, on the lake, to Marsabit. As the faint outline of the mountain appeared on the distant horizon, we strained our eyes to see if the cloud mass sitting on Marsabit was above or below the level of the airstrip. It was difficult to be sure. We were running short of fuel, and could take no risks – the craters and lava rock of Marsabit's slopes do not make a good alternative landing site. Anne called up Foundation Control, the Flying Doctors' radio base in Nairobi. 'Foundation Control, this is Alpha Juliet Echo! We have Marsabit in sight' she reported, 'but because of cloud I am diverting to Maikona, and will be landing at Maikona in ten minutes.' 'Roger! Roger!' came the reply. We had caught Foundation Control just a few minutes before they closed down for a one hour lunch break. I knew that Rosemary would call them at 2 p.m. from Marsabit to find out our ETA. We landed at Maikona, had a leisurely lunch with Father Tablino, topped up with a couple of cans of aviation fuel, which were kept at the mission, and soon after 2 p.m. took off in the expectation that Marsabit would now be clear of mist.

Anne turned on the radio to give Foundation Control our ETA for Marsabit. We found ourselves in the middle of a distressed dialogue between Rosemary in Marsabit and Foundation Control. The exchange went something like this: Rosemary: 'But when I called you just before 1 p.m. you told me that they had Marsabit in sight and would be landing here in ten minutes!' Foundation Control: 'Roger! Roger! That is correct. They should have arrived a long time ago!' Rosemary: 'They are NOT here! They have NOT landed!' Foundation Control: 'Roger! You say they are not there. They should be there!' Rosemary: 'I repeat they are not here! What has happened to the plane? Have you heard anything from them?' Foundation Control: 'No, we have not heard, but we have been closed down for an hour. They should be there!' It was as though, if only Rosemary were to try harder, and look around a bit more, she would find us! Anne tried to break in to the conversation. 'Marsabit! Marsabit! Alpha Juliet Echo calling Marsabit!' But the dialogue Rosemary was having with Foundation Control left no gaps, and Anne couldn't be heard. By now we were only ten minutes flying time from Marsabit, and we decided to leave it. Soon we were sweeping low over our house. There below was the tiny figure of Rosemary in the garden, waving like mad, and even from our elevated position and in the seconds available I think I could see a look of the most enormous relief on her face. By the time we flew over the house Rosemary had convinced herself that Anne and I were in a crumpled heap in the bottom of a crater somewhere. It turned out later that the Kenyan lady manning the radio that day was new to the job, and had not yet mastered the skill of hearing rightly radio messages – especially when very crackly, as they often were from a plane in flight.

And so I was home again. Rosemary could relax for another month, until the next safari. It was so hard for her, and experiences like the one just described did nothing to boost her confidence. Yet she knew, as I did, that there was no other way to cover such a vast district, as well as to be responsible for the District Hospital. We had to rest ourselves in God's care, and pray constantly for safety in all our travelling. Anne Spoerry tirelessly and generously gave so much to Marsabit District, as well as to Maasai District and her beloved Lamu Island. She continued to fly for the Flying Doctor Service until she was eighty years old. She died in 2001, and was buried near her home on Lamu. To quote Anne from her own book (entitled *They Call Me Mama Daktari*): 'I have seen Africa at its best and at its worst. I have known it in joy and in sorrow. These last few years have been dire, but I believe the best is yet to come, and that come it will.'

Chapter 30
DROUGHT AND FAMINE

The unremitting background to life in Marsabit in those middle 1970s was drought. We had rain from time to time, but it was not sustained. Kenya has two rainy seasons – the 'long rains' in March/April and the 'short rains' in October. At that time the rains were consistently late and unreliable. Clouds would build up, and tantalise us, and then as suddenly disperse. The people on Marsabit mountain would plant their maize and sorghum when the rain came, it would germinate, and then the rain would stop, and the young shoots shrivel up. It was heartbreaking. Drought inevitably led to two consequences – famine and severe water shortage. Cattle began to die, then camels, then people – beginning with the little children and the frail elderly. Within a few months of our arrival in Marsabit we became aware of the crisis that was brewing. Each day hungry women with their small children would gather around our house, begging, crying out, for food. 'Sagale na ken! Sagale na ken!' ('Give me food!') was the constant cry. We began to buy in sacks of dried milk powder and gave what we could, but it was never enough, and giving to some only drew more to the house, until we were inundated. We felt guilty about eating food ourselves. How could we sit down to a meal, however simple, when the house was surrounded by starving people, calling out and peering in at the windows?

By March 1974 Rosemary was feeding over one hundred women and children at the house each day. Dennis and Priscilla, at the High School, had begun to feed hungry people, buying in sacks of maize meal. Before long they were feeding three hundred people, and it was beginning to get on top of them. We did not want to end up in the same situation, and yet wanted to do something. For us the answer was simpler. We were well aware that many of those begging were completely genuine, but some were rogues, who begged for food and then sold it on at extortionate prices. We decided to centre all our famine relief at the hospital, and to give it on a more scientific basis – we would weigh children, and calculate the body mass index of adults, and also use skin-fold measurement, to identify those in greatest need.

At the hospital we were admitting an increasing number of patients suffering from severe malnutrition. Most of the malnutrition was marasmus (protein and calorie deficiency – in other words, starvation) as opposed to kwashiorkor (caused by deficiency of protein alone). One typical three-year-old boy we admitted weighed just six kilos. His parents and grandparents had died of starvation. He had forgotten how to laugh or cry – he just sat in his cot, like a shrivelled little old man, staring impassively with his big, round eyes. Over the weeks it was wonderful to see his wrinkled little body filling out, and a mischievous smile appearing on his face. He turned out to be a lovable rascal, who eventually went home to relatives. Our nutritionist and I visited one of the Marsabit Primary Schools, and examined all the children. Many were emaciated and anaemic, and some were suffering from pellagra, caused by vitamin B deficiency. The lucky ones were living on one cupful of maize porridge per day. Others depended on their parents' begging, and on some days went without any food at all. One little girl fainted while we were visiting the school. She had had nothing whatever to eat for twenty-four hours. We went on to a *manyatta* just outside Marsabit township. An old lady had died of starvation there a few days before, and two more old folks, a man and a woman, were sitting outside their grass huts, too weak to move. Babies in the village were obviously severely malnourished. Billows of red dust, blown up by gusts of hot, dry wind, swirled around the huts. The bare ground was littered with the skeletons of cattle and camels. We were indeed on the edge of a catastrophe.

I wrote a strongly worded memorandum to the District Commissioner, and also an urgent request to Oxfam for help. Somehow the media got wind of my report, and I had a radio call from a national newspaper, the Daily Nation. I spoke freely to the paper. Two days later I had a stern telegram from my boss, the Provincial Medical Officer, telling me that on no account was I to speak to the media again. Officially there was no famine. It was seen as a criticism of the Government to report that the rains had failed and that people were starving. I kept up the pressure on our local administrators. I discovered that five hundred bags of maize meal were sitting down country, awaiting transport to Marsabit, but nobody would accept responsibility to bring them. Meanwhile every Government lorry and Landrover in Marsabit (including our hospital Landrover) had been commandeered to carry a large delegation of people, and a gift of three thousand shillings, to President Kenyatta, at his home at Gatundu near Nairobi. The purpose of the delegation was not in order to put to the President the needs of Marsabit – rather it was to sing to him, and to make flattering speeches. Those vehicles could have transported all that maize, and the money would have provided famine relief for a month.

In March 1974 rain at last came, with thick, cold mist enveloping the mountain. As so often happens in famine situations, things initially got worse. Cattle, weakened by starvation, now began to die from the cold and pneumonia. In one week over one hundred and fifty cows died at Marsabit. The other frustration was that there was no seed available in Marsabit, for love or money, for planting. People had been forced to eat their stocks of maize seed. The agricultural officer had not had the foresight to keep seed for planting. The 'long rains', which should have lasted six weeks, in the event only lasted ten days. Now there was no prospect of rain until the next October. With the help of Enda Byrne, of Catholic Relief, a good supply of maize seed was donated, and lodged with the agricultural officer, in readiness for free distribution if and when the 'short rains' came. We did not want to be caught out again. Rain did come in October, people needed seed to plant – and the agricultural officer refused to release it. He had various reasons and excuses – the main one being that the seed was 'the wrong variety'. He found it difficult to explain why he had not mentioned this fact during the six months that he had had the seed in store. The Catholic priest and I offered to take the seed down country, and exchange it for the 'right' variety, but he would not release it to us either. In due course the real reason for his reluctance emerged – he had sold it, for personal gain, to contacts in Nairobi.

Water shortage was the other result of the prolonged drought. Marsabit township's water supply came from the springs at Barkuli, deep in the forest. It was pumped to the town. It was not a plentiful supply, and at times of drought the stream at Barkuli was reduced to a trickle. In colonial days it was recognised that the water supply was finite, and therefore strict rules applied to prevent the township growing above a certain size. People living outside the township drew their water from various wells and waterholes. During my childhood our water supply at Karantina was from rainwater tanks, filled from the roof of our house. They had to last us from one rainy season to the next. All that had changed. By the 1970s Marsabit township had grown to about four times its colonial size – from a population of three thousand to twelve thousand. There were new buildings everywhere, none of them with rainwater tanks. Whereas once everyone had used pit latrines, now many of the new houses had flush toilets, and baths instead of showers. The consumption of water by the population of Marsabit had increased enormously. And water became desperately short.

Yet the lesson had not been learned. I was astonished when a delegation from the Ministry of Water Development called at the hospital, not to discuss ways of increasing the water supply, but to discuss plans for a town-wide sewage system. I asked them incredulously, 'How can you have sewage without water? Give us enough water for people to drink, and cook, and even to wash, and then we can discuss water-borne sanitation.' There were occasions when even the hospital ran out of water, and many times when we were the only place in Marsabit to have it. An everyday sight in Marsabit was of crowds of people with kerosene tins and plastic containers waiting forlornly at standpipes, in case water might come.

I used to bang on tirelessly about famine and water at every opportunity – at the District Famine Relief Committee, which eventually got established, and at every Heads of Department meeting. My African colleagues must have thought me a very tiresome fellow. Maybe I should have said less, but I was the one who had to watch people, and children especially, die of hunger. One day we were told that the Assistant Minister for Water Development was coming on an official visit. All Heads of Department were to meet him. I relished the opportunity. I wrote a full and strongly worded memorandum to him, about Marsabit's water shortage, and the effect this was having on the health of the population. I was told that my memorandum could not be presented to him as it was, and that it would be 'incorporated' with the memoranda of other Heads of Department. I knew exactly what that meant. The Assistant Minister was going to be 'protected' from me, and I could do little about it. The morning of the meeting came. The Assistant Minister was staying at the tourist Lodge, and we all gathered at District Headquarters at 9 a.m. to await his arrival. The time came and went. No Minister. Then I was called out of the room. The Minister was ill at the Lodge, and needed a doctor. I drove in to the forest, to the Lodge, and found him still in bed, suffering from a severe attack of gout. I returned to the hospital to get the necessary medication, and took it to him. 'Come and sit on my bed,' he invited me 'while the medicine takes effect.' And so for the next hour and a half I had the Minister all to myself. While my fellow Heads of Department waited at District Headquarters, I sat on his bed and told him everything that had been in my memorandum, and more. He was appalled at how misinformed he had been. He had understood that the population of Marsabit was still three thousand, and all their planning was based on it not reaching twelve thousand for another twenty years. He asked me many questions, and took careful notes. By the time we arrived together at the meeting he knew most of what he wanted to know, and a lot that he had not expected to know. It was a God-given opportunity, and it was productive in that real thought began to be given to water supply and consumption in Marsabit. Thank God for gout!

Oxfam, as always, came up trumps with money for famine relief. The District Famine Relief Committee was all for buying with Oxfam money dried vegetables, and cooking oil, and fancy foods. I persuaded them not to – what we needed above all was milk powder for the children and elderly. We could supervise the drinking of milk, and make sure that it went into the right mouths. Any other kind of food that was distributed would have been wide open to abuse, and to sale on the black market. We continued to distribute milk at the hospital through a Nutrition Clinic, and it was allocated purely on clinical need. I was upset to hear that at the Roman Catholic Mission in Marsabit the Verona Fathers had said that if anyone wanted food they must come to church first. They got seven hundred to church the next Sunday.

I had another remonstration with authority when our Provincial Commissioner came on a flying visit to Marsabit. He had been twice before on lightning visits in which he took care not to meet me, or anyone who might want to talk about famine or water. I called each of these visits a 'Flying Evasion'. He was one of those most responsible for denying that we had a problem – his Province did not 'fail' by having famine. It was a head in the sand approach. On this occasion, however, we were told that all Heads of Department would meet him, and that we would (of course) give him a lunch party, and could we please donate twenty shillings each towards it. A lunch party, with local people dying around us! I donated twenty shillings instead to famine relief, and gave the lunch party a miss.

At every level it was difficult and frustrating to ensure that the really needy people got appropriate help. Throughout our time in Marsabit we had two domestic helpers in our home – Naomi, who helped Rosemary in the house, and kept the wood-burning Dover stove stoked, and did the ironing with a heavy iron filled with glowing charcoal; and Jarso, her brother, who helped in the garden. When crowds of people begging for food invaded the garden Naomi would help with translation. When milk distribution was moved down to the hospital, Rosemary continued to supply a small number of women and children with food. 'These,' Naomi assured her, 'were real *maskini* [very poor].' It was enlightening, therefore, when some time later we took a sack of maize meal to Naomi's house, as a gift for her family, to discover that the entire group of 'genuine *maskini*' were living at Naomi's – they were all, without exception, her relatives! We did quite a lot for Naomi and Jarso, but in return they gave us so much more in terms of generosity. She invited us to tea in her little mud house on two or three occasions. In honour of our visits she re-mudded the inside walls, decorating them with patterns in pigment, and put a fresh layer of cow dung on the floor. She got out her very best cups, and made mandasis for us (deep-fried doughnuts). We had African tea, 'chai' – tealeaves boiled with milk and sugar, and sprinkled with cinnamon. She and her poor relatives insisted on giving us of their precious belongings, such as gourds and a home-made knife. On our first Christmas we discovered that Jarso had given us his one remaining chicken. In their poverty their generosity was very moving.

The hospital Nutrition Clinic thrived, and in time we expanded its role to that of a health centre, with child health and immunisation, family planning, nursery school and 'Maendeleo wa Wanawake' (parentcraft and skills for mothers). Very much involved with this was our dear friend Mary Solomon, wife of my childhood friend Solomon Daudi. Mary was a Burji from Ethiopia, tall and elegant. She trained as a family worker, and was a perfect role model – her own family and home were shining examples of what could be. And her sincere Christian faith gave her a love for people, and a radiance that was so attractive. David Wiseman, a paediatrician working with Nairobi University, helped to set the health centre on its feet. By the time I left Marsabit over one hundred and fifty children a week were attending the centre, with their mothers. Over sixty severely malnourished children were receiving regular milk supplies. Oxfam, happy with what we had set up, provided financial support.

The problems of drought, famine and water shortage in a district like Marsabit are not short-term. They are ongoing and likely to get worse. (In 2006 the area suffered an even severer drought than that of the 1970s.) Crazy ideas about the long-term water supply of Marsabit were bandied about at our District Development meetings. It was suggested that water be piped across the desert from Lake Turkana, or even from the snow caps of Mount Kenya. It was only when I said that without adequate water soon the hospital would have to shut down, and my comments were reported in the press, that realism prevailed. The Director of Water Supplies and his consultant engineers were in Marsabit within a week. Alternative water sources, such as boreholes, and other springs on the mountain, were seriously looked at. But the fact remains – Marsabit, though forest-clad, is actually a very dry mountain. It is mists that maintain the forest. The burgeoning population has put enormous pressure, not only on the water supplies but also on the fragile forest and thus in turn on the wild life population. Not long before we left Marsabit I noted in my diary my gloomy prophecy for its future. I speculated that within a time-scale of fifty to a hundred years the following sequence would take place:

Steady erosion of the forest edge by encirclement of *shambas* (gardens), pole-cutting for building, etc., as the population increases and there is increasing pressure for land.

The man/animal conflict will therefore increase, with elephant migration routes blocked, increased raiding of *shambas* by elephants, and more being shot.

The Marsabit elephants will finally be killed off, followed by other game, until the forest no longer serves any purpose as a national park.

Continuing demographic pressure will lead to increased clearing of the forest for cultivation, until no significant forest is left.

The rainfall will decrease, and Marsabit mountain will eventually become like the Huri hills to the northwest – now barren and waterless, but once covered with thick forest.

So much for my gloomy predictions about the mountain. What about the rest of Marsabit District – the desert, semi-desert and lava plains? How can such a harsh district maintain an increasing population? Historically one thing alone has enabled people to eke out a living in this desert and semi-desert area – nomadism. It is due to the people constantly moving on, following the grazing, that the sparse vegetation has survived. Nowhere was over-grazed. The fragile ecology was preserved. The people respected the land, and did not abuse it. Much of that has changed. The Government now encourages people to settle. Nomadism is considered to be primitive and shameful. Police posts, and schools have been built near to permanent water supplies, such as boreholes or oases. Missions too have been part of the process, building permanent bases to which people are attracted. So slum-like settlements have sprung up. The people in such settlements inevitably keep goats. The goats live permanently in that place, and before long destroy every bit of vegetation within range of the settlement. So a mini-desert is created. The people then depend permanently on some sort of famine-relief. They become permanent *maskini*, the beggars of the desert. My prophecy for these areas was as follows:

The Government policy of settling nomadic desert people in centres where they can have schools, dispensaries, police protection, and be 'civilised' will have borne full fruition. Places such as Kargi, Maikona, Loglogo, Laisamis, Bubissa etc will have become settlements of *maskini* living in newly-created, goat-produced deserts, and depending entirely on hand-outs. The nomad, with his sophisticated way of life, utterly adapted to this hostile area, will be no more.

The Government will decide that it cannot feed the people in the man-made desert settlements for ever, so will move them to Marsabit, to become agriculturalists – thus further opening up the now redundant forest on Marsabit, patch by patch, for clearance for *shambas*.

Marsabit, having followed the way of the Huri Hills, will be deserted.

My pessimism has been shown to be excessive by the passage of time. But perhaps it was only the time-scale that was wrong. We now have the added factor of global warming, and the steady southward advance of the Sahara. Africa is getting drier. And the population of Kenya is exploding – one of the fastest growing in the world. Can arid areas like Marsabit District continue to support a population?

I had my pet solution to the problem, which I occasionally dared to mention at District Development Committee meetings. I suggested a return to a form of 'organised nomadism'. My proposition was to sink boreholes all over the District, to ensure clean water supplies. Then to shut most of them down, and only to open them when rain had fallen in that area, and there was grazing for the livestock. The people would then be encouraged to move with the grazing, as they traditionally have done, but wherever they went they would have clean water within reach. Then came the crunch. With them would move travelling police, dispensers and teachers – 'barefoot' workers from their own tribes, willing to move with them. The people would have the advantages of security and education and treatment, but without destroying the finely balanced ecology. Whenever I dared to suggest my proposed solution at a meeting, my ideas were met with incredulity. I could almost read the thoughts of my African colleagues – 'He just wants to take us back to the dark ages!' They were very patient with me, and, in true African style, tolerant and forgiving.

Something we all did during those days of drought was to pray regularly for rain. Sometimes I rather gave up, but Andrew and Paul never forgot, in their bedtime prayers. On one occasion, after a long, very dry spell, we had a sudden and unexpected downpour. The rained teemed onto the thirsty ground. Huge drops thudded into the dust. It drummed on the tin roof of our house, so that we could hardly hear one another speak. Water poured down the gutters. Rivulets turned to streams, and the garden became a lake. We rushed out to watch it, and stand in it, and celebrate it. Suddenly I realised that eight year old Andrew was missing. We found him in his bedroom, on his knees, thanking God for the rain. It took a child to remind us, not just to ask, but to say 'Thank You' to God.

Chapter 31
THE CHURCH IN MARSABIT

St Peter's Anglican Church in Marsabit is a very simple affair – just a long cement-block building, with corrugated iron roof, furnished with benches, and with a small vestry attached. It stands at the foot of a dusty hillock on the edge of the town. Prior to independence the Kenya Colonial Government kept a tight control over the activities of missionaries, especially in the Northern Frontier area. My father had set up the Anglican mission at Marsabit in 1931, but no other denominations were allowed to work in the area. On the eve of Independence Day, in 1962, the Roman Catholic bishop is said to have been waiting at Isiolo, at the entrance to the Northern Frontier, and the moment independence was declared he set off for Marsabit, to establish a Catholic Mission. There are now Catholic missions dotted throughout the area. During our time in Marsabit a Pentecostal Church opened in Marsabit. The Africa Inland Mission and Church, have work scattered throughout the area, but had not build a church in Marsabit itself out of consideration for the Anglican Church already there. This fragmentation of the church is, as always, sad, and a poor witness to the Muslim population – but they too are divided into sects.

When my father left Marsabit in 1956, to take up work as Kenya's Senior Prison Chaplain, he was initially replaced by the Reverend Bernard Brown, but the Reverend Stephen Houghton (and later his wife Eve) soon followed – all BCMS missionaries. Stephen had been born of missionary parents in China, and had, as a boy, been interned for a while by the Japanese. He was in the same prison camp as Eric Lidell, of 'Chariots of Fire' fame. Stephen was a linguist, and following his arrival in Marsabit he very quickly learned the Boran language. My father examined him on behalf of the Mission, and he passed with distinction. Stephen's main aims and achievements (apart from preaching the Gospel and building up the Church) were to complete and revise the translation, which my father had begun, of the New Testament into Borana; and to train up African leadership in the Church, so that it was not dependent on expatriate missionaries. This policy has been the strength of the Anglican Church throughout East Africa. During my father's time the first ordination of a local Christian had taken place – that of the Reverend Petro Oce, one of the very first converts to Christianity. Petro was sincere, and devoted to his ministry. I can picture him now, at the beginning of a service, standing at the front of church, head tilted back, peering over his glasses at the congregation, to see who was and was not there. He resembled a senior camel reviewing his herd. By the 1970s he was old and frail, and died in our hospital in 1975. I had known Petro and his wife Ruth all my life, and his death was the end of an era, and the end of a link with my parents. I took Petro's body back to his home from the hospital. Ruth insisted on coming with us in the Landcruiser. All the way she kept up a song of lament in Boran – 'My loved one is gone! What shall I do? My eyes are gone! How shall I see? My hands are gone! What shall I do?' It was a broken-hearted song, and very moving.

Meanwhile a young Gabbra Christian, Andrew Adano, was showing great promise as an evangelist. Stephen Houghton encouraged him, and he trained for the ministry, and was ordained in 1974. Following Stephen's untimely death from cancer some years later, Andrew became Vicar of Marsabit, and then Bishop – the first Anglican Bishop of Marsabit. He showed great leadership, and there were high hopes for the future. However it was not to be – Andrew was tragically killed, along with a number of Government ministers, in a helicopter crash on Marsabit Mountain. The question of sabotage arose, but the final verdict was mechanical failure. (As previously mentioned, Andrew's successor, Bishop Waqo, also a local man and a person of great promise, was likewise killed in a plane crash on Marsabit Mountain in 2006. On that occasion it was Marsabit's notorious mist and poor visibility that was to blame.)

On most Sundays St Peter's Church was full for its two services, Swahili and Borana. The custom in the Boran service was for the women and children to sit on one side of the church, the men on the other. On special occasions, such as Christmas, Easter and Harvest, the congregation would number well over a thousand, and the services would last for two hours or more. Christmas was traditionally celebrated with a feast, to which all were welcome. Two oxen would be killed and roasted outside the church. I discovered that, in my role as MOH, it fell to me to inspect the carcasses, and declare if they were free from parasites, and fit to eat. One Christmas I went along at the appointed hour to carry out my inspection. One ox had already been killed and was being skinned. The other, however, was still very much alive, and had obviously decided that it did not wish to be part of the Christmas celebrations. It broke free, and careered round the church compound, chased by Stephen Houghton, the church evangelists and others. One man got hold of its tail and was pulled along at high speed. Then the ox shot out of the compound, and down the road towards the market and the mosque, an evangelist still clinging desperately to its tail, and the others in full pursuit. I did not have the heart to wait to watch its final capture and execution.

None of the local tribes is particularly musical. The hymns sung at the Boran service were the old Moody and Sankey hymns translated by my parents back in the 1930s and '40s. They were sung with more gusto than harmony. The Swahili service, attended by many from down country, and representing some very musical tribes, was a different matter. There was a choir which sang with that beautiful, spontaneous close harmony for which African choirs are famed. They sang with heart and soul, sometimes acting out the words. The prisoners in Marsabit Prison ('Hoteli ya King George') also had a choir of sorts, which occasionally sang in services. They filed through the town to church. There was little fear of any escaping – after all, who would want to run away from free board and lodging? The simplest of instruments accompanied their singing – the tapping of a soft drink bottle with a bottle top, or the rattling of a gourd containing dried beans.

Harvest Festival services were tricky during those years of drought. How do you celebrate a harvest that has failed? Yet the Christians were so generous with what little they had. There might be a few sad-looking vegetables, or maize cobs, or pawpaws, or the odd scrawny chicken. Mainly those who could gave money for famine relief. I vividly recall one Harvest service at that time. Those who had any produce or money to offer were asked to bring it forward and place it on the Communion table. People filed up to offer their gifts. Then an old Boran woman, who had been sitting near the back of church, got up. She was wizened and stick-thin, and was wearing a very dirty and tattered robe. She appeared to have nothing to offer in her claw-like hands. But she shuffled forwards in her bare feet, and when she reached the table she lifted the corner of her robe, and began to undo a knot. There, carefully secured in the cloth, was one egg. She gently removed it and placed it on the table – her offering to those even less well off than herself. I guess it was her only egg. She shuffled back to her bench. It made whatever we gave seem so paltry in comparison. She, like other African Christians, gave her all.

The busyness of medical work made it difficult to spend much time with Stephen Houghton, but we went together on one or two combined medical/evangelistic safaris. One such trip was to Kalacha, the oasis on the Chalbe desert between Maikona and North Horr. Six of us, plus boxes of food and medicine, set off down Marsabit Mountain in our Land Cruiser. As well as Stephen there were two evangelists (Galgalo Shonka and Daniel Huqa) on board, together with Steve Richardson (medical student) and a Catholic catechist hitching a lift back to Maikona. As we slowly wound our way down the rock-strewn road, towards the Chalbe Desert, we passed a group of Rendille tribesmen, armed with spears. A few miles on and we met a lone Boran man, walking towards Marsabit. We stopped and he told us that he had walked from Ethiopia, and was on his way to Marsabit to find work. We assured him that there was little likelihood of work in Marsabit, but that there was a group of Rendille ahead who would very likely spear him. We gave him a drink, and persuaded him to cram in with us and have a lift back to Maikona.

The sparse thorn bush of Marsabit's lower slopes got even sparser as we neared the foot of the mountain, and the desert. The heat was intense. Then, in the midst of the black rocky wilderness the shiny tin roofs of Maikona appeared, like small ships lost in a vast sea of lava. We called at the Catholic Mission, to drop off the catechist, and to see if Sister Serafina had any medical needs. In fact she was about to send a very ill lad up to Marsabit. He had amoebic dysentery, and I was able to leave treatment for him. Soon we were speeding across the salt-encrusted sand flats of the Chalbe, a billowing cloud of dust in our wake. Constantly ahead of us, filling the featureless landscape, was a vast lake of water – or, at least, a mirage of one. From time to time we passed camels, whose outlines were distorted by the heat haze, so that they appeared to have very long legs and to be walking on water. The tiniest bush took on the proportions of a tree. At last palm trees that were not a mirage appeared in the distant haze, and soon we were winding our way through the doum palm groves and pools of Kalacha. An evangelist, Andrew Haro, was already based at Kalacha, and he was delighted to see us. We bedded down that night in a small tin hut, the hot desert wind howling around it and rattling the corrugated iron walls.

The next day began with a service to which about forty people came. Daniel Huqa spoke about the Boran man we had met the day before – in a strange land, without food or water, and with enemies ahead. He compared his situation to that of the person travelling through life without Christ. I held a clinic, saw about sixty patients, and extracted a tooth. Then we trekked to a *manyatta* six miles away. There were only women in the village when we arrived, and they gave us a very suspicious reception. Soon the men of the village returned, and they were verging on hostile. The chief made it clear that theirs was a 'Hayana' village – a sect in the Gabbra tribe which believes in, and worships, evil spirits. Galgalo and Daniel asked if they could talk about Jesus Christ, who has power over evil spirits. The chief shrugged, as he went into his hut, and said, 'You can talk as much as you like, but nobody will listen!' So they did talk, and it was clear that the people of this village had never heard the Christian Gospel before. Gradually the village folk, men and women, did listen, and finally the chief emerged and made tea for us all. They said they would like to hear more about Jesus, and agreed for Andrew Haro to follow up our visit. So back to our tin hut in Kalacha. After the heat and dust of the day it was wonderful to plunge into the clear but somewhat camel-smelling water of one of the oasis pools. Then a meal of roast sheep and maize cobs, as we sat under the breathtakingly beautiful night sky.

Another clinic the next morning, then we set off back for Marsabit. As we passed one of the most polluted and offensive-smelling pools of the oasis, Galgalo Shonka asked me to stop the car as he wanted to fill a bottle with water. 'Why this water?' I asked. 'It is a very good medicine, a strong purgative!' he said. From the smell of the water I believed him.

His medicinal needs were not quite satisfied. Once we got out onto the desert we had to stop again to fill two sacks with salt crust from the desert surface. This time it was for his cows. And so the long, slow drive back up the rough mountain track began, with zebra, Grant's gazelle, giraffe and ostrich to add interest to the tedium.

It was a privilege to work closely with my fellow Anglicans, as on the Kalacha safari. I also cooperated, as MOH, with the AIM and Catholic missionaries working in the district. We were personally on very friendly terms with a number of the AIM folk. The one denominational group that I did find a little trying were the Pentecostals. A group of American Pentecostal missionaries built and opened a church in Marsabit during our time there. They did so without any reference to those Christians already working in Marsabit, and clearly regarded any version of Christianity other than their own as invalid. It was the visit of Margaret that really irritated me. Margaret was an eighteen-year-old Kikuyu girl from near Nairobi. She was said to have miraculously healed her grandmother, and the media got hold of the story. So did a group of American Pentecostals, who took Margaret under their wing, proclaimed her to have the gift of healing, and started to fly her around Kenya, holding Healing Services, at which miracles were to be expected. They arranged to fly her to Marsabit, and to hold a mass rally on the football field. I planned to go, more out of curiosity than anything. But Robbie Gurney was away from Moyale at the time, and on the evening of the Healing rally I was called up to Moyale to do an emergency operation. I was away for two days, and missed Margaret's visit, though I heard all about it, and witnessed the aftermath. A large crowd had attended, including many Muslims. There was a lot of hype, with loud music, shouting, exhorting and Hallelujahs. At that time Marsabit had a high incidence of poliomyelitis. There were many people with withered, paralysed limbs from childhood polio. Some could only crawl around on hands and knees. Others hobbled with the aid of home-made sticks. One of our medical priorities was to get such people fitted with appropriate callipers, boots, crutches etc, to give them a measure of mobility, independence and self-esteem. It was a slow process. The Flying Doctors would bring a physiotherapist who assessed and measured patients. On her next trip from Nairobi she would bring with her the callipers and crutches for trial fittings. She might have to take them back for modification. Finally, perhaps after several months, patients had their aids fitted, and then had to be taught how to walk with them. A huge amount of time, effort and expense had gone into helping each individual.

At Margaret's rally the cry, once she had laid hands on people, was, 'You are healed! God has done a miracle! Now throw away your callipers and crutches! You won't need them any more!' And in the heat and emotion of the moment many did just that. And, as they rode on the crest of a tide of elation, and the adrenaline flowed, they found they could walk (or hobble) a few steps. Meanwhile the local blacksmiths were moving amongst the crowd, gathering up any discarded metal, and it was not seen again – at least, not in the shape it had been. During the following days a steady stream of embarrassed and disillusioned patients crawled back to the hospital, wanting to be re-fitted with callipers, crutches etc, and the whole long process had to begin again. One man, with no history whatever of mental illness, was brought to the hospital by the police. He was shouting, gesticulating violently, and telling all and sundry that he had been 'saved' at Margaret's meeting. He said that he wanted to marry a girl in place of his wife, and that he was not mad, but simply suffering from Love. 'Love! Love!' he roared, sniffing deeply at a Vick inhaler (which, he informed me, helps love). I gave him some 'love pills' (a sedative), and he had to be sectioned and sent down-country to a mental hospital. The Muslim community laughed at the whole charade.

Meanwhile the patient at Moyale to whom I had been called had made a remarkable recovery. She had had a severe ante-partum haemorrhage. By the time I had made the gruelling four hour drive to Moyale her blood pressure was unrecordable. She had a severe degree of placenta praevia. We could only get three pints of compatible blood off relatives, and she was losing blood faster than we could run it in. Reluctantly I had to operate on her as she was, in a very shocked state. Amazingly she survived the operation, and the following morning was already gathering strength. That, to me, was the real miracle of that weekend. So too were the people who were, once again, lovingly and painstakingly measured for new callipers and crutches, to restore to them the dignity which had been taken from them.

Chapter 32
THE MIRACLE ROCKS

From time to time we made the long journey down country – on school runs, or for supplies, or on holiday. Those journeys were often spiced with incident. Half way between Isiolo and Marsabit was the (usually dry) Merrille riverbed. It marked the southern boundary of my District. When returning to Marsabit the Merrille bridge reminded us that we still had eighty-five back-breaking miles to go, including the crossing of the Kaisut Desert. It was at Merrille bridge that we had camped with June, following her aborted visit to Amudat. About a mile south of the Merrille bridge lies a long outcrop of rocks, running parallel to the road. We called them the Miracle Rocks of Merrille, and whenever we passed them my mind went back to 1949.

It was the Easter holidays. I was aged seven and Dennis nine. Our father, with a helper, Galgalo Bilala, had come to collect us from Nairobi Primary School, and we were driving home to Marsabit – where our mother was waiting for us. We were in our ex-army Dodge station wagon. Even before we reached Isiolo, the gateway to the Northern Frontier District, we had had two punctures. With the second Eric had to repair it at the roadside. The puncture repair outfit, with its patches and rubber solution, was nearly finished, so in Isiolo he bought another repair kit in one of the corrugated iron *dukas*. We signed the book at the barrier, and entered the NFD. About thirty miles on we had yet another puncture – or rather it was the previous patch coming off. While repairing it again our four gallon emergency jerry can of water was accidentally knocked over, and the water spilled. We continued our journey, but a few miles short of Merrille the tyre yet again went flat. Eric opened the new repair kit – and discovered that the rubber solution was solid. It must have been on the shelf in the hot *duka* in Isiolo for ages, and had perished. We had no way of repairing the puncture, nor did we have any water. We were in the middle of scorching, arid bush country. We knew of no water supply in the area. The Merrille riverbed, five miles ahead, was at that time of the year just dry sand. We tried packing the tyre with bushes, cramming them in as tightly as possible. On releasing the jack the bushes just crumbled to dust. We were hot, sweating, dirty, and there was not a trace of shade anywhere.

Eric decided to try to drive on, with the flat tyre, to Merrille river bed. At least there we would have shade, under the doum palms, and there was a chance of finding water by digging in the sandy riverbed. But as we drove the stony road began to slice the flat tyre into shreds. Sparks flew from the metal wheel rim. There were ominous grinding sounds. We were wrecking the car. We came to a full stop alongside the ridge of rocks mentioned above. The outcrop was about half a mile long and thirty feet high with just one spreading thorn tree at the base of the rocks. We decided to stay there. Eric recalled that someone had once told him that water could occasionally be found in holes in these rocks. Dennis and I immediately set off to explore. The heat was intense, reflected off the black, flaking rock surface. We climbed to the top – and there, in a hollow, about three feet in diameter and one foot deep, was a pool of water. It was the last thing we would have expected to find. The water was green, and had larvae of some kind swimming around in it – but it was water. We raced down the rocks, shouting 'Water! Water!' Eric and Galgalo came up to see for themselves. We had food in plenty in the car – our supplies for Marsabit. Now we had water too. We were safe. That water kept us supplied until we were rescued. Many times since I have checked that same hole in the rocks. It is still there. But never again have we found water in it. A freak rainstorm must have filled it for us in 1949. That night, as we sat around our campfire under the thorn tree, and sipped our rather oddly flavoured tea, we thanked God for that pool.

Vehicles on the Marsabit road were few and far between in 1949. We knew that we might have a long wait. But we also knew that Ruby, in Marsabit, would be worrying as to what had happened to us. Several times a day we would climb to the top of the rocks and look for any telltale dust clouds, which might herald the coming of a vehicle. But nothing came. Dennis and I occupied ourselves by concocting a paint, out of a mixture of car oil and ash. We painted our names, 'D. AND D. WEBSTER', in four feet high letters on the rock face. We lit fires in the crevices in the rock, causing it to split with satisfying bangs. We watched for hours a colony of rock hyraxes, who disported themselves in the nooks and the crannies. In the heat of the day we dozed in the thin shade of our thorn tree. An elephant browsed a few hundred yards away, apparently disinterested in our plight. Before settling down for the night we would once again climb the rocks to look out for any approaching vehicle lights. We were sitting around the campfire one night when from the surrounding darkness there came a sudden, loud snort. I made a spectacular dive into the car. A large animal thundered off into the night. Morning revealed the footprints of a rhino, very close to our camp.

On the evening of the fourth day we made our ascent of the rocks – and saw, far away to the north, the dust of a vehicle, heading in our direction. Dennis and I scrambled down the rocks, shouting 'A rescue! A rescue!' It was probably an hour before the vehicle arrived – a lorry from Marsabit. The driver had been alerted by Ruby to look out for us, and he had on board a basket of fruit and other food. She had also sent an assortment of tyres and inner tubes from the mission store – in case that was our problem. Unfortunately none was the right size. The driver promised to send a telegram to Ruby from Isiolo, to tell her where we were, and what our problem was. He would also alert our Pathan trader friend, Mr Khan, in Isiolo. In due course the lorry left, and we settled down for another night and day. It was late in the evening of the next day, our fifth, when we saw a moving column of dust, far to the south, coming from Isiolo. It moved very slowly indeed, which led us to think that it might be the lorry of Khan, noted for his extremely careful driving. Three hours later, after sunset, he arrived. It was indeed Khan. He was ill, with an acute attack of malaria, but on hearing of our dilemma from the previous lorry he had immediately risen from his sick bed, found spare tyres and tubes of the right size for our Dodge, and set out. It underlined to us the kind and generous nature of this gentleman. Soon after Khan arrived from the south, a convoy of no less than six police lorries arrived from the north. They were on their way from Moyale, on the Ethiopian border, and had by-passed Marsabit. They had not heard that we were missing. Our lonely campsite rapidly turned into a busy picnic site. There were now eight vehicles. Men spilled out of the lorries, lit fires, and started to brew tea and to cook injira pancakes. There were murmurs of conversation, and bursts of laughter, as the flames from the campfires flickered on the faces of our new-found companions. It was a homely scene. Life had been transformed.

Khan helped to fit the new tyre, supplied a new puncture repair kit, and saw us on our way. It was by now late at night, as we resumed our long delayed journey home. But our adventures were not quite over. We soon had yet another puncture, and successfully repaired it. We stopped on the edge of the Kaisut Desert for Eric to have a nap, as he found himself falling asleep at the wheel. While he slept a hyena circled the car, snuffling at the tyres, but fortunately did not chew them. We arrived at Marsabit in the early hours of Easter morning. A welcoming pressure lamp was glowing in the window of our home – Ruby had had one there every night since we went missing. The house was, as always, unlocked and she was asleep. We crept in, and gently woke her. We were home from school. We were safe. It was not long before the Dover stove was stoked with blazing wood, and the kettle was boiling. We gathered round the pressure lamp with our cups of tea, excitedly recounting all that had happened. As we did so Easter Day dawned.

The Merrille rocks featured also in the lives of Dr Graham and Jan Fraser (who had stayed with us in Amudat shortly before Graham's tragic death in a car crash). In the mid-1960s, before they moved to Kapenguria, Graham was the BCMS doctor seconded to Marsabit Hospital. It was at a time when *shifta* were particularly active in northern Kenya – pursuing Somalia's claim to northeast Kenya. They mounted regular attacks on vehicles travelling between Marsabit and Isiolo, which therefore had to move in convoy. They had recently ambushed and murdered the District Commissioner of Isiolo, David Dabassso Wabera (a former pupil of my mother). Jan Fraser was expecting their first baby, and needed to travel to Nairobi for an antenatal check, but Graham and she had to wait until a convoy was organised from Marsabit. The day arrived, and a convoy of about twenty vehicles, several of them containing armed police, set out for Isiolo. Graham and Janet were travelling in the Marsabit hospital Landrover. About a mile short of the Merrille rocks Graham's Landrover hit a boulder. It cracked the sump. The whole convoy had to stop while the damage was inspected. It was decided that they could not proceed, but must all turn around and return to Marsabit. No part of the convoy was allowed to proceed alone. All the vehicles turned and started to retrace the eighty miles they had come. A few days later, after repairs, they set out again, and had an uneventful journey. No more was thought of the sump incident until several months later, when a Somali bandit was captured. During interrogation he asked, 'How did you know about us, that time at Merrille?' 'Know what?' 'Know about our ambush.' It turned out that on that day of the broken sump the *shifta* had laid an ambush along the length of the Merrille rocks. They had mined the road, and would have shot up the column with guns placed in the rocky ridge. But when they saw the convoy stop, just a mile short of their position, and then turn round and return to Marsabit, they thought that their ambush had been detected. They quickly dug up their mines and disappeared with their weapons into the bush. Graham and Janet felt they had experienced a miracle at Merrille rocks.

And so we return to 1974. Rosemary and I, with the three children, were on our way back to Marsabit from a trip down country. It was the middle of the day, and the heat beat down mercilessly on our Landcruiser. There was a shimmering haze over the parched landscape. If we opened the windows of the vehicle to catch a breeze we were smothered in dust. If we shut them we baked. Our teeth vibrated with the corrugations. We were passing Merrille rocks, and feeling glad to be nearly half way from Isiolo to Marsabit, when in the heat haze ahead I saw what appeared to be a body lying in the road. Although *shifta* activity was not nearly as bad as it had been, and travel by convoy was no longer required, yet still ambushes occurred. One way of getting vehicles to stop was with a 'body' in the road. I was worried, and had to make a quick decision as to what to do. Then, in the shimmering heat, I saw that there were people standing openly at the side of the road, waving us down. We drew to a juddering stop. The body in the road was that of a young Rendille boy who was unconscious, frothing at the mouth, and convulsing. He was very hot. His parents said that their village was in the bush about a mile away, and that he had become ill just two hours before. They had brought him to the road in the hope of a vehicle to take him to Marsabit, but he was getting worse by the minute. Clearly the boy had cerebral malaria, and was dying fast. There was no possibility that he would have survived a further wait, or the journey to hospital. But it so happened that we had come along almost immediately, that I was a doctor, and that I had with me all that was necessary to treat cerebral malaria – intravenous chloroquine and hydrocortisone. I injected him there and then at the roadside, and we squeezed him into the Landcruiser, on top of the luggage. Before we had proceeded many miles he had stopped fitting, had regained consciousness, and by the time we reached hospital was very much better. Over the years God seemed to have a way of timing things at Merrille – the Miracle Rocks.

Chapter 33
MOUNTAIN AND LAKE

My brother Dennis and Priscilla and family originally went out to Kenya with the Church Missionary Society to a government post at Thika High School, north of Nairobi, where Dennis was school chaplain. They renewed contact with our childhood friend, Luka Galgalo, who was at the time an administrative officer south of mount Kenya. They came to an arrangement whereby Luka's son, John, and his daughter, Anne, went to live with Dennis and Priscilla, so that they could attend nearby Imani School, along with their own children, Timothy and Peter, as day pupils. Dennis also renewed contact with other childhood friends from Marsabit, who were now in positions of influence in Kenya. Elisha Godana was a cabinet minister in the Government. Solomon Daudi worked for the Teacher Services Commission in Nairobi. These friends all had vested interests in Marsabit, and wanted the best for Marsabit Secondary School, which had difficulty retaining teachers because of its remoteness. Luka approached Dennis, and asked him if he would consider a move from Thika to Marsabit, to teach at the Secondary School. Dennis was delighted to apply for the move, and CMS and the Kenya Ministry of Education were agreeable. For Dennis, as for me, it would be a going home, a logical full circle. For Priscilla too it would be a return to the place of her early childhood. For them, as for us, it seemed so right.

As already noted, by the time we moved to Marsabit in 1973 Dennis and Priscilla were established there at the Secondary School, on the slopes of a hill on the outskirts of the township. Drought and famine were, by then, taking their toll. Dennis and Priscilla came under great pressure from the sheer numbers of hungry people begging for food at their house on the school compound – they were supplying maize meal to about three hundred people twice a week. But in spite of that they were enjoying being back in Marsabit, were busily involved in school life, and Dennis was able to help with services at St Peter's Church.

Unfortunately a visit to the school from a top level team of government officials resulted in the school Head being transferred, and Dennis was, without prior consultation, appointed as Headmaster in his place. This post brought with it a load of problems and administrative responsibilities. The pressures on Dennis, and the tensions, and the political wheelings and dealings, were enormous. All that would have been challenging enough, without drought and famine in addition. Water, such a basic requirement for a boarding school, was increasingly unavailable. The school taps often ran dry. It was not just a case of no water for washing – there was on occasion none with which to make tea for the boys, or to cook their meals. Dennis could have left the boys to go off and find water for themselves, and lose time from school, but he felt a responsibility as Head to provide it for them. He travelled to a well a few miles away, his Volkswagon Kombi laden with water drums, to fetch water for the students' next meal.

Examinations brought yet more pressure. The day before School Certificate exams were due to start the papers had not arrived in Marsabit. An overnight trip by Dennis to Isiolo and back to collect them was necessary – three hundred and fifty exhausting miles, to enable the boys to sit down to their first paper the next morning. On an earlier occasion, when the Biology Practical paper was received shortly before the exam, it became clear that tadpoles would be needed. Tadpoles in Marsabit! Another Head would perhaps not have bothered, and would have told his students to miss that question, and lose marks. But not Dennis. He lent his car to the Biology teacher, who drove all the way to Mount Kenya and back, a return journey of four hundred and fifty miles, to search for and collect tadpoles from a river there. Dennis's car was abandoned in Isiolo after a breakdown, and it took him weeks to retrieve it. But he was determined that his pupils would have the chance to do their best. They needed to, because tertiary education in Kenya, and worthwhile jobs, were so very competitive. All these factors added greatly to Dennis's stress, and his efforts were not always appreciated by the pupils and other staff. Throughout 1974 the pressures on Dennis mounted, and we could see the toll that this was taking on his health. In January 1975 I had to sign him off work. He and Priscilla spent time recuperating at a farm at Solai, near Nakuru, and then returned to England to a school chaplaincy.

Dennis had done a wonderful job as Head, and nobody could have cared more for his school than he did. On a personal level we missed their presence in Marsabit so much. It had been a very special time being back there together.

While Dennis was convalescing at Solai, Rosemary and I fulfilled one of my lifetime ambitions – to climb Mount Kenya. I had driven round its base so many times during my life, and had looked up at its glacial peaks. Now, at last, I determined to climb it. One special factor had to be taken into consideration – Rosemary was pregnant. We arranged to meet up with John and Gill Malcolm, and other friends, to form a climbing party. Dennis and Priscilla would meanwhile look after Stephen at Solai, where he and his cousin John (born during their days in Thika) would no doubt enjoy one another's company. So it was that in February 1975 a group of us set off from the meteorological station on Mount Kenya. Climbing from the end of the vehicle track, at ten thousand feet, we made our way up through dense forest. Already, as we had driven up the track in the Landcruiser, we had passed buffalo, and we knew that elephant were also prevalent. We kept our eyes skinned. Gradually the beautiful indigenous forest gave way to thickets of bamboo, which arched above us and shut out the light. We followed a tortuous pathway between the impenetrable yellow-green clumps. The air was getting noticeably colder. Upwards we trudged, emerging quite suddenly from the bamboo belt on to moorland. Tufts of coarse grass were interspersed with wild gladioli and giant lobelias. We had reached the notorious 'vertical bog'. Fortunately the weather had been dry, and the going was steep but not too slippery.

An hour's steady climbing brought us to the Teleki Valley, named after the mountain's first explorer. Now the vista unfolded. The wide valley, its slopes scattered with candelabra trees, swept up to a massive scree slope at the foot of the Lewis glacier. Above the glacier, and to one side of it, rose the sheer snow-capped twin peaks of Batian and Nelion, over seventeen thousand feet high. To the other side was the lesser peak, Lenana, at over sixteen thousand feet, which was to be our final destination next day. As we made our way up the Teleki Valley we passed wild flowers in profusion, and fascinating and fearless rock hyraxes, which emerged from their holes in the ground to take sweets from our hands. We camped that night at a permanent tented site, Mackinder's camp, at fourteen thousand feet. The glaciers, glistening in the evening light, towered above us. An icy stream burbled its way past the camp. The air was cold and crisp, and once the sun set the temperature plummeted. That night we snuggled close. Though I was wearing two vests, a thick shirt, three sweaters, an anorak, three pairs of trousers and a balaclava, all inside a sleeping bag, I still shivered. A bitter wind howled down from the glaciers, and shook our tent.

We were up and off at 4 a.m., having broken the ice in the stream to wet our faces. Rosemary felt sick, and in view of her pregnancy we decided it would be wise for her to stay at camp. Up the steep scree slope the rest of us trudged, by the light of torches. It was very heavy going, and we could feel the effect of the altitude. As we neared the top of the slope the tips of the mountain peaks began to light up with a delicate pink glow, which spread down to the glacier at their base. Soon the whole mountain top was aglow with the reflection of the huge orange orb of the rising sun. Its rays spread down the mountainside, lighting in turn the Teleki valley, the forested slopes, and finally the plains and desert below. It was a breathtaking sight. We pressed on up the side of the Lewis glacier, sometimes walking on the ice, sometimes on rock. At one point two of us ventured on to the glacier, to investigate an ice grotto – bathed in blue light and festooned with icicles. It was hard to believe that we were almost exactly on the Equator. Finally we reached our goal, Lenana. Our hands were frozen stiff, but our hearts glowing with satisfaction. As we looked down on the vista below we could clearly see the curve of the earth's surface. From our frozen height we were looking down on to scorching desert, and, far away to the north, Marsabit mountain. We were in another world.

The descent was many times faster than the climb. I came down the long scree slope with an exhilarating scree run. As I approached the campsite Rosemary was sitting outside our tent scanning the Lewis glacier with the binoculars, trying to spot me, and to see how near to the top I might be. She was astonished to find me standing in front of her. That night, as we all sat around a roaring log fire at our base camp, sharing our feelings and experiences, we felt not so much a sense of pride (after all, it was no great achievement) but rather a sense of privilege that we had been able to experience this other face of Kenya – such a beautiful country, and so full of contrast.

The Mount Kenya climb was not the only adventure of that pregnancy. We also made a journey by road from Marsabit to Lake Turkana. John and Gill Malcolm, and John and Libby Wattis (who were now at Amudat) joined with us in the expedition. We debated as to whether it was wise for Rosemary, in her pregnant state, to make such a rough journey to so remote a part. But we realised that, if she were to stay in Marsabit, she would have little medical cover, whereas if she came she would have three doctors and two nurses to care for her. She came! We stopped at the Catholic Mission at Maikona, for me to see patients, then sped across the flat Chalbi desert to the oasis of Kalacha. We camped under the palms at one of the pools of the oasis. Our peace was shattered next morning by the arrival, across the desert, of a stampeding herd of camels, eager to get to the water. Their arrival was heralded by a rapidly approaching cloud of dust, and the growing thunder of hundreds of hooves, followed by a cacophony of bellows and roars of protest as the camels jostled for position at the water's edge.

We continued across the desert to North Horr, where again I saw patients at the dispensary, and the children romped on a large sand dune. The 'road' from North Horr to the lake was not really worthy of that name. It was a deeply rutted track which in places became a deep dust bowl. Our vehicles lurched from side to side in an enveloping cloud of dust. Eventually we came over a rise in the land and there below us stretching as far as we could see from north to south lay the waters of Lake Turkana. The road down to the lakeside can only be described as a staircase, and a steep and rough one at that. We eased our four-wheel drive vehicles down the rocks. The baby nestling inside Rosemary must have wondered where it was going.

Our plan was to camp on the lakeshore, then I would drive in to Loiyengalani the next day to check out the dispensary. The shore was very rocky, but we found an area of relatively flat smooth sand, in a slight hollow. We pitched our tents, lit a camp fire, and sat back to admire the sunset across the lake. Jarso, who had come with us, and who had never seen a lake before, stood speechless on the shore, astonished at the sheer quantity of water. An enormous anvil cloud filled the evening sky. That night we were woken by the sound of thunder, rumbling across the lake. Then flashes of lightning lit up the sky. Heavy drops of rain began to fall. ('You told us it never rains at Lake Turkana!' protested John Malcolm, who had come to escape from a long spell of miserable wet weather in Nakuru. This was, in fact, the first rain at Lake Turkana for eight years.) By the next morning our sandy hollow had turned into something of a mud bath. We were not too worried, as we were confident that the heat of the day would soon dry everything out. With some slipping and sliding, and with the aid of four wheel drive and low ratio, we made the journey in to Loiyengalani and back.

During the second night thunder and lightning returned, but even more so. Rain drummed relentlessly on the tents. We became aware that items in the tent were beginning to float and water lapped around our camp beds. We huddled, miserable and cold, waiting for dawn. Daylight revealed why our camp site was sandy and smooth – the hollow in which our tents were pitched had turned into a small lake, and we were in the middle of it. Drenched to the skin, we dismantled our tents and carried them to higher, rocky ground. (A Biblical text about wise and foolish men came to mind!) We slipped and squelched in glutinous mud. Low cloud and mist swirled over the lake surface – we could well have been on the shores of a Scottish loch. We became aware of a roaring sound coming from our left, between us and the road. Further investigation revealed that we were cut off from the world by a raging torrent of water, about one hundred yards wide and three feet deep, and quite impassable. Branches, even whole trees, were being swept down to the lake. We were stranded. Now was not the time for Rosemary to go into early labour. By the following day the spate had subsided somewhat, and we were able to extricate ourselves from our 'idyllic' campsite.

Hot showers and a good breakfast at Loiyengalani Mission restored our spirits, and we continued our journey south along the lake shore. The stark, rocky shore, and the green-blue water of the lake, made a stunningly beautiful sight. It was with regret that we left the lake and turned inland to Mount Kulal. Standing at over eight thousand feet,

Kulal dominates the southeast shore of Lake Turkana. It is a fascinating mountain – remote, rugged, bisected by a deep and sheer ravine, crowned with primaeval forest, it is home to Samburu people, and to a small AIM mission. The track up Kulal to the mission at Gatab had been carved out of the mountainside by the American missionaries who live there. In places the road was very narrow, and the unguarded drop from the roadside was sheer. It was a breath-taking, at times heart-in-the-mouth, drive. But even more memorable was the view from the mission when we got there – far below sparkled the waters of Lake Turkana, the 'Jade Sea'. If ever one had to choose an idyllic place to establish a mission, this was it. Being Americans the missionaries there were relatively well funded, and seemed (to our poor Anglican eyes) comfortably provided for. We were intrigued by the number of vehicles they possessed – from jeeps, to JCB diggers, to Yamaha motorcycles. But we also admired the faithful, consistent work of the missionaries in this incredibly isolated place. They used Gatab as a base for outreach work, both evangelistic and medical, into the desert below – much as my father had done in Marsabit. The forest was very much like that on Marsabit, but being higher there were more cedar trees. I treated patients at the dispensary, and we joined about sixty Samburu worshippers at their Sunday service. Our two days at Gatab were restorative after the rigors of camping at the lake. And so we returned to Marsabit, making our cautious way down Kulal, and then speeding across the Koroli desert. It had been a fascinating trip, and one that we repeated again with Dr Robbie and Priscilla Gurney. But I was glad that my regular trips round my district were done by air. We were also glad that Rosemary had survived the journey intact, and wondered if the unborn baby would become an explorer.

Chapter 34
AN EVENTFUL BIRTH

Life did not consist entirely of exciting road journeys and mountain climbing. For the most part it was, for me, the daily routine of clinics, ward rounds, operations, administration and personnel problems. In September 1974 Paul (aged six) joined Andrew at St Andrew's School, Turi. Being more gregarious than Andrew, and having his older brother already at the school, he settled in better, but he was nevertheless very homesick. Andrew was certainly most caring and solicitous for his little brother. Paul's first letter home arrived on our tenth wedding anniversary. He wrote: 'Dear Mummy and Daddy, I wonder if you are sad. I am not sad. But I am a bit sad. I like my teacher. End. I love my Mummy and Daddy. The End.' We missed the boys so much, Rosemary particularly. So, too, did Stephen (now aged three) miss their companionship. He had a vivid imagination, and invented a whole world for himself. His brothers were replaced by two imaginary friends, called Bibi and Dogo, with whom he had long conversations. In time they were joined by two more, called Jiggers and Jericho. One day he solemnly announced that Dogo (whose gender until then was uncertain) had had a baby, called Baby Dogo – found, apparently, under a bush, though whether a gooseberry bush he did not specify. Farmer Junko joined the growing family in due course, and his role in life was to make scrambled egg and bottletop sandwiches for the others. Tragedy struck when Baby Dogo died – of 'diarrhoea' we were told. The happenings and sufferings of the real world were reflected in Stephen's imaginary world.

'Jiggers' was a familiar word in the house. Marsabit is plagued by jigger fleas, which burrow into the toes and lay their eggs, often around the nail bed. The toe becomes red and intensely itchy. The jigger, with its sack of eggs, has to be dug out with a pin – and many an evening was spent removing jiggers from the children's or our toes. We continued to be pestered by somewhat larger creatures too – elephants. They frequently broke through the fence round our garden to feast on our pawpaw and banana trees, right outside our back door. I devised an EEWS – an Elephant Early Warning System – which consisted of tin cans strung around the garden. The clattering of cans announced the arrival of yet another pachydermal raiding party, which had to be driven off with shouts and torches. On occasion I pinged the rear end of a retreating elephant with my air gun, but I doubt if it was even aware of being shot.

Rosemary's pregnancy progressed, and she booked in for her delivery at Nairobi Hospital. The baby would be born within a few hundred yards of my birthplace, the former Eskotene Nursing Home. We were returning to Marsabit from her final antenatal check up, a few weeks before the baby was due. It was well after dark by the time we reached Marsabit mountain. The red earth road stretched ahead, carved out of a hillside, with a steep bank down to the road on the right, and an almost sheer drop to the left. I was driving at about fifty miles per hour, to ride the corrugations. We were discussing possible names for the baby, and had concluded that, if it was a girl, we would call her either Lynette Joy or Lindsey Joy – but we could not decide between the two. Suddenly, in the headlights of the Landcruiser, we saw ahead of us an elephant slithering down the bank on to the road. It was closely followed by a second elephant. As I jammed on brakes, and we began to shudder to a stop, the first elephant came to a halt broadside on across the road. It filled the road. I had to make an instantaneous decision. If I were to veer to its left, we would plunge over a sheer drop. If I were to steer to its right we would mount the steep bank, hit the second elephant, and overturn. And yet I knew that we could not come to a stop before colliding with the elephant in the road. The thought flashed through my mind that if, as seemed inevitable, we ploughed into the first elephant we and it would, at best, be seriously damaged. But what would the second elephant then do? It might finish us off. As we juddered relentlessly towards the brown, wrinkled mass in front of us he suddenly – perhaps disturbed by our headlights – swung his massive, tusked head round to face us. This left just about a car's width between the side of his head and the drop on our left. 'Go for it!' Rosemary shouted at the same moment that I pressed the accelerator to the floor. We surged forward through the gap. I remember vividly a fleeting glimpse of the elephant's baleful eye, just inches from my face through the car window. We must have literally brushed against him. But we made it! We were stunned to silence, and said little for the rest of the journey home. The baby's name was not discussed again.

Three weeks before the baby was due Rosemary and the children took the opportunity of a flight down to Nairobi in a Sight by Wings plane. The plan was that I would follow by road a week later, to be sure of being with her for the birth. Their flight was variously described as 'terrifying' (Rosemary) or 'exciting' (the boys). They flew through a thunderstorm, with lightning flashing around them – yet another adventure for the unborn baby. The chaplain to Nairobi University, who was on leave, had kindly made his home available to us over the time of the birth. Rosemary settled in with the children, and kind neighbours offered help. I meanwhile had a hectic week in Marsabit in preparation for my impending absence. An important day in my calendar was an official visit by my boss, the Provincial Medical Officer, scheduled to take place two weeks before the baby was due. After that I would be free to join Rosemary in Nairobi. It was a time of broken nights – every night woken by an almighty clattering of tins and beating of drums. On the first occasion I woke with a start, thinking it was my EEWS operating. Then I realised – it was Ramadan, and the noise was the call to the Muslim faithful to get up and eat their middle-of-the-night meal.

The day of the PMO's visit arrived. Soon after 8 a.m., when the radio-telephone link to Nairobi opened up, I was called by a policeman to take an urgent call. It was from Rosemary's neighbour in Nairobi, Derek Wilkes. Rosemary had given birth to a little girl during the night on 12 September 1975, the day after Andrew's ninth birthday. I felt a mixture of utter elation and yet of bitter disappointment that I had not been there for her. I could not leave immediately – the PMO was waiting to do his inspection. This was finally over by 11 a.m. and I set off for Nairobi at midday. Apart from having to slow down for a lion to cross the road near Marsabit, and a stop for petrol in Isiolo, I drove at full speed all the way to Nairobi. I covered the three hundred and sixty gruelling miles in exactly six hours – a land speed record for that journey. At 6 o'clock I was at the chaplain's house, where neighbours were looking after the boys. Soon after I was at Nairobi Hospital, longing to see Rosemary and our daughter.

Visiting time was officially over, but such a triviality was not going to prevent my seeing the two ladies now in my life. Rosemary had had to name the baby, and she was Lynette Joy – the choice I would also have opted for after our unfinished discussion. I had a glimpse of her – so small and feminine in comparison with her brothers at birth, and with a shock of black hair. I spent a little time with Rosemary, then as I made my exhausted but happy way back along the silent hospital corridor, a figure with the looks and dimensions of Hattie Jacques approached. It was none other than Matron, carrying a furled umbrella. Fortunately just ahead of me was one other person, an Asian gentleman, who had also broken the curfew of visiting time. As matron approached him she raised her umbrella, and, prodding his stomach with each word as though to add emphasis, she said to him, 'What – do – you – think – you – are – doing – here?' I by-passed the scene and went on my way, fearing how I might have responded if she had prodded me like that.

The rules of Nairobi Hospital were indeed old-fashioned. Children were not allowed to visit. But Andrew and Paul were due back at boarding school, and would have gone by the time Rosemary and Lynette were discharged. They wanted to see their baby sister, and it was so important that they did. Not to be outdone by rules I took them along to the hospital, led them through a hole in a hedge near Rosemary's ward, and then passed them in through an open window. Fortunately Matron was not around. Andrew, who maintained that all babies are born bald, was astonished at how quickly Lynette's hair had grown.

The house in which we were staying in Nairobi was adjacent to the home of the Anglican Archbishop of Kenya. Stephen was aware of this, and would spend considerable lengths of time peering through the hedge, hoping to catch a glimpse of the Archbishop. One day he came running in a state of great excitement. 'The Archbishop is there! Come and see! Come quickly!' We went – and there, in a tatty old raincoat and bare feet, sweeping leaves off his drive, was the Archbishop's gardener. 'There!' said Stephen triumphantly. Over the following days he made good friends with the gardener through the hedge, and would come in and tell us nonchalantly, 'I've just been speaking to the Archbishop again!'

In due course we made the long journey back to Marsabit, though this time much more slowly, and in stages. Lynette travelled in a Moses basket. We spent two nights on the slopes of Mount Kenya with Richard and Joan Carles at their beautiful farm. Now as we looked up onto the snow-clad peaks of the mountain it felt familiar, like an old friend who had shared his secrets with us. We could imagine the Teleki Valley, and the Lewis glacier with its blue ice grottos and the malachite green Lewis tarn at its base. It was strange to think that little Lynette had also been up there, in utero. And so she came home to a royal welcome in Marsabit, with a succession of our African friends calling at the house to see the little one with her mop of black hair. Our family was complete.

Chapter 35
KWA HERI

I was now well into the final year of my contract with Kenya's Ministry of Health. The question had to be faced as to whether to apply to renew it. Our time in Marsabit had been good. We had made medical progress in the hospital and district. We had made a dent in the famine situation resulting from drought. We had made many friends. In my capacity as Medical Officer of Health in charge of a large staff there had inevitably been some tensions. Some staff understandably resented having a white boss. It was too reminiscent of colonial days – after all, it was only just over ten years since Kenya's independence. I too had misgivings about the place for an expatriate head of department in independent Kenya. So long as the likes of me filled such posts in the remoter parts of Kenya, then the longer it would be before Kenyan doctors took up the challenge of working in the tough areas. It felt to be the right time to step aside.

On a personal level it also felt to be the time to return to England. Andrew was within sight of secondary school, and Paul not far behind. Primary schooling, at St Andrew's, Turi, had been excellent, but suitable secondary education, which would prepare the boys for university in Britain, was not at that time available in Kenya. This was a priority. We also had a sense of responsibility to Rosemary's mother, who had moved to Malvern to be near June, and was beginning to feel her age. We wanted her to have some time with her grandchildren. We concluded that it would be right to leave Marsabit in 1976.

Our concern for Amudat continued. We had kept in regular touch with the folks there through the Flying Doctor radio. The situation in Uganda, under General Amin, remained tense. Dr John Wattis and his wife Libby (a nurse) were looking after Amudat Hospital, together with Ruth Stranex. John, on an emergency call to the hospital one day, was shot at by the Uganda army soldiers manning the roadblock in Amudat. Fortunately they missed, but when he stopped to protest they nearly shot him again. Then we heard that Ruth had been arrested and taken to prison in Moroto. She was subsequently put under house arrest at Archbishop Janani Luwum's house in Kampala, and then deported from Uganda. The Wattises completed two years in Amudat towards the end of 1975, and left. The future of the hospital remained uncertain. But it then became clear that Keith Knox, now qualified, was ready to go back to Amudat on a long-term basis as soon as he had completed his current house jobs. He would be available in February 1976. Keith had already spent two periods in Amudat – as a medical student with us, and as a newly qualified doctor filling in until the Wattises were available. He was already much loved and respected in Amudat. He was very aware of the political situation in Uganda, and yet felt strongly that that was where God was calling him. The people in Amudat looked forward to his coming enormously.

Keith arrived in Amudat towards the end of February 1976. Morale in the hospital soared. Just two weeks later we were given the shattering news over the Flying Doctor radio that he had had a serious road accident. Apparently he, with one of the dressers, Francis Mbotela, had taken the hospital Landrover down to Kampala to collect much needed supplies. On the return journey Keith took a bend in the earth road too fast and the Landrover overturned. (Ironically it was the very same bend on which George Barnley's wife had been killed.) Keith sustained a head injury, but was initially conscious. Francis was not badly hurt. Keith said to him, 'Francis, could you pray for me, then go for help.' He did just that, but by the time he returned with help Keith had lost consciousness. They took him in another vehicle through Amudat and up to Kapenguria Hospital in Kenya, where Dr Peter Cox was. This was a one hundred mile journey over rough roads. By now Keith was deeply unconscious. Peter immediately did a tracheotomy, and for two days shifts of staff ventilated him by hand (there being no mechanical ventilator). The Flying Doctors were loathe to evacuate him because of the risk that air travel might exacerbate his head injury. After two days, however, with no sign of improvement, it was felt that the risk must be taken. In the event Keith died as he was taken to the airstrip. He was buried at Kitale cemetery next to Graham Fraser.

The question inevitably rang out, 'Why, God, why?' Keith's father,

Neville Knox – town clerk of Harrogate and a well-known Christian speaker – flew out to Kenya for the funeral. He gave the address at the funeral, and very movingly spoke of Keith's faith, and how Keith would have said, with St Paul, 'For me to live is Christ; to die is gain'. After the funeral, and in spite of the risk of entering Amin's Uganda without a permit, Neville Knox insisted on being taken to Amudat. He said he must meet the many folk who loved Keith so much, and tell them to grieve for themselves, but not for Keith. There, to a huge gathering, he spoke again of how, in Christ, death holds no fear, and how, for Keith, it was pure joy to be with his Lord. Many that day found comfort and faith through Neville Knox's message.

But the question still remained – what about Amudat Hospital? BCMS made a policy decision that, until the situation in Uganda improved, they would not send further doctors or nurses to Amudat. The hospital would meanwhile be run as a health centre by the Ugandan staff, whom we knew to be so capable. They worked on through difficult times. The wife of Paulo, one of the dressers, was shot dead by the army. Pressure was put on them repeatedly by aggressive soldiers and officials, but they stood firm in their practice of good medicine and in their faith.

One of the last things that I organised in Marsabit was a District Maternal and Child Health Seminar. It was a great success. The Flying Doctor Service flew eminent speakers up from Nairobi. Health workers, both Government and Mission, Protestant and Catholic, came from all over the district, even from the remotest parts, to gather for those days in Marsabit. When so often Government and Mission medical services competed rather than cooperated, and when Catholics and Protestants would have no dealings with one another, it really warmed my heart – and was a fitting conclusion to what I had strived for in the District – to see health workers learning together, and sharing their problems together. That seminar forged a new spirit of teamwork and friendship. After all, the medical challenges we faced were huge, and to face them successfully we all needed one another.

I began to make enquiries about a partnership in General Practice in England. We wanted somewhere within reach of Malvern, so as not to be too far from Rosemary's mother and her sister June. Such jobs seemed few and far between, and anything that looked suitable was – by the time I received my medical journal, and my application arrived back – already filled. Then one GP, in his reply to my unsuccessful application, advised me to spend a year as a Trainee in General Practice. It was soon to become compulsory, and it would re-orientate me to medicine in Britain. After all, the incidence of lion maulings and kala-azaar, even in rural England, was not great! June, a Girl Guide Commissioner, discovered, in conversation with one of her fellow Commissioners (who was the wife of Dr George Wilson, a GP in Upton-upon-Severn) that the Upton practice was looking for a Trainee. I applied immediately, mentioning that my only experience of General Practice had been with Dr Tony Barnie-Adshead in Nuneaton, during our home leave in 1973. It so happened that Tony had trained together with the senior partner in the Upton practice, Dr David Jennings. David rang Tony, who gave me a kind reference, and I was accepted by the Upton-upon-Severn practice – just seven miles from Malvern. It was a wonderful relief to have the next step in place. (In due course I was invited to join the Upton practice as a partner, and so followed thirty very happy years, in a practice reputed for its excellence. During that time I saw cases of malaria, tick fever, jiggers and giardiasis. On occasion other tropical diseases had to be excluded. In these days of worldwide travel and back-packing a knowledge of tropical medicine is useful even in England.)

Our time in Marsabit was drawing to an end, and there was the inevitable and painful round of goodbyes. We were invited to a succession of farewell meals with our African friends. It was hard saying goodbye to people such as my gentle childhood friend Solomon, and his lovely wife Mary and family. Then there were Naomi and Jarso, who had worked for us in the house and garden. Naomi had spruced up her house in our honour with a new layer of mud, decorated by her daughter with pictures in ash. Jarso proudly showed us the calf born to a cow we had given him. Our concern for them was that our departure left them with no employment. Life for them was so precarious, for us so secure. They had to contend with drought and famine and locusts, with elephants and with baboons. We just had the taxman.

We made a final visit to the old mission site at Karantina. Once more

I recalled those magic days of childhood. No doubt they had become romanticised in my memory by the passage of time. Memories were of wandering free, with Dennis and Luka and Solomon and Elisha and our other friends. Barefoot days, with forest to explore, trees to climb, dens to make. In my mind I saw once again the swirling mist, and my parents hurrying to office and school. I could smell the acrid wood fire in the Dover stove, and the cool, musty mud walls of our home. As we stood on the remains of the floor of my childhood home little Stephen wanted to know what each room had been, and how I wished I could make it live again for him. What a privileged childhood it had been, and now I had come full circle, and it was time to leave again.

We returned to England, in that June of 1976, from a situation of drought to a situation of drought. We came from a water shortage to a water shortage. The difference was that nobody here was suffering or dying. Here they were just inconvenienced. The lawns were an unsightly brown, and garden plants were annoyingly wilting. But shopping trolleys in the supermarkets were, to our culture-shocked minds, obscenely full. It was something that we had to readjust to – the plethora of choice of food; the sheer amount that people seemed to need. And we thought of our friends in Amudat and Marsabit, struggling to survive.

In Uganda things went, for a while, from bad to worse. In due course an invading Tanzanian army drove General Amin from power. We heard that Amin's retreating soldiers had ransacked Amudat hospital. We heard that our house had been stripped of its corrugated iron roof, and was in a state of ruin. The garden had been decimated by goats and had reverted to bush. Then again, in time, we heard that the hospital was back in action, still manned by the faithful staff of dressers. It is now run as a health centre, and is currently manned by medical workers from Medecin Sans Frontiers. The whole of northeast Uganda is still a no-go area, due to roaming bands of raiders, armed now with automatic rifles. The only safe way in and out of Amudat is by air. Pray God peace and security will come once more, and that Amudat Hospital will again be the centre of healing that it once was.

Before Amin was ousted the stories coming out of Uganda of murder and violence were horrific. But worst of all was the murder of the Anglican Archbishop of Uganda, Janani Luwum. I remembered him from the time when we sat together on the Provincial Medical Board. He was a tall, very black, gentle, soft-spoken man, with a radiant smile. He had, as Archbishop, courageously spoken out against the excesses of Amin's soldiers. He and his fellow Anglican bishops appealed to Amin to stop the violence, the massacres, the disappearances. Amin's response was to summon him and his fellow bishops to his presence. A rigged trial took place outside the Nile Hotel in Kampala. Weapons were produced which, it was alleged, had been found at the Archbishop's house. A crowd of three thousand soldiers who had been bussed in for the 'trial' shouted for Janani's death, in a manner reminiscent of another staged trial two thousand years ago. The Archbishop and bishops were taken indoors, and kept waiting for four hours. Then Janani was told that the President wanted to see him. As he was taken from the room he turned to Bishop Festo Kivengere and smiled and said, 'I can see the hand of the Lord in this.' They were his last known words. It is believed that Amin himself shot him in a rage shortly afterwards.

As the news of his death ('in a car accident' according to official sources) became known the people of Uganda, and Christians in particular, were stunned. This really was a step too far. Preparations were made for a funeral service at Namirembe cathedral, and thousands converged on Namirembe hill (Luganda for 'The hill of peace' – the hill on which our Paul had been born). But at the last minute the regime banned a funeral. The body would not be released. Nevertheless the service continued, and thousands gathered in the cathedral and then around the grave site. At one point a soldier came into the cathedral and tried to stop the proceedings. 'This funeral service has been forbidden!' he told the clergy. 'No!' said the minister 'This is just an ordinary service, but it is going on for an unusually long time!' Outside, at the empty grave, the former Archbishop, Erica Sabiti, spoke of the first Easter, and the empty tomb – the symbol of hope and new life. Pointing to the empty grave he said of Archbishop Janani, 'Whether we have our brother's body here or not does not matter. He is not here! He has gone to be with the risen Christ! He is risen! Praise God!' And gradually the crowd took up the revival song 'Tukutendereza Yesu!', 'Glory! Glory to the Lamb!', until it resounded around Namirembe hill. That day many in Uganda came to faith in the risen Jesus Christ, and the faith of many others was strengthened and revived. As Janani Luwum had said, 'I can see the hand of the Lord in this!'

Our story does not compare in any way with that of martyrs and saints like Janani Luwum, and the many before him whose lives and whose blood were the seed of the church in Uganda and Kenya. But in a small way, as we look back to our years in those beautiful countries, and among such lovely people, we feel deeply humbled and privileged to have had the opportunity to do what we did. We experienced a way of life that has all but gone. We lived and worked in situations where one could make a real difference – where one's presence could mean the difference between life and death for many people. That is a huge privilege, and a great responsibility. We lived among people for whom the Gospel was truly liberating, and who were hungry to hear God's word. People whose lives were precarious, and who lived from day to day with the possibility of death. How different from our materialistic, apathetic, comfortable, self-serving society in the West.

Our experience was by no means all one of giving. We received and learned so much from those we lived among – lessons in loyalty, responsibility, and courage. And from our Christian brothers and sisters we learned lessons about openness; about 'Christ-ianity', as opposed to 'Church-ianity'. We experienced faith that is real and practical, not just cerebral. Our own part in the story of mission in East Africa was not even a sentence, barely a phrase. At times we felt we were not even planting the seed of the Gospel, we were just clearing the stones from the field. But now, in His time, God has brought a harvest. As we look back on those precious years we too can say, in all humility and inadequacy, 'We can see the hand of the Lord in this.'

If you have enjoyed this book you may also like to read another title by David Webster, *Mishkid: A Kenyan Childhood.*

Available from:

Dr D. Webster,
The Grange, Longdon Hill End, Upton-upon-Severn, WR8 ORN.
Email: namirembe@btinternet.com

Aspect Design, 89 Newtown Road, Malvern, WR4 IPD
Website: www.aspect-design.net

Also available from Amazon or to order from all good bookshops